MALTA

MALTA

A TRAVELLER'S ANTHOLOGY

Edited by

Deborah Manley

Signal Books

OXFORD

First published in the UK in 2010
This edition published in 2017 by
Signal Books Limited
36 Minster Road
Oxford
OX4 1LY

www.signalbooks.co.uk

A catalogue record for this book is available from the British library

ISBN 978-1-909930-57-5 Paper
Cover Design: Bryony Newhouse
Cover Image: © Richard Goodrich/istockphoto
Images: istockphoto: i, xiv, xxi, 1, 17, 19, 31, 39, 53, 55, 71, 104, 107, 134, 147, 233, 261;
             Deborah Manley: 66, 81, 140, 143, 168, 180, 190, 207, 211, 244

This edition prepared for print by
Andrews UK Limited
www.andrewsuk.com

CONTENTS

3 Once Ashore   39

4 Some History   55

MALTA UP TO THE SIEGE OF 1565   59

6 Valletta   147

7   Elsewhere on Malta, and the islands   211

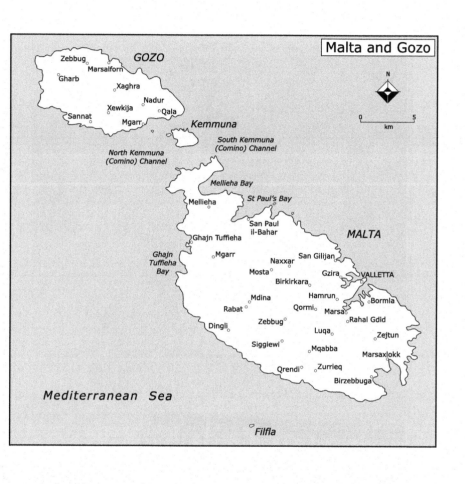

Malta and Gozo

GOZO

Zebbug
Gharb
Marsalforn
Xaghra
Nadur
Xewkija
Qala
Sannat
Mgarr

N

0   5
km

Kemmuna

North Kemmuna
(Comino) Channel

South Kemmuna
(Comino) Channel

Mellieha Bay

Mellieha
St Paul's Bay

San Paul
il-Bahar

Ghajn Tuffieha
MALTA

Ghajn
Tuffieha
Bay
Mgarr
Naxxar
San Gilijan
Mosta
Gzira
VALLETTA
Birkirkara

Mdina
Hamrun
Bormla
Rabat
Qormi
Marsa
Dingli
Zebbug
Luqa
Rahal Gdid
Zejtun
Siggiewi
Mqabba
Marsaxlokk
Qrendi
Zurrieq
Birzebbuga

Mediterranean Sea

Filfla

INTRODUCTION

'Somewhere ahead of us in that cobalt sea must be the island of Malta. Two hours later we were entering one of the most exciting harbours in the world. "Under the guns of St. Elmo" is a phrase that reverberates in one's mind from recesses of past reading, and here was St. Elmo and the Ricasole fortress of a creamy yellow against the blue of the harbour, seeming to make for us like great battleships about to bear us down. A brilliant sun was pouring a warm tremulous light upon waters, forts, and shipping, and suddenly Valletta, a radiant orange-coloured city, touched up with green like some successful stage setting, began to cascade backward before us, to lure us up the rock, to lure and to invite.

"So this is Malta," we concluded brilliantly, and a great sense of cheerfulness, of jubilation almost, flamed up in our minds. For, like only a very few spots upon the earth – like Venice, Taormina and possibly Bruges, reading and pictures and postcards had failed to ruin it for us. It surpassed our most elaborate expectations. It is beautiful with a beauty that no one can render upon canvas or paper. It has a sense of life, a soul and a mystery, that cannot be reproduced.

At once all the discomfort and hardship of attaining it are wiped out like a sum upon a slate.'

(Henry James Forman, *Grecian Italy*, 1927)

Malta is a nation of three islands, Malta, Gozo and Comino, situated at the crossroads of the Mediterranean, some sixty miles south of Sicily and 200 miles north of Africa. Together the islands cover only 122 square miles; and being small and low lying, they have not been able to offer much resistance to invaders over the centuries. This critical location therefore helps explain Malta's uniquely diverse and significant place in European history.

I went there first almost by chance, en route to Sicily. But I have returned—and will return—because Malta offers such intriguing variety with so much to see and learn and to enjoy. Malta also has the advantage that, in addition to its own language, both English and Italian are widely and easily in use.

Above all Malta is easy to get around—not just because it is small, but because of its famed public transport system, with yellow buses fanning out from just outside the city gate of Valletta to every village and small town. On Gozo the buses are grey with a red stripe and have their centre at the capital Victoria (Rabat), from which they meet the incoming ferries all day. You soon acquire a knowledge of the system and the destinations it can take you to.

Malta's history is intertwined with the history of all the powers of the Mediterranean: with the Phoenicians and others in the Neolithic age, with the Normans from Sicily, with the Arabs of North Africa, with all the nations of Europe through its period as home to the Knights Hospitaller of St. John from 1530 to the end of the eighteenth century. And after that, for a century and half, Malta's history was closely linked to Britain's.

From this intermingling has come the distinctive Maltese language, said by some to be the living legacy of the Phoenicians, with Arabic influences and words borrowed from the Romans and other Europeans. Sit on a Maltese bus and listen. You will understand some sense from these roots, though you may not understand a great deal. But do not worry if you don't: all Maltese speak English fluently, giving the extra benefit to travellers that you will always be able to ask your way.

Malta's history starts in the mists of time. On the archipelago are what are thought to be the oldest free-standing structures in the world. They are massive, solid buildings, made of huge boulders to create curved chambers, thought to be linked to the worship of vast female godlike figures. More recently discovered and identified is the Hypogeum at Hal Saflieni—a complex of interlinking subterranean chambers, hewn by hand out of the native rock some 5,000 years ago. Only discovered in 1902, the Hypogeum was excavated under the direction of the Maltese historian Sir Themistocles Zammit, whose description of it I include.

To help you understand this prehistory, visit the Museum of Archaeology in Valletta. Such a visit has the double advantage of the collection itself and its setting, in the *auberge*, or residence, of the Knights of Malta of Provence, which thus provides insight into the lives of the Knights who so influenced the country and its buildings.

Everywhere, but especially in Valletta, one is aware of the impact of the Knights on the history of the islands. The founding of the order of St. John of Jerusalem goes back almost a thousand years to 1085, when the Knights Hospitaller were brought together to care for the health and welfare of pilgrims to the Holy Land. Over the decades, as confrontation between Christians and Muslims grew, the Knights took on an added role as protectors of the pilgrims. These more warlike knights were drawn from the great families of Europe—from France, Italy, Spain, Portugal and England—and were divided in their daily lives into the *langues* or tongues of their origins.

Eventually the Knights were driven out of the Holy Land by the forces of Islam and sought refuge first in Cyprus and then, from 1310, on the island of Rhodes. There the Order developed into a force strong enough to threaten and harry the mainland and to deter Islam from moving westwards. After the fall of Constantinople to Sultan Mehomet II in 1453, Turkish attention was focused on these offshore Christian enemies. The struggle was long, but in 1523 the Knights on Rhodes had to accept defeat under their Grand Master de L'Isle-Adam, and made an honourable surrender to Sultan Suleiman the Magnificent. The couple of hundred remaining Knights, with a few thousand Rhodians, set sail with no sure destination. The rulers of Europe sent sympathetic messages but offered no welcome, until Charles V, Emperor of Spain, offered the Order permanent sanctuary on Malta. It seemed to the Knights a poor place—an infertile land, threatened constantly by corsairs, difficult to defend, and inhabited by an impoverished people. But there was no alternative. De L'Isle-Adam accepted the Emperor's offer, and the Act of Donation (which now lies in the Bibliotheca Archives in Valletta) was signed in April 1530. Six months later the Knights arrived to take over the islands.

They were there only three decades before the forces of Islam came after them again. On 18 May 1565 a vast and carefully chosen Muslim army—described by one Francisco Balbi di Correggio as being about 35,000 fighting men—approached the islands of Malta to face the Knights under their Grand Master La Valette, whose combined forces totalled only some 9,000 assorted men. It was inevitable, despite splits in the Muslim leadership, that Fort St. Elmo fell—on the very eve of the feast of St. John the Baptist, patron saint of the Order. There followed a horrific retaliation of medieval warfare through the long, hot summer. At long last, in September, a promised force of some 8,000 men reached Malta from Sicily, and after a further terrible battle in St. Paul's Bay the siege at last came to an end. The enemy forces departed and the Knights of the Order of St. John of Jerusalem of Rhodes and, now, of Malta took over the role of rulers of the island— and maintained that role for three centuries.

Once the invaders had gone, the Knights turned to rebuilding the fortifications of the island and building the small Renaissance city that bears the name of their Grand Master—Valletta. The great and the good—and the grateful—of Europe were eager to reward the Knights for their achievement in turning back the 'Turks', and within six years the newly fortified city of Valletta that we see today had risen around the Grand Harbour of the island. For the next 233 years the islands prospered: the population (no longer harried from across the Mediterranean) increased; agriculture was greatly improved, and new industries were created. The potential of Malta as a trading port between Europe and the East and onward to India could at last flourish. The Knights poured money into the infrastructure of the island, constructing splendid buildings like Fort Manoel, the Opera House and the Manoel Theatre, palaces and great town and country houses, including the seven *auberges* of the Knights, churches and other buildings, such as the National Library which is still in daily use, and of course fortifications. Perhaps the most important construction was the aqueduct built by Grand Master Wignacourt and admired by the French intellectual Vivant Denon, which brought much needed water to the cisterns of the city of Valletta. Those who visited Malta enthused about Valletta—once those arriving from the East had been released from serving quarantine in the offshore Lazaretto.

But as time went on the high-minded principles of the Order relaxed into an undisciplined and ostentatious way of life. Unwisely, but perhaps understandably, at the approach of the French Revolution, the then Grand Master, de Rohan, gave financial succour to Louis XVI and brought the enmity of revolutionary France down upon the islands.

In 1798 Napoleon Bonaparte was on his way to conquer Egypt and cut off European and British links to the East when he anchored his fleet of nearly 500 ships off the Grand Harbour. The Knights feared to stand against such a force so, on board Napoleon's great flagship *Orient*, they agreed to a humiliating defeat. They were ordered by the French to pack up and go—leaving behind the French knights if they wished to stay. Napoleon fully understood the importance of Malta, and is reputed to have said that he would rather see 'the British on the heights of Montmartre than in Malta'. But to Malta is just where they would come.

The French who were left to guard the island quickly alienated the Maltese—robbing their churches, looting other properties, and generally pushing their 'republican' ideas upon the unwilling and very religious people. Even half a century later travellers were still told how the French looted the treasures of the great church of St. John the Baptist in Valletta.

On 5 September 1798 the Maltese turned on the French. The French force retreated into the fortified city of Valletta, and both the Portuguese and British navies came to the aid of the Maltese, blockading the harbours and the city. Napoleon's forces, defeated at the Battle of the Nile, could give no help. The French on the island submitted and the Maltese called upon Britain to support their cause. Captain Sir Alexander Ball of the Royal Navy took over responsibility for the islands on behalf of Britain—and his monument on the Lower Barracca Gardens is still one of the sights of Valletta. He was joined by the young Samuel Taylor Coleridge as his secretary, and Coleridge's journals give descriptions of Malta at this time.

In 1802, when the Napoleonic Wars were over, Malta was offered back to the Order by the Treaty of Amiens; but the Maltese refused. It took time to resolve the impasse, but in 1814, by the Treaty of Paris, the Maltese islands were formally added to King George III's possessions and most of the Knights departed—although an occasional traveller, like Anne Katherine Elwood in 1825, would report meeting an elderly Knight attending a formal dinner or wandering the streets of Valletta in his ancient garb.

Britain and Malta became increasingly dependent upon one another. Malta was the centre of British naval power in the Mediterranean—with a bakery that made the bread for the whole Mediterranean fleet, in a building that is now a delightful naval museum. The streets rang to the voices of the British army and navy, and the *auberges* of the Knights and the Opera House and Manoel Theatre were centres of social life. There were important shipyards, employing many, many Maltese. Various proposals were made for the sharing of government responsibility, as described in 1879, and eventually in 1921 a Maltese government for Maltese affairs was agreed. However, it was not entirely a smooth move from colony to independence through the 1930s.

Then with the Second World War came the second great siege of Malta, with the Germans and Italians attempting to starve Malta and the British forces stationed there into submission—an aim they nearly achieved in the summer of 1942. But the Maltese stood firm under horrific onslaught from the German Luftwaffe flying out from Sicily— sending up to three raids a day during 1941. The Maltese suffered terribly, as the novelist Joanna Trollope describes in her empathetic account of the period. Food was scarce, and rations were tiny; and there was much illness alongside the fear and constant exhaustion. At last, in August 1942, a convoy of merchantmen limped into the Grand Harbour and broke the siege.

The damage to the islands during the siege was terrible. It is estimated that some 30,000 buildings were destroyed, but somehow these wounds have healed and a modern visitor scarcely notices the damage that was done. But go to the Lascaris War Rooms burrowed into the rock below the Baracca Gardens, where Malta's response was plotted, to get a chilling sense of the time and context of the resistance.

The bravery of the Maltese people was imaginatively recognised by the award of the George Cross by King George VI—the highest award for civilian bravery, which can be seen today in the National War Museum in Valletta.

As Malta rebuilt it also prepared for independence—won eventually in 1964 with a place in the Commonwealth. In 2004, after a referendum, Malta joined the European Union and confirmed its position as an important member of the European nations, in whose history the Maltese have played such a strong part. With a strong and valued historical relationship with Britain, Malta now prides itself in its own distinctive culture—linguistic, artistic and literary. A new generation of writers, mostly writing and publishing in Maltese, look back to the origins of an indigenous literature in the fifteenth century as well as expressing the vitality of contemporary society. While the large Maltese diaspora continues to flourish in many parts of the world, a strong sense of cultural identity is to be found among Valletta's many bookshops and publishers.

~

Beyond Valletta unfolds a fascinating country—but not one from which it was ever easy for the hard-working Maltese peasant to earn a living from the soil. Yet it is land from which spring abundant precious flowers—like darkly bright anemones and little irises—pushing eagerly up towards the warmth of the sun. The Irish naturalist Andrew Adams described the changing seasons and their impact on the land, as he watched migrating birds pass overhead on their way south or north. Each Maltese village has a well supported church, and each village celebrates with an annual *festa* on their saint's day with parades of joyfulness and magical displays of fireworks—so loved by the Maltese.

xxii Malta: A Traveller's Anthology

This collection of writings about Malta can only serve as an introduction to the literature and experience of Malta; it is the tip of an iceberg, for there are far, far more gems for those inspired to research more. We include as many Maltese writers and historians as we were able, often translated from their own language, and their insights are uniquely valuable to us. Many of the British writers included are familiar names: the young Benjamin Disraeli, Sir Walter Scott near the end of his life, but longing to write a novel about the Knights and their Malta, William Makepeace Thackeray, voyaging to the East, Edward Lear, the novelist Joanna Trollope, Vera Brittain and David Niven, to name but a few. But others who travelled to Malta are little known today—although often deserving of more attention. Spellings are left as in the originals, with all their intriguing variations.

I was fortunate enough to do some of my research in the Maltese National Library in Valletta, set up by the Knights themselves five centuries ago. The building is almost unchanged from the days of the *Malta Penny Magazine* in the mid nineteenth century. Much of my research was done in the changeless rooms of the Bodleian and Rhodes House Libraries in Oxford, where I have spent many hours travelling through the literature of Malta, Gozo and Comino. This collection introduces both the Malta of the past and the Malta of today—for they are inseparable.

Deborah Manley, Oxford, 2010

ARRIVAL IN MALTA

I first came to Malta almost by chance. I was flying on holiday to Sicily with Air Malta, and they took us to Malta both going and coming en route. There was a sense of excitement on seeing those islands lying below us in the sunny sea, and we greatly looked forward to coming back after our week in Sicily. Since then I have returned twice—for weeks rather than days—to become comfortably familiar with the place.

Caught by the wind: the shipwreck of St. Paul

NEW TESTAMENT: ACTS 25–7

St. Paul was sent before the Roman governor by Jews because of his claims about Christ's resurrection. Paul answered, 'Neither against the law of the Jews, neither against the temple, nor yet against Caesar, have I offended anything at all.' He appealed to be sent before Caesar to answer the charges against him. So he was delivered with other prisoners to a centurion, named Julius, to be transported to Rome.

The ship met contrary winds and, near Crete, a tempestuous wind arose, called Euroclydon. 'And when the ship was caught, and could not bear up into the wind, we let her drive.' The ship was 'exceedingly tossed with a tempest' (Acts 27: 14–18), but Paul assured them, 'Be of good cheer; for there shall be no loss of any man's life among you, but of the ship... Howbeit,' he added, 'we must be cast upon a certain island.' (Acts 22: 22–6)

At last they knew they drew near land, but feared they would be driven onto the rocks. They cast four anchors out of the stern, and wished for the day.

39 And when it was day, they knew not the land; but discovered a certain creek with a shore, into which they were minded, if it were possible, to thrust in the ship.

40 And when they had taken up the anchors, they committed themselves unto the sea, and loosed the rudder bands, and hoisted up the mainsail to the wind, and made towards shore.

41 And falling into a place where two seas met, they ran the ship aground; and the forepart stuck fast, and remained unmoveable, but the hinder part was broken with the violence of the waves.

42 And the soldiers' counsel was to kill prisoners, lest any of them should swim out, and escape.

43 But the centurion, willing to save Paul, kept them from their purpose; and commanded that those who could swim should cast themselves first into the sea, and get to land:

44 And the rest, some on boards, and some on broken pieces of the ship. And so it came to pass, that they escaped all safe to land.

Passing Malta in bad weather, 31 July 1718

LADY MARY WORTLEY MONTAGU

En route from Italy on her way East, Lady Mary did not land on Malta…

We pass'd Trinacria without hearing any of the Syrens that Homer describes, and being neither thrown on Scilla nor Charibdis came safe to Malta, first call'd Melita from the abundance of Honey. It is a whole Rock covered with very little Earth. The Grand Master lives here in the state of a Sovereign Prince, but his strength at sea is now very small. The fortifications are reckon'd the best in the world, all cut in the solid Rock with infinite Expence and Labour. Off of this island we were toss'd by a severe storm, and very glad after 8 days to be able to put into Porta Farine on the Africk ship, where our Ship now rides.

We discover the isle of Malta, 1765

PATRICK BRYDONE

Brydone arrived from Sicily, which he had found not all to his liking; Malta, by contrast, was far more pleasurable.

We had a fine breeze, and about two o'clock we discovered the island of Malta; and in less than three hours more, we reached the city of

Valetta. The approach of the island is very fine, although the shore is rather low and rocky. It is everywhere made inaccessible to an enemy, by an infinite number of fortifications. The rock, in many places, has been sloped into the form of a glacis, with strong parapets and entrenchments running behind it.

The entry into the port is very narrow, and is commanded by a strong castle on either side. We were hailed from each of these, and obliged to give a strict account of ourselves; and on our arrival at the side of the quay, were visited by an officer from the health-office, and obliged to give oath with regard to the circumstances of our voyage. – He behaved in the civilest manner, and immediately lent us Mr. Rutter, the English Consul, for whom we had letters of recommendation.

On getting on shore, we found ourselves in a new world indeed. – The streets crowded with well-dressed people, who have all the appearance of health and affluence. ... Mr. Rutter immediately conducted us to an inn, which had more the appearance of a palace. We have had an excellent supper, and good Burgundy; and as this is the King's birth-day, we have got almost tipley on his health. We are now going into clean, comfortable beds, in expectation of the sweetest slumbers. – Think of the luxury of this, after being five long days (at sea from Sicily) without throwing of our clothes. Good night.

People may say what they please, but there is no enjoyment in living in perpetual ease and affluence, and the true luxury is only to be attained by undergoing a few hardships. – But this is no time to philosophise. So adieu.

Aspect of the Maltese islands from the sea, 1860

ANDREW ADAMS

The Maltese islands appear to the traveller approaching them as long, low, and narrow strips of land broken up here and there by gaps and channels, giving them much the aspect of a small archipelago formed of many insular fragments running in a south-east and north-west direction. This is owing to their small elevation above the sea, and the deep indentations in their coast-lines; gradually, however, as the vessel draws nearer, we begin to define the true state of matters, but the high stone fences hiding the verdure give a very desolate and barren appearance to the surfaces. Moreover, even to the eye of the casual observer, they present very much the appearance of fragments of a sea-bottom that had been upheaved and long subjected to the denuding influences of the waves as they slowly emerged from the deep; and a closer study of their physical characters furnishes more definite conclusions on this head. As will be shown ... the Maltese islands are assuredly mere fragments of what had once been an extensive sea-bottom, which, when first up-heaved, formed portion of Europe and Africa, or both; and, lastly, that after oscillations of level, the greater portion was submerged, leaving only these small remnants now known to us as Malta, Gozo and Comino.

Gateway to the East, 1857

WILLIAM C. PRIME

The American traveller William C. Prime came to Malta from the West rather than the East, and saw it as a stepping stone to that other world, not as St. Paul had experienced Malta as a step towards Rome and the West. A priest whom Prime had met in Italy explained Malta to him...

He who goes to the East should always go by way of Malta. It is a stepping stone between Europe and the Orient, where the last wave of the Crusades rolled back from the walls of Jerusalem and sank in the foam.

No place in the Mediterranean is so intimately connected with the history of the East as this island of Malta, and there is scarcely any part of the Orient where you will not be reminded of it. This fact alone, that is in the place of the death and burial of that mighty order who for so great a period swayed the sceptre of power in Europe, is enough to connect it with Egypt and the Holy Land, indeed with all the possessions of the Turks.*

Here, when Valetta was Grand Master, the arms of the Muslim had their first great check, and the followers of the false prophet learned that their invincibility was a fable. Here, too, but yesterday, when the great leader of the French had garrisoned the island, your stout cousins of England, who followed his swift fleet as the hounds follow after the deer, drove out his soldiery. ...

---

* 'The Turks' was the collective term for the Ottoman Empire—ruled from Constantinople.

There have been valiant deeds done on this rock. If the sea could have a voice, it would tell of men of might, and deeds of might done here, that are themes for bards who love to celebrate the great acts of men. But the sea is the only living thing that knows them. For there are no trees, or ancient vines, nor anything here but the great rock, and the living, moving, throbbing sea around it."

I don't know that my friend would have talked on all day, had not a gun from the harbour announced that the steamer was heaving up her anchor.

First sight of Malta, 1805

GEORGE, VISCOUNT VALENTIA

Valentia had been travelling for some years when he arrived back into Europe through Malta—and was sent straight to quarantine in the lazaretto, but, as a nobleman, with less exclusion than other travellers met.

The weather became extremely pleasant, and on 26th July, for the first time, the wind came round to the eastward, and by ten o'clock this morning conveyed us to the port of Malta.

Soon after a boat was sent along side, empty, attached by a cord to another, in which were four men. We entered the former with our baggage, and were towed by the latter to the Quarantini, where we took up our abode in several very lofty stone apartments, with large windows looking over the harbour. The whole building is of the same materials, and surrounds a quadrangle; it is built on the solid rock, with a flight of steps down to the water, and is kept exceedingly clean. The lower storey is used to receive goods that are unclean.*

In consequence of its being known that no plague had existed in Egypt for three years. It was only for the sake of form that we were obliged to perform quarantine. Had a King's ship arrived under similar circumstances, she would have been immediately allowed pratique, or free access to the town, but this indulgence is in no circumstances granted to a merchantman. The Board of Health met, and sentenced us to confinement in the Lazaretto, for twenty days; but, in consideration

---

* 'Unclean' because they had come from Alexandria where plague could have been rife, and therefore they could not be safely landed for some time.

of our clean bill of health, and long voyage, gave us two days of grace, and left it to the discretion of the captain of the Lazaretto to give us two more, if we all continued well.

Our imprisonment was by no means a punishment, after so long having been confined to a merchantman; the Governor (Sir Alexander Ball) and many other gentlemen paid us visits in the presence of an officer, whose duty it was to take care that they did not touch us, nor any article belonging to us, that could communicate infection. With books and newspapers we were plentifully supplied, and the luxuries of ice and fruit, to which we had long been strangers, assisted in consoling us for the want of permission to visit the town.

An amazing approach, 1814

JAMES SILK BUCKINGHAM

As a merchant naval captain, Buckingham's experience of entering the harbour, though similar, is different in kind from those travellers who were passengers.

At length, about sunset, we were abreast of the opening to the harbour of Valetta, and entered it soon after. Nothing can be conceived more imposing than the scene presented to the navigator who for the first time sees this magnificent port. Though the entrance is extremely narrow (a great advantage to its strength of defence), the depth of water is everywhere sufficient for the largest ships of war that float; and the fortifications and batteries that guard the entrance on either hand, where the guns rise tier over tier in countless numbers, seem to threaten instant annihilation to any enemy that should dare to approach it. As you go further up the harbour, the public and private buildings of the city add greatly to the effect, and produce an impression of strength, durability, and opulence, which few island settlements can boast. Lateral harbours, in creeks leading from the main harbour into the land, afford shelter for smaller craft and vessels under repair; and, as an island fortress, a splendid naval station, and an imposing city, I had never yet seen anything to equal Malta as a whole.

At last we opened Malta, 1831

SIR WALTER SCOTT

The great historical writer Sir Walter Scott travelled in the Mediterranean for his health, escaping the northern winter. He also had plans for a book on the Great Siege of 1565, and was making observations accordingly. He recorded his experiences in his journal, but sadly did not survive to write what might have been his greatest book ...

Monday. Indifferent night. In the morning we are running off Gozo, a subordinate island to Malta, intersected with innumerable enclosures of dry stone dikes similar to those used in Selkirk shire, and this likeness is increased by the appearance of sundry square towers of Antient days. In former times this was believed to be Calypso's island and the Cave of the Enchantress is still shewn: we saw the entrance from the deck, as rude a cavern as ever opened out of a granite rock. The place of St Paul's shipwreck is also shewn, no doubt on similarly respectable authority.

At last we opened Malta, an island or rather a city like no other in the world. The sea port, formerly the famous Valetta, comes down to the sea shore. On the one side lay the Knights, on the outer side lay the Turks and finally got entire possession of it while the other branch remained in the power of the Christians. Mutual cruelties were exercised: the Turks seizing on the remains of the knights who had so long defended Saint Elmo, cut the Maltese cross on the bodies of the slain and tying them to planks let them drift with the receding tide into the other branch of the harbour still defended by the Christians. The Grand Master in resentment of this cruelty caused the Turkish prisoners to be decapitated and their heads thrown from mortars into the camp of the Infidels.

Newcomers from distant shores, 1840

MALTA PENNY MAGAZINE

'It is,' wrote the editor of the Malta Penny Magazine *of 17 October 1840, 'interesting at all times, to hear the remarks of newcomers from distant shores on foreign things and customs, especially as they strike them at first sight.'*

My dear friend,

I believe we last parted company just as we were approaching the island of Malta. Some of our passengers were romantic enough to sit up till two o'clock to see our steamer enter the harbour of Malta, which certainly appeared truly picturesque beneath the rays of the moon, which streamed down in silvery lustre upon the shore. I was not one among the number, however; I went quietly to bed at the usual hour, and knew not that we had reached the place of our destination, till the chime of a hundred bells from the numberless churches and convents around us, roused me at early dawn from my slumbers. When I first went on deck in the morning, and looked around upon the encompassing city, with its houses of stone, its flat and terraced roofs, and all the unique appearance of its streets rising one above another, crowned with castles, and convents, and churches, I felt for a moment as though I had been transported by some unknown power into a scene of enchantment – a place of which I had never before heard. I was soon awoke from my reverie, however, by the voice of a servant, reminding me that it was necessary to get my baggage in a state of preparation for landing.

~

As we stood upon the deck, in front of us rose the lofty, embattled shores of Valetta, sweeping down by terraces in the rock on which it stands, to the waters brink, its summit crowned with fortifications, towers, castles, convents, and churches. On our right lay the densely populated Senglea, with its own peculiar fortifications, and on the left, the steep and guarded banks of Burmola and Borgo, the first residence of the Knights, and which, from a great victory they gained over the Ottoman forces in 1565, was originally denominated Vittoriosa. On our rear, sweeping around the head of this little haven, were a series of houses and streets, forming connecting links between Senglea and Vittoriosa, backed and flanked by the Cottonera – a fortification of immense strength, built in 1676 by the Grand Master Nicola Cottoner

– and which joins by its two extremities Senglea on one side, and Vittoriosa on the other.

From the sea, 1972

NIGEL DENNIS

Approached from the sea, as it always should be but rarely is today, the sight is one of the most astonishing in the world and almost justifies the clerical school in its insistence on Malta as the last bastion of Christianity. It rises out of the Mediterranean like some wonder from the sea in classical legend, at once lemon-yellow and pale grey, often with a pinkish glow, it makes the volcanic stone of Syracuse seem infinitely shabby and grimy in comparison. On deck in the early morning, D.H. Lawrence saw this beauty immediately,

Picking up the pilot, 1840

GEORGE ANGAS

Sept. 19 – At sunrise the captain called me on deck to witness a most magnificent spectacle. The sun rose surrounded with long rays, forming a complete glory of most dazzling brilliancy, whilst the scattered fleecy clouds shone like burnished gold upon the exquisite light blue of the morning sky. On our left was the coast of Sicily, with Mount Etna towering proudly above it, at the distance of 120 miles; and far before us, cradled in the Halcyon seas, the Maltese islands themselves appeared like dark specks on the horizon.

~

The temperature of the atmosphere was greater today than yesterday, the thermometer at noon was 87°.

~

Eight o'clock. – The new moon is shining with great brilliancy, and a Sicilian speranoza has just passed us. The lights of Valetta are visible, distant about fifteen miles.

Eleven o'clock – One of the native Maltese boats has come alongside to put a pilot on board; the moment he neared us, he jumped upon deck without any ceremony ....

✳

Close under the land, 1840

GEORGE ANGAS

Sept. 20. Long before day-break a crowd of small boats surrounded us, whose crews begged that they might tow our vessel into the Grand Harbour. We are now fast approaching it, pulled long by about a dozen of them.

With this extra assistance we soon neared the Maltese shores, which speedily became visible through the dim light of early morning. It was a truly pleasant and refreshing sound, after a five weeks' tedious voyage across the briny sea, to hear the murmuring of the waves as they dashed at intervals against the rocky shores, a sound to whose gentle music we had been strangers ever since we had watched the sweeping breakers hurry confusedly along the Race of Portland (in the English Channel).

As the water rapidly deepens at the distance of a few yards from the shore, we sailed along close under the land, and the first ruddy hues of morning discovered to our view the towering fortress of St Elmo, with its impregnable buttresses and turrets, bristling with cannon.

The moment we rounded the promontory of St. Elmo, all was gaiety and animation. Myriads of little boats were darting in every direction across the harbour, and the graceful *palechi* and *speronazos* with their curved lateen sails, the men of war lying at anchor, and the crowd of yachts, schooners and other vessels, rendered the waters of the Grand Harbour a very lively scene.

On the Valetta side, the dark green foliages of the feathery trees, and the broad spreading leaves of the bananas, the sombre cypresses contrasting strongly against the unstained purity of the white buildings as they rose up one above another from the water's edge, and the line of domes, turrets, and varied fortifications, added to the bright sky and strangely foreign air of the whole scene, bursting at once upon the sight, produced a fairy-like panorama, – a real picture with all the vivid novelty of some city seen in dreams; and the charm was not a little augmented by its contrast to the monotonous but silent grandeur of the ocean, where all around, as far as the eye can reach, nothing breaks the distant horizon but a sail dimly seen, or a solitary sea-fowl skimming over the restless water.

By sailing vessel, 1804

SAMUEL TAYLOR COLERIDGE

On 5 June 1804 the poet Coleridge arrived in Malta and soon took up a post as secretary to the first British governor, Sir Alexander Ball. It had been a long, slow, weary journey and Coleridge had been quite dangerously ill. ('Whoever,' he wrote, 'makes a sea voyage should above all things provide themselves with aloetic pills, castor oil, and several other purgatives—as sometimes one will answer when others disagree—& everything depends on keeping the Belly regularly open.')

The Harbour of Valetta is narrow as the neck of a bottle in the entrance, but instantly opens out into a Lake with tongues of Land, capes, one little Island &c &c, where the whole Navy of England might lie as in a Dock in the worst of weathers – all around its banks in the form of an amphitheatre rise the magnificent Houses of Valetta, and its two over-the-water Towns Bormola and Floriana (which are to Valetta what the Borough is to London) – the Houses all lofty & built of fine white free-stone, something like Bath, only still whiter and newer-looking, yet the Windows from the prodigious Thickness of the walls being all out of sight, the whole appeared to me as Carthage to Aeneas, a proud City well nigh but not quite finished.

I walked up a long street of good breadth, all a flight of Stairs no place for beast or carriage – each broad Stair composed of a cement (Sand & Terra Possolana) hard & smooth, as the hardest pavement of smooth rock by the Sea side – and very like it.

Thankful to arrive, 1851

WILLIAM MAKEPEACE THACKERAY

The novelist Thackeray was on his way to the Levant and Egypt—an experience he would describe in From Cornhill to Cairo. In many places he was disappointed or critical; Malta obviously enchanted him.

On the 15th, to the inexpressible joy of us all, we reached Valetta, the entrance to the harbour of which is one of the most stately and agreeable scenes ever admired by a seasick traveller. The small basin was bust with a hundred ships, from the huge guard-ship, which lies there a city in itself, – merchant-men loading and crews cheering, under all the flags of the world flaunting in the sunshine; a half score of busy black steamers perpetually coming and going, coaling and painting, and puffing and hissing in and out of harbour; slim men-of-war's barges shooting to and fro, with long shining oars flashing like wings over the water; hundreds of painted town-boats, with high heads and white awnings, – down to the little tubs in which some naked, tawny beggars came paddling up the steamer, entreating us to let them dive for halfpence. Round the bust blue water rise rocks, in blazing sunshine, and covered with every imaginable device of fortification: to the right, St. Elmo, with flag and lighthouse; and opposite, the Military Hospital, looking like a palace; and all round, the houses of the city, for its size the handsomest and most stately in the world.

A superb prospect, 1789

VIVANT DENON

When the French came briefly to Malta en route to Egypt, Vivant Denon observed the islands with enthusiasm.

… We now got sight of that superb prospect, the inside of the harbour, its innumerable forts, and the two towns built in an amphitheatre; a prospect, resembling that of no other city in the world, and second perhaps in magnificence to none. There is not a single beautiful edifice; but being all remarkably well built, and appearing as if founded on vast and noble bastions, nothing can be more striking than their external aspect. The inner part of the New Town on the right, built by La Valette, after the famous siege of the Turks, bears the name of its founder. Beautiful and spacious flights of stone steps conduct to large streets, perfectly straight, and exceedingly well paved. The houses are built of free stone, of so peculiar a beauty, as to appear always new, and the earth and dust are so white, that instead of soiling the walls, they seem perfectly to renew their colour. ….

Arriving on the *Sunbeam*, 1877

LADY ANNIE BRASSEY

The Brassey family—Thomas Brassey, M.P. (later the first Earl Brassey), his wife Anna (Annie), their four children, two friends, three naval officers (and a crew of 23 plus four stewards, two cooks, a nurse, a lady's maid and a stewardess)—set sail from Cowes on the Isle of Wight on 1 July 1876 and sailed around the world. They sailed home through the Mediterranean, reaching Malta on Tuesday 8 May 1877.

A fine morning, with a cold strong head breeze. At noon we rejoiced to think that Malta was not more than a few miles ahead, or we should assuredly have failed to reach our port before nightfall. About three we closed in with the land about Marsa Scirocco and Delamara Point, and, after one or two tacks, rounded the point of Ricasole, and, leaving Port St. Elmo on our right, we swiftly glided into the grand harbour of Valetta. We have been here so often that it feels quite like reaching home. We soon found ourselves in our old quarters in the Dockyard Creek, and had scarcely moored before one of the officers came on board with the usual complimentary offers of assistance, whilst directly afterwards came an invitation to a farewell ball at the Palace, given to the Duke of Edinburgh. Our old boatman, Bubbly Joe, took us ashore to dinner, and we found everything looking as bright and cheerful and steep as it always does and always will do; not the least bit altered or modernised. The landlord of the Hotel d'Angleterre was delighted to see us again, and so were his servants, who came flocking from all parts of the house, nearly pulling the children to pieces, and plying our own servants with questions in their anxiety to know all about us.

So much of interest, 1879

REVEREND WILLIAM LOFTIE

Now, Malta is a place full of interest for many different kinds of travellers. Soldiers may want to see the forts, artists to sketch the up-and-down-stairs streets. The ordinary tourist even may have many things to see in the three little islands which form the group. He has read St. Paul and Josephus, and would visit the scene of the wreck of "a certain ship of Alexandria". He may have an interest in the history of the orders of chivalry, and desire to examine St. Elmo, and fight over on the spot the famous siege of 1565. He has studied architecture, and would verify Mr Ferguson's account of the wonderful dome of Mosta.]

If he is a botanist, he may propose to judge for himself as to the genus of a so-called Centaurea about which Linnaens are in doubt. The language of the natives has not yet been successfully reduced to writing. The statistical problems offered by the thickly populated islets are but half worked out. There are, in short, few places of the same size in Europe. – for the Maltese reckon themselves Europeans[*] – in which so many objects of interest, social, political, geological, geographical, or only picturesque, may be found; and the traveller easily makes up his mind to land, and, after seeing something of Valetta and its environs, to go on by the next steamer. He may be sorry to leave pleasant company on board, but pleasant company may be encountered again, and there is but one Malta. There may even be melancholy pleasure in persuading himself that bright eyes are a little dimmed as he announces his heroic intention. He is not altogether displeased to find that he will be missed, and his own sorrow in much mitigated by the regrets he hears at the prospect of parting.

Cheerful and animating sights, 1810

DR. CHARLES MERYON

Few cities are more striking at first sight than La Valetta, the capital of Malta. It happened to be Easter Day; and the ringing of bells and firing of crackers and guns, as we entered the harbour, about ten in the morning, with the varied appearance of English, Moorish and Greek ships, with their different flags mingled in a most agreeable confusion, and reflected from a green water, transparent to the bottom, at the

---

[*]   Malta joined the Council of Europe in 1965; became an associate member of the European Community in 1970; and a member of the European Union in 2004.

foot of stupendous fortifications, altogether rendered it one of the most cheerful and animating sights we had ever beheld.

Today, of course, the comings and goings in the Grand Harbour are less exciting and colourful, but still fascinating. From our hotel terrace we watched the comings and goings of a vast American war ship, a cruise ship bringing tourists to spend the day on the island, two French submarines, their sailors saluting on deck as they entered the harbour, a somewhat decrepit oil servicing ship from Benghazi, and still, as in the past, the scuttering little boats of Malta, carrying people and goods back and forth across the harbour.

THE LAND, THE CLIMATE
AND WATER

My first impression of Malta was of a land surrounded by water, but with only just enough water to refresh the land and make it green. It was late spring and already the sun was drying the land, revealing the stone which underlies all one sees. Here the stone walls seemed more significant than the fields they surrounded. Later, in late winter, I would see rain flooding down and washing across the land and into the sea. This is clearly not a land where it is easy to scrape a living...

Malta's place in the world, 1792

LOUIS DE BOISGELIN

The island of Malta is situated between Sicily and Africa, in 330° 40 minutes of east longitude from Ferro (150° 54 minutes east of London) and 350° 44 minutes 26 seconds north latitude. It is the most southern island in Europe: distant 66 miles from Cape Spartivento in Calabria, the nearest point on the continent of Europe; two hundred from Calipia, the nearest point on the continent of Africa; and two hundred and seventy from Tripoly. It is sixty miles in circumference, twenty long, and twelve broad. It faces on the east the island of Candia (Crete); on the west, the small islands or rocks of Pantalcria Linosa and Lampedosa; on the north, Sicily; and on the south the kingdom of Tunis.

Malta as it is, 1839

THOMAS MACGILL

The Island of Malta (as everyone knows or ought to know) stands in north latitude 35 54 and in east longitude 14 31. The length of the Island is 20 miles, in breadth 12, and its circumference 60 miles. The quidnunc of ancient days, picked each others eyes out, to determine whether Malta was in Europe or Africa; but John Bull (before he allowed himself to be dictated to) in his own gruff way, put a stop to all further dispute on the matter; and by act of Parliament, told the world that Malta is in Europe, and there she must remain.

The land is high towards the north; the highest hill *Bengemma* is only 590 feet above the level of the sea. The ports and harbours are all on the north side; the southern and western parts are bounded by inaccessible cliffs, forming a barrier against all debarkation. The first port or harbour on the east is called Marsascirocco, then comes Valletta, St. Julian, the Salines, St. Paul, and lastly Meleha.

The basis of the Island is limestone rock, generally soft, but hard in some parts; quarries of marble are even to be met with; the air of Malta is salubrious, her people of sound constitutions; there is no running water on the Island and every house in town or country is furnished with cisterns, into which the rains are carefully collected; the soil is part natural and part artificial, rendered fertile by extraordinary industry; the fruits ate exquisite.

The products of the land consist in cotton, cumin, and anise, fruit and vegetables, corn for from 3 to 4 months supply of the inhabitants, potatoes, not only sufficient to supply the inhabitants …

✳

The climate, 1926

SIR THEMISTOCLES ZAMMIT

The climate of Malta is temperate, surrounded as it is by a vast extent of water it is not subject to the sudden changes of temperature which occur on the Continent. In winter the average temperature rarely falls below 60 degrees Fahrenheit.

Snow is practically unknown and frosty weather is rare. Sunless days are an exception, and Malta in the winter months is as pleasant and healthy as any of the famous resorts on the shores of France and Italy.

The summit of heat is trying only when the damp southern winds prevail. The temperature does not usually exceed 85 degrees in the daytime, and at nightfall a cool breeze blows from the sea.

The rainy season occurs between October and April, but it rarely rains continuously for days or even for many hours. The average annual rainfall varies between 21 and 22 inches and, though this amount falls in about six months, it is sufficient to enable the husbandman to raise all his yearly crops and to furnish the ever-increasing population with an adequate supply of water.

Water (still) in the well does not quench the thirst.

Don't foul the spring from which you may have to drink.

Heat and health, August 1804

SAMUEL TAYLOR COLERIDGE

The poet Coleridge worked as secretary to the first British Governor of Malta, Sir Alexander Ball. Here he writes to Sir George and Lady Beaumont.

I live at the Palace of St. Antonio in the country, four miles from La Vallette, & when in town, in the Palace at La Vallette. A Parent could scarcely be kinder to me than Sir A. Ball, the Governor: – Great as the Heat has been on the Thermometer, 85 to 87 degrees, yet there is always a free Air here, & I have never once felt the Heat oppressive. I take care not to expose myself – and take my exercise from 5 to 7 in the morning, & not till after 7 in the Evening. The Climate to me appears heavenly; & the Sirocco a mere Joke compared with our close *drizzly* weather, in England. On the whole my Health is, I hope, better. I am scarcely ever ill, & very seldom am tormented with distressful Dreams.

An inhospitable island, 1792

LOUIS DE BOISGELIN

Account of Malta given to the full council of the Knights of St. John in Louis de Boisgelin's History of Malta.

That the island of Malta was merely a rock of soft sand-stone, called *tufa*, about six or seven leagues long and three or four broad; that the surface of the rock was scarcely more than three or four feet of earth, which was likewise stony, and very unfit to grow corn and other grain;

though it produced abundance of figs, melons and different fruits; that the principal trade of the island consisted in honey, cotton and cumin, which the inhabitants exchanged for grain; that, except a few springs in the centre of the island, there was no running water, nor even wells; the want of which the inhabitants supplied by cisterns; that wood was so scarce as to be sold by the pound; which forced them either to use cow-dung dried in the sun or wild thistles, for dressing food; that the capital of the country, named *Citta Notabile* [Mdina] was situated upon a rising ground in the centre of the island; that the greatest part of the houses were uninhabited; and the circumference not more than thirteen hundred and three paces; that the miserable walls that surrounded it were only thirty paces in breadth; that there were neither ports, bays nor coves, on the western coast of the island; that the shore in that part was full of great rocks and shoals; but on the opposite coast there were many points or capes with indentures in the form of bays and coves, in which ships might anchor: that there were two spacious and very good ports in the island, capable of receiving the largest fleets; but with no other defences than a small castle, named St. Angelo, which was partly in ruins – its whole artillery consisting of one small cannon, two falcons, and a few iron mortars; that the island contained about twelve thousand inhabitants of both sexes; the great part of whom were poor and miserable, owing to the barrenness of the soil, and the frequent descents of corsairs, who, without the smallest sentiment of compassion, carried off all the unfortunate Maltese who happened to fall into their hand; in a word, that a residence in Malta appeared extremely disagreeable – indeed, almost insupportable – particularly in the summer.

Aspect of the islands in Springtime, 1860

ANDREW ADAMS

A few extracts from my journal will suffice to convey some idea of the spring and autumnal … climate of Malta at these seasons.

April 15th Studying nature in such a climate as this during the winter and spring months is certainly most delightful. The temperature continually mild, renders exertion pleasant, and one never feels overdone by walking fast, or the necessity of doing so in order to keep up the animal heat. I often stroll along the roads, or the terraced fields, over the interminable stone fences, up the valleys among ripening crops of barley and budding pomegranate groves; the rich red flowers of the latter are just appearing, and long since the fig has thrown out its broad leaves to shelter many a bird-wanderer from the south. The pods are green on the stems of the carob, and the bulrush is springing up rapidly in dank places near the sea-shore. It is harvest; the red vetch has been cut, dried, and stacked, and the yellow taint commences to tinge the corn fields. Summer is coming, but indeed, as regards verdure, it is truly winter, for in another six weeks a grey mantle will have covered the islands, and their surfaces will appear as bare an unburnt as if no plant could flourish there. The green meads will become howling wastes, and the fierce and tropical heat will imprison us from June to September,. The gay songsters now crowding every available bush and tree and field, will have flown to more northern climes.

Summer in Malta, 1827

REVEREND WILLIAM JOWETT

Reporting to the Church Missionary Society in London, Jowett who lived with his family in Malta wrote in May 1827:

We sometimes have a more distinct and positive suffering from the *approach* of Summer heat, than from its continuance. If I may so express myself, the Months of May and June knock us down; the months of July, August, and September simply leave us languishing on the ground.

Bleached by the heat, 1942

JOANNA TROLLOPE

From her novel about Malta, The Brass Dolphin *(written in 1997 under the name Caroline Harvey), the novelist Joanna Trollope describes Malta in wartime.*

It was a hot day, already the sky the pale whitish blue it seemed to be in Malta in summer, lacking those northerly breezes that keep other parts of the Mediterranean sky so deeply blue. All Malta looked bleached out by the heat: the broken streets and the rubble heaps that were once houses, the roads, the dusty countryside where farmers and off-duty soldiers struggled to grow at least something for the coming winter. It was, Lila thought, pedalling on while the sweat ran down her in rivers, as if Malta had been sucked dry and left out to bleach to a husk in the sunlight. The lion sun, the Maltese called it, as if it was some greedy beast, sucking the marrow out of the island, and leaving only the dry bones behind.

Aspects of Malta in Autumn, 1860

ANDREW ADAMS

About the last day of October, Malta commences to put on her winter robe, and doff her greyish-brown garments of summer. Now it is that the grass begins to sprout, and the farmer turns up the soil; the leaf is slowly dropping off the fig, vine, and Persian lilac: thus, while the sap is descending in them, it is rising in the herbs of the field. The ripe red fruit of the pomegranate hangs pendant from the branches, whilst the Napoli Japonica is seen in flower, and will bear its luscious fruit in March. Again come back our spring-feathered visitors from the north, the migratory young birds of the year predominating; but the bared, sunburnt slopes in September afford nothing tempting to the passers-by, and were it not for the vegetable gardens in the valleys of the Marsa, Boschetto, and suchlike, I verily believe not one bird in a thousand would then condescend to alight on the islands. It must be the fields of cabbages, tomatoes, pumpkins, cotton, and Indian corn that tempt them, or the few fig trees, now laden with delicious fruit, with which the market is stocked at this season.

It is an interesting occupation for the naturalist to repair to any of these localities during the calm evenings, and witness the birds, one after another, or in flocks, descending from their lofty aerial highway, and note those that come in singly or in groups, some stooping to reconnoitre, whilst others, apparently satisfied that this is not the land they are seeking, continue onwards, and are lost to view in the sea-haze.

✳

The produce of the land and sea, 1839

EMMA ROBERTS

The shops and cafes of Valetta have a very gay appearance, and the ingenuity of the inhabitants is displayed in several manufactures; the black lace mittens, now so fashionable, being particularly well made. Table-linen, also of superb quality, may be purchased, wrought in elegant patterns, and, if bespoken, with the coat-of-arms or crest into the centre or the corners. In the fashioning of the precious metals, the Maltese likewise excel, their filigree work, both in gold and silver, being very beautiful; the Maltese chains have long enjoyed a reputation in Europe, and other ornaments may be purchased of equal excellence.

To the eye of a stranger, Malta at this season of the year (the end of September) seems bare and destitute or verdure; yet, from the quantity of every kind of vegetable brought to the market, it must be amazingly productive. The growth of cotton, lately introduced in Egypt, has been injurious to the trade and manufacture of Malta, and the attempt to supply its place with silk failed... How many goodly schemes have been ruined from want of scientific knowledge upon the part of their projectors, and how frequently it happens that a moment of impatience will destroy the hopes of years!

Fruit is cheap, plentiful and excellent at Malta, the figs and grapes being of very superior quality, while the island affords materials for the most luxurious table. The golden mullet and the *Beeca fica* are abundant; and all the articles brought to market are procurable at low prices. I can scarcely imagine a more agreeable place to spend a winter in, and I promise myself much gratification in the sojourn of a few weeks at this delightful island upon my return to England.

Emma Roberts died after only a few months in India, so never came back to enjoy Malta.

Aspects of Malta in Mid-winter, 1860

ANDREW ADAMS

As far as verdure is concerned, Malta may be said to be in its prime in February. It is then the daisy and the dandelion deck the meads, grassy lanes, and waysides; wheat is ripening, and the luxuriant tops of the purple vetch adorn the terraced fields, and commingle their flowers with the red poppy, yellow marigold, daffodil, crimson pheasant's eye, and purple anemone, where the painted lady, cabbage, clouded saffron, and other butterflies are sporting.

The evergreen of the stunted locust or carob tree consorts well with the scene, whilst the bare boughs of the fig stand out in inanimate ugliness against the stone fence around the terraced fields. Here and there a small, flat-roofed barn occupies a corner of the little flat, for the Maltese huddle together in villages, and rarely is a solitary house to be found in the cultivated districts.

A land without water, 1804

SAMUEL TAYLOR COLERIDGE

June 1804: For 8 months in the year the Climate of Malta is delightful; but a drearier Place eye never saw. No stream in the whole Island, only one Place of Springs, which are conveyed by aqueducts & supply the Island with about one third of its water under the Houses, Walls, &c &c, to preserve the Rain are *stupendous*! The Tops of all the Houses are flat, & covered with that smooth hard composition; & there and every where, where Rain can fall, are channels – & pipes to conduct it to the Reservoir –

Malta is ... – a mere rock of free stone, in digging out this they find large quantities of vegetable soil – they separate it and the stones build their Houses, & garden and field walls – all of an enormous thickness – the fields seldom so much as half an acre, one above another in that form so that every thing grows as in huge garden Pots, & the whole Island looks like one monstrous fortification. Nothing *green* meets your eye – one dreary grey-white, & all the country Towns from the retirement and invisibility of the windows look like Towns burnt out and desolate. – Yet the fertility is marvellous – you almost see things grow – and the population I suppose unexampled ...

Water, 1809

JOHN GALT

Although the island is but one great rock, thinly covered with soil, the inhabitants are well supplied with water. A small stream, which rises in the interior, is brought to Valetta by an aqueduct, and distributed by public fountains. Every house in the city, as well as in the country, has also a cistern, capable of containing a quantity of water sufficient to serve the family six months. These cisterns are filled by the rain from the roofs of the houses.

The Aqueduct, 1765

PATRICK BRYDONE

The great source of water that supplies the city of Valetta takes its rise near this place (Bosquetta in central Malta); and there is an aqueduct composed of some thousand arches, that conveys it from thence to the city. The whole of this immense work was finished at the private expense of one of the Grand Masters.

The Aqueduct, 1789

VIVANT DENON

We returned to the town, passing by the bottom of the bay where St. Paul was shipwrecked, and after crossing the handsome villages of Rabatto and Kercava, went under the aqueducts by which the Grand Master Vignacourt brought the water from the only fountain belonging to the city. This scarcity of water at Malta is remedied by a prodigious number of cisterns, which are easily made, as nothing more is necessary than to arch over and convert into reservoirs the excavations that serve for quarries, and the foundations of their houses, so that each house has its own, and not a drop of rain water that falls upon the city is lost.

*

A whole land subdivided, 1809

JOHN GALT

The aspect of the country of Malta is, perhaps, more wonderful to a stranger, particularly to one who has come from a land of verdant fields, groves, and hedge-rows, than the fortifications of Valetta, amazing as these are. The whole island appears to be subdivided, by walls, into innumerable little properties, of not more than an acre or two in extent. Nothing that approximates to the definition of a tree is to be descried within the whole range of view, form the highest watch-tower on the battlements of the city. The appearance of the landscape, so destitute of refreshing green, so intersected with stone walls, every where studded with churches crowned with domes, and with the flat-roofed and windowless cottages of the peasants, is not to be previously conceived. To me, it constantly suggested the idea of a great cemetery, subdivided into family portions, and crowded with tombs and mausoleums. Malta has, in fact, reached that point of cultivation and population, which a wrong-headed disciple of Maltus would be apt to consider as affording the most melancholy subject of reflection. Every inch is tilled, and yet the produce has long been inadequate to the maintenance of the inhabitants; notwithstanding which, the very labouring class of people are still so inconsiderate as to marry and beget children, as merrily as if they had all sinecures. Cows were long ago expelled; and the frugal-feeding goat supplied a competency of milk till the English came; but these epicures had again recalled these huge vegetable-devouring creatures; and, in the year 1908, I was told, that there were three milch cows in the island of Malta! As a compensation, however, for the provender of the cows, our countrymen have introduced the cultivation of potatoes.

Using the hard land, 1792

LOUIS DE BOISGELIN

The ground in Malta is never suffered to remain uncultivated, but constantly sown every year. Each season yields its peculiar crop, and the produce is abundant.

~

The colour of the soil varies in the different districts of Malta, and is seldom more than one foot deep above the surface of the rock. It is irrigated chiefly by the night dew; but the rock, being porous, retains and keeps the ground constantly fresh. The earth is always removed once in ten years, in order to clear the rock of a thick crust, which forms and prevents the moisture from sufficiently penetrating.

When the ground is properly prepared, it produces, the first year, water-melons and garden plants; the next, an excellent fruit, which is preserved during the winter and distinguished by the name of melons; and afterwards barley, the straw of which furnishes fodder for the cattle. The ground is ploughed the third year, and planted with cotton; the fourth sown with corn. The land afterwards yields these different crops alternately; but care is always taken to prepare the ground, particularly the cotton-tree is to come into bearing, when it is necessary to reduce the earth into a kind of powder.

~

Each field is enclosed with walls to shelter the different plants from the effects of the wind, rain and storms, during the spring and autumn.

What may be called the country, 1844

WILLIAM MAKEPEACE THACKERAY

Although Thackeray's two visits to Malta—as he went East and then returned on his way back to Britain—were brief, he found time for 'a drive into what may be called the country'.

The country, where the fields are rocks, and the hedges are stones. I passed by the stone gardens of the Florian and wondered at the stone villages and churches rising everywhere among the stony hills. Handsome villas were passed everywhere and we drove for a long distance along the sides of an aqueduct – quite a royal work of the Caravaggio in gold armour, the Grand Master De Vignacourt.* A most agreeable contrast to the arid rocks of the general scenery, was the garden of the governor's country house, with the orange trees and water, its beautiful golden grapes, luxuriant flowers and thick cool shrubberies. The eye longs for this sort of refreshment, after being seared with the other Malta, as Malta was after the sea.

The domestic animals of Malta, 1860

ANDREW ADAMS

The domesticated animals of Malta, more especially cattle, sheep and goats, deserve notice. The native cattle and sheep of the islands being few, and belonging to the poorer classes, what between constant interbreeding, and no selection whatsoever, there is a marked deterioration of race; thus the cattle are all fawn-coloured, tall, with gaunt, lanky bodies, and large bony limbs, and precisely the same appearance characterize the sheep. Only sufficient bulls and rams are preserved to propagate the race, the cows being kept for the combined purposes of labour and any little milk their small udders may supply. The sheep and goats are the chief milk producers, the latter participating to a great extent in the physical characters of the former. Nowhere else, however, are goats to be seen with more enormously developed udders, thus affording a good example of constant use in

---

* He refers to the portrait of De Vignacourt by Caravaggio in the Palace.

enlarging organs. I have seen their udders so exaggerated as to trail on the ground during progression. A good milk goat will furnish one-third of a gallon of milk at one milking.

The planting of the garden, 1806

GEORGE, VISCOUNT VALENTIA

The Maltese, under the protection of the British flag, are rapidly rising in prosperity, by the success of their commercial speculations [which he believed to have been discouraged by the Knights and the French], and every inch of their little island will soon be cultivated like a garden. Sir Alexander Ball has wisely established a botanic garden, and actively exerts himself to procure every article which he thinks will flourish, and add to the comfort or the luxury of the inhabitants.

Another garden visited, 1804

SAMUEL TAYLOR COLERIDGE

Coleridge's entry in his Notebook for 22 April, Tuesday morning, extends this picture. The month was actually May. San Antonio is now the principal residence of the President of Malta; the gardens are open free to the public every day until sunset. The house was built in 1625 as the country house of the sybaritic French Grand Master Antoine de Paule. Here, during the summer of 1810, the affair of Lady Hester Stanhope and her lover, Michael Bruce, ripened.

Was on horseback and rode to St. Antonio. Fields with walls (parallel) to keep the Soil from the rains – mere desolation seemingly, & yet it is fertile. St. Antonio a pleasant Country House, with a fine but unshaded Garden, save among the low Orange and Lemon Trees, still thick with Fruit on many of the Trees, Fruit ripe, blossoms, & the next years Fruit – Pepper Tree very beautiful & the Locust Tree not amiss.

Colours and perfume in a garden, 1929

ELIZABETH SCHERMERHORN

Of all the beautiful gardens, public or private, for which Malta is famed – hidden jealously away, many of them in mean, narrow streets behind high, shabby walls – the loveliest are the gardens of St Antonio – surrounding the villa of Grand Master de Paule, about four miles out of Valletta. From a white, empty street that winds between yellow walls and blue-green doors, pass cosy villinos buried in flowers, a low, dark vaulted passage leads to a terraced parterre, overlooked by the stately loggia and tower of the villa, with glimpses through arched openings in the wall of a spacious courtyard draped with jasmine and honeysuckle, with long, pale tassels of dropping pepper trees and gaudy fan-shaped splashes of pink and crimson bourgainvillia. Through the elegant gateway at the bottom of this spacious court the carriages of Grand Master de Paule's guests used to enter and at the great stone basin, ornamented with the peacock and stars of his Arms, the horses were watered; and the grooms of the Grand Crosses sunned themselves on the stone benches that stretch along the enclosing walls.

Those glistening groves of orange-trees whose fragrance is wafted through the grilled openings of the tunnel bear the far-famed Luscious fruit which it was the Grand Master's pleasure to present to the Sovereigns of Europe, still reckoned the finest in the world. In the Eighteenth Century the buildings formed from it have remained perfect for centuries. From its being so easily cut, the buildings are much and beautifully ornamented with tasteful carving. The entire sides of the church of St John is made of this stone, carved so that the figures stand out in relief and are gilt, with the ground work painted blue, having the finest effect imaginable.

Following the plough, 1972

NIGEL DENNIS

...The spluttering little rotary hoe seems to have been invented precisely for these tiny fields. It replaces the children who have fled to the factories and hotels and does the week's work of six daughters in half a morning. It is the greatest boon that has come to the Maltese farmer since Roman days, and even the most stubborn enemy of progress would not deny the farmer his gift. Work on those hot, stony fields is hard and exhausting; the old plough is little more than an extension of the farmer's own arm and he must use one hand to control his yoke-animals, stopping and turning them every half-minute in those minute spaces. One must be very romantically minded to find beauty in so much bestial effort and to deplore the arrival of the efficient little machine.

Pollution by plastic, 1972

NIGEL DENNIS

The British contribution to rural ugliness has been immense, and extremely well received; the rusty coils of barbed wire discarded by the soldier are laid proudly on top of field walls by the farmer; backed by a hedge of prickly pear, and intermingled with broken beer bottles, they would make any Turk hesitate to ravish the inhabitants. Old oil-drums are also immensely popular; in an island that has no wood, a row of upended drums makes an excellent gate, easily rolled aside when the farmer himself wants to use the roadway; when well rusted, they can also be bashed flat and worked in with barbed wire and broken glass on the wall tops. One exceptionally beautiful area in the south-east of the island has been devoted exclusively to the leavings of the Tin Age; rusting tins, numbering millions, serve as a broad, brown verge to some two or three miles of cart-roads. The Plastic Age, which we are now entering, has already made a sizeable contribution to the landscape, but its bloated containers, toilet accessories, and armless dolls have far to go before they overwhelm the honest tin.

A ride, 1843

ELLIOT WARBURTON

Leaving La Valetta for Citta Vecchia, we passed over and through fortifications of extraordinary strength, consisting principally of vast excavations made in the solid rock. The pretty gardens of Florian partly shelter the open space between these and the outer lines of fortifications.

Thence we passed through what would be the dreariest country I ever beheld but for the brilliant sunshine always sailing over it. Scarcely a particle of vegetation shaded the brown burning rock. Almost all the soil upon the island had been brought from Sicily, and is retained in little trays or shelves of terraces, built up with dull grey stones.

We rode by the side of a well-built aqueduct, by which Valetta derives its supply of fresh water, except whatever may be caught and contained in tanks within the walls.

The hot glare of the place, 1846

WILLIAM MAKEPEACE THACKERAY

We took a drive into what may be called the country: where the fields are rocks, and the hedges are stones – passing by the stone gardens of the Florian, and wondering at the number and handsomeness of the villages and churches rising everywhere among the stony hills. Handsome villas were passed everywhere, and we drove for a long distance along the sides of an aqueduct, quite a royal work of the Caravaggio* in gold armour, the grand master de Vignacourt. A most agreeable contrast to the arid rocks of the general scenery, was the garden of the governor's country house...

The land becomes the place, 1843

SARAH HAIGHT

The Island furnishes from its own rocky foundations beautiful building materials of yellow limestone, so soft that it may be cut with an axe or hatchet into blocks, and almost carved with a pen-knife, yet so durable that they contained seven hundred orange trees and one thousand lemon trees, and the terrace was "covered with strawberries producing three crops a year." The air is languid with the heavy

---

* He refers to the portrait of the Grand Master

perfume of strong-scented flowers, and faint with orange blossoms and roses; and something of a pensive wistfulness of old Moorish gardens lingers about Paule's fair pleasance, where, beneath the drooping fringes of glossy palms and sweet thickets of roses, other, and yet other, gardens are half-revealed between wreathed arches and vine-smothered walls; and the dark quiet vistas end in a crumbling fountain, or a softly dripping stone basin, or a round, quiet pool where swans "float double".

Another garden visited, 1804

SAMUEL TAYLOR COLERIDGE

Coleridge called on General Valetta at his country house, just outside the city gates, near the end of the Botanic Gardens.

General V's the pleasantest place I have ever been here, the multitude of small Gardens & Orangeries among the huge Masses of fortifications, many of them seeming almost as thick as the Gardens inclosed by them are broad. – Pomegranate in beautiful scarlet, Flower under a Bridge over a dry Ditch, saw the largest Prickly Pear elk horns for Trunk, & then its leaves, but go & look & look. Hard rain we sheltered in the Botanic Garden, yet reached home not unwetted ...

Wed. Morning July 11th *[Coleridge having slept at St. Julian's walked back in the dawn and observed and noted some of the stranger plants of the island.]*

The Locust Tree and Fruit deepest verdure, most efficient shade of any but the Tree all made up of branches, like Ivy, these branches oddly bossed or scabbed, looks as if meant to be a climber, and to stand up per se only by compulsion – The fruit looks exactly like the pods of the Scarlet Bean when grown to their full size; and it is a pod, but full of a austere dulcacid Juice, that reminds me of a harsh Pear. These Pods grow out of the Branches, out of the very *wood* of the Tree, at the bottom of each of these twisted upright branches, in a large Assemblage – Pomegranate, prickly pear, pepper tree, Oleander, Date Tree (with its Wheel of Plumage a complete circle including the enclosed part of the Stem) Myrtle Bowers, Arbour of a scented Butterfly-flower...

ONCE ASHORE

Not all who arrived could land. Malta was until 1843 a quarantine island and travellers from the East were put straight into 'pratique':* either kept on their ship—with a yellow warning flag flying—or sent to isolation in the Lazaretto rather than into the fun and flurry of Valletta. Isabella Romer, coming from England, was relieved to be ashore at all in 1845. The *Government Gazette* laid down, in 1828, the rules for shipping in Malta. Reverend Charles Swan's ship was in quarantine for only a week—others were held far longer.

The Lazaretto still stands on Manoel Island in Msida Creek, its graceful arcaded frontage facing toward Valletta. It is an important historic site and one hopes it will be preserved as such. By the mid eighteenth century up to 1,000 people could be accommodated there, although not all in the comfort which our travellers enjoyed. The island was used as an isolation hospital up until 1936. John Howard, the great prison reformer, was one of the travellers who went straight into quarantine in 1786; he studied the arrangement with an expert eye. Lord Valentia was in the Lazaretto in 1806, and Sir Walter Scott, though only briefly, in 1831. Samuel Bevan made the most of the experience in 1830. The New Yorker Sarah Haight took the whole matter more seriously. William Eton doubted the effectiveness of quarantine as early as 1809. Quarantine was completely ended by mid-century and Murray's Guide of 1873 gave advice for those arriving that did not include it.

Once fully ashore, John Galt described the hostelries of Valletta in 1812; as did Evelyn Waugh in 1929—with great satisfaction. In 1804 Samuel Taylor Coleridge noted his first impressions.

---

* Pratique—a term used in southern Europe from *c*.1609 indicating cleared to communicate with the port of landing.

Regulations, February 1828

MALTA GOVERNMENT GAZETTE

III Every merchant ship or vessel entering either of the Harbours, as above, shall become liable to the payment of all Port charges, on receiving on board or landing any article or passenger, or on performing any operation calling for the adjustment of her papers.

IV All merchant ships and vessels, in pratique, entering the Great Harbour of Valletta, with an intention to avail themselves of the exemption from the payment of Port Charges, shall be bound to anchor in such place as may be pointed out by the Department of the Intendant of Marine Police, and be subject to such orders and restrictions, during their stay in Port, as Government may be pleased to impose, through the said department of Collector of Customs.

All withheld, 1828

REVEREND CHARLES SWAN

Charles Swan was chaplain to HMS Cambrian during her service in the Mediterranean 1825–6, and visited Malta three times, warming to the country more on each visit.

Tuesday evening, 8th March 1825. Arrived at Malta, that 'military hot-house', as it has been, not inaptly called. The appearance which it presents from the sea is always new and inviting. We had today rather a different aspect, and I thought La Valetta resembled a town chiselled out of the rock, to which the skilful hand of the lapicide had just given the finishing touch. Malta is famous for vases cut from the same soft porous stone; and I could easily have fancied that the clean yellow cast of the houses and churches, rising over this most precipitous part of the island, was devised by a sculptor, and executed con amore!

Tuesday 15th March, 1825. We were released from quarantine – a most joyful circumstance. To be cooped up in our 'winged citadel' at sea is nothing; we expect no other, and our minds are made up to the endurance; but to be so imprisoned in harbour, with the prospect of an augmented society before us – with the power of roaming at pleasure from place to place – "from flower to flower", just as inclination prompts; all in sight, yet all withheld, is realising the fable of Tarantulus, and tempting us to wish the right honourable Board of Health a hearty ducking!

Communications from quarantine, 1840

DAVID L. RICHARDSON

We started from Alexandria on board the *Oriental* on the 24th and reached Malta on the 28th. As we hoisted the yellow flag, we were not permitted to land anywhere but at the lazaretto. The lazaretto is a barrack-like building near the shore. Articles were brought there for sale, and the sellers were divided from the purchasers by a single bar or rail, which it would have been easy to leap over or creep under. It was like a bazaar or a fair. Fruit, ices, paintings, canary birds, lap-dogs, and all sorts of nic-nacs were temptingly displayed before us. We were allowed to handle gold and silver ornaments, (amongst which were innumerable Maltese crosses, beautifully worked) and to return if disapproved of; but other articles we were compelled to keep or pay for if we laid our fingers on them. I could not understand the reason of the exemption in favour of gold or silver ornaments, when it was necessary to pass gold and silver money through vinegar and water, and curious stones and other hard and polished materials were carefully kept from all contact with non-purchasers. There was an odd inconsistency too in the way in which the jewellers presented and received back their goods. They presented them to us with a pair of tongs, but on receiving them back with the tongs in the right hand, they dropped them carelessly from the tongs into the left hand, and re-arranged them on their shop-board.

It excited in us a curious feeling to find ourselves each marked and suspected people, and to know that strangers were so horrified at our touch. It was enough to convince a hypochondriac that the plague was in his blood.

The Lazaretto of Malta, April 1786

JOHN HOWARD

Most travellers coming in from Egypt and the Levant had to spend weeks in quarantine, isolated as far as possible from the island. This quarantine allowed them to cross from the East into Europe. The British prison reformer John Howard spent two years visiting prisons and places of confinement in Europe and wrote a substantial report comparing conditions in different places.

At Malta there are two types of quarantine performed: one by ships with clean bills of health, and the other by ships with foul bills. The first, called the petty quarantine, lasts eighteen days, and the ships which perform it lie at the entrance of the port near the health office. (There were arrangements for provisioning and for crews to converse with their friends with "two soldiers stationed to prevent improper communication".) At a little distance there was a church, situated on high ground, and intended for the accommodation of the persons who perform this quarantine.

The other, called the great quarantine, is performed in a lazaretto, which is situated on a peninsula near the city. It was not a convenient building: "too close to admit of proper ventilation of cotton and other merchandise. It has sixteen rooms on two floors. On the higher floor there are eight, which open onto a balcony and have opposite windows, but all were dirty".

In the other part of this building there are two courts, with rooms and sheds much more convenient for the passengers and airy for merchandise. Two other buildings and a chapel are just begun, and these erections when finished, will make the lazaretto capable of allowing a proper separation of the cargoes of six or seven ships on the quay together.

At the end of the lazaretto is a large court, with stone troughs for beasts with often come from the Barbary coast. At the upper part of this court, on a pleasant rising ground, there are several large and good sheds, with stone mangers, and two or three rooms over them.

There is here a burying ground, where they seemed to have some recent burials, and also a place for burning the bodies of such that die of the plague.

✳

Into a Spanish palace, 1831

SIR WALTER SCOTT

Sir Walter Scott was held unusually in quarantine on his way to the East because of a cholera outbreak in Britain.

22 Tuesday. Today we entered Malta harbour and to Quarantine which is here very strict; we are condemned by the board of Quarantine to ten days imprisonment or sequestration and go in the Barham's boat to our place of confinement built by a Grand Master named Manuel for a palace for himself and his retinue.

It is spacious and splendid but not comfortable, the rooms connected out of one into another by an arcade into which they all open and which forms a delightful walk. If I was to live here a sufficient time I think I could fit the apartments up so as to be handsome and even imposing but at the present they are only kept as barracks for the infirmary or Lazaretto. A great number of friends come to see us who are not allowed to approach nearer than a yard. This, as the whole affair, is a farce, is ridiculous enough. We are guarded by the officers of health in a peculiar sort of livery or uniform with yellow necks who skip up and down with every man that stirs ...

Murray's Guide to Lazaretto life, 1847

JOHN GARDNER WILKINSON

Many travellers coming from the East and planning to travel across Europe chose to stop at Malta—finding quarantine there 'less irksome than in most places'. Passengers were collected on arrival from their steamer and transferred to the Lazaretto.

When numerous, there is often a scramble for rooms, and two people are put in the same bedroom. A sitting room is not given except as a favour, or when there are few passengers, but it is not refused to parties of five or more who intend to dine together. *[Arrangements could be made for the hire of servants who then joined their employer in quarantine.]* The necessity of a servant is very evident, when it is remembered that no guardian is allowed to render the stranger any services beyond those demanded by lazaretto duties, and there is no one to bring him a drop of water. This is sufficiently explained in the quarantine regulations...

* In the lazaretto each passenger will be provided with two chairs, a table, and a wooden bedstead, for which no charges are made; but any damages done by the passengers to the apartments or furniture is to be made good by them before pratique.

* All letters and parcels, or other effects brought by passengers, must be given up, in order that they may be fumigated or depurated separately from them as the occasion may require...

* All cases of sickness must be reported immediately by the physician to the lazaretto, after which official visit passengers are at liberty to avail themselves of any medical attendance they may think proper.

The Murray's Guide listed the meals offered in the Lazaretto and the prices for such meals. Passengers were supplied with table linen and dinner services, but had to pay for any item missing or broken, or in any manner destroyed. An important warning was about contact with other people.

Great care must be taken to avoid touching any one not in quarantine, as he would be condemned to pass the same number of days in the lazaretto as the person so compromising him, who would have to pay all the expenses ... Equal care should be taken not to come in contact with any new comer, ...as the person touched would be doomed to an additional imprisonment, or the same number of days that the other had still to keep quarantine.

When the quarantine term was over, one could, on taking pratique, send your things down to a boat, and across the harbour to the Marsa Muchett stairs, from which they will be carried by porters to the hotel.

✳

The Lazaretto today and yesterday, 1965

PETER MCGREGOR EADIE

A bridge on the right leads to Manoel Island, where Fort Manoel, built by the Tigné and de Mondion in 1723–32 for Grand Master Manoel de Vilhena, was designed for a garrison of 500 men. Here in 1800 the French garrison was interned until (after the Treaty of Amiens) the men were returned to France in British ships. The island, previously called Bishop Island, was first used as a quarantine station by the Knight, who erected an infectious disease hospital, the Lazaretto of San Rocco, before 1643, much of which still stands. Its graceful arcaded frontage on the sea makes a familiar landmark from the ramparts of Valletta.

Into the Lazaretto, 1806

GEORGE, VISCOUNT VALENTIA

Viscount Valentia and his companion, Henry Salt, had been four and a half years away from home on a great tour of South Africa, India, Ceylon, Abyssinia, the Red Sea region and Egypt and were eager to reach Malta on their way home. Caught by both wind and calms, their journey was frustrating and sometimes disagreeable, and they were greatly relieved to make port in June 1806. They climbed from the ship into a boat with their belongings and were towed by another boat to the 'Quarantini'.

We took up our abode in several very lofty stone apartments, with large windows looking over the harbour. The whole building is of the same materials, and surrounds a quadrangle; it is built on solid rock, with a flight of steps down to the water, and is kept exceedingly clean. The lower storey is used to receive goods that are unclean.

They were sentenced by the Board of Health to twenty days in the Lazaretto, which might be relaxed 'if we all continued well'. For a personage of such rank, the rules anyway were relaxed.

The Governor and many other gentlemen paid us visits in the presence of an officer, whose duty it was to take care that they did not touch us, nor any article belonging to us that could communicate infection.

With books and newspapers we were plentifully supplied, and the luxuries of ice and fruit, to which we had long been strangers, assisted in consoling us for the want of permission to visit the town.

Days in the Lazaretto, 1840

SAMUEL BEVAN

Samuel Bevan was a lively young man, with a very positive attitude to the adventures he met in his work in Egypt, helping to improve the Overland Route to India, and in his travels in Europe on his return. Time lost in the Lazaretto was all part of the adventure.

The first approach of the Lazaretto is by no means pleasing to one who knows that he must there undergo a three week imprisonment, but I have often heard it affirmed, and can in my own case bear ample testimony, to the truth of the assertion, that under ordinary circumstances, the terms of pratique may prove a great enjoyment. Of course, much depends upon the chance of the persons with whom you associate, but it would be strange indeed if, among the large and mixed party thus thrown together, there were not some one more gifted than the rest with the power and will to amuse and instruct his companions, whilst for the development of character, few places are better situated than Fort Manoel.

Our steamer's boats landed us and our baggage at the stairs; from whence we were escorted, by our guardians, through a formidable sort of fortification and across a large quadrangle, to an opposite building, where we were all shown into a series of empty rooms and required to make our selection. I found one in the angle of the building, containing an iron bedstead and table, and no sooner had I thrown my bag upon the brick floor, in token of right of possession, than a functionary from below put into my hand the price current of the furniture-broker of the Lazaretto, who undertakes to supply, for a trifling sum, the wherewithal to furnish the chamber.

Having made my selection, I was next waited upon by a cuisinier of the establishment, who likewise solicited my patronage. I got rid of him by ordering dinner. Then my own particular guardian arrived (and went through all his belongings most minutely).

The dinner served was disappointing and Bevan sent out for hampers, as did others; and by dining with each other the inhabitants supplemented the fare.

Our walks and rambles were necessarily very limited being confined to the ramparts and fortifications which surrounded us, and the spacious courtyard in front of the Lazaretto. We had books from Muir's Library to read, and, as Murray (guidebook) says, 'drawings to finish and journals to fetch up', and these resources occupied the hours of daylight, whilst our evenings passed away around the tea-table of one or other of our company, either in social chat, and the relation of bygone experience, or in the enjoyment of embryo tales and poems from the portfolio of one of our party who has since given them to the world.

Inspection and views, 1842

SARAH HAIGHT

After a terrible and 'sickening' journey from Navarino, the American traveller Sarah Haight, 'a Lady of New York', was more than usually cheered by the cry of 'Land ahead!' as numerous sails began to dot the horizon, 'accumulating rapidly as we neared our harbour'. They were soon installed in Fort Manoel, the Lazaretto.

We had scarce taken possession of our apartments in Fort Manoel, here we were visited by the guardians, who required us to take everything out of our trunks, bags and boxes, and spread them on wooden frames, given us for the purpose. The next morning another came to see that it was done, and to place his hands on each article, to imbibe any infection they might contain; after this, we were left to amuse ourselves as we could best find ways and means.

I took my Bible, turned to the Acts of the Apostles, and read from the twenty-third to the twenty-eight chapter, where is given the account of St Paul's being made prisoner at Jerusalem, his appeal as a Roman to Caesar, his speech before Agrippa, and his voyage from Caesarea, and his shipwreck on the island of Melita (Malta), every word of which seems as much more impressive after journeying, as we have done, his track along the sea.

*Sarah amused herself gazing from the window of the Lazaretto or climbing
higher to extend her view.*

On our left was a small but safer and pretty harbour where vessels
from the north flee for shelter from the coming storm, guarded on one
side by Fort Tigne, and on the other by our residence, Fort Manoela.
These also guard the quarantine harbour on our right, which we look
down upon from the bastions, and can almost grasp the yellow flags
that are fluttering from the masts of many vessels lying quietly in its
basin. ...Vessels of all kinds are constantly passing and re-passing and
it is delightful to watch the huge waves, way off in the open sea, and
see them all roll onward till they dash and break themselves (on the
rocky shore).

The practicalities of the place, 1873
MURRAY'S GUIDE TO EGYPT

*By the early 1870s the quarantine of incoming passengers had been lifted and
travellers who had read of the experience were relieved to find they did not
have to undergo this restraint.*

If on arriving at Malta you intend staying there for any time, either in
going to or returning from Egypt, and have to land any luggage, it is
agreeable to find there is no custom-house examination; all you have
to do is to hire a boat as soon as the officer from the Board of Health
has pronounced the steamer to be in pratique.

In returning to Malta from Egypt there is no longer any quarantine,
except that when cholera happens to be in Egypt travellers are subject
to a quarantine of 15 days.

✳

Ashore at last, 1846

ISABELLA ROMER

Mrs. Romer was coming from Europe, so was not delayed in the Lazaretto, but was still very glad to be ashore.

Safely landed at Valletta! Let those who suffer physically and morally in the same degree that I do at sea imagine the delightful contrast of finding oneself in the clean, spacious, airy rooms of a Malta Hotel, after being 'cabined, cribbed, confined', three mortal days and nights in the berth of a steamer, even although that steamer be a first class English Mail packet ... But, alas! Such are the absorbing effects of sea-sickness, that nothing is thought of or the time being, but one's own selfish quota of sufferings, and it is only when they are over, that one remembers gratefully, how much was done to alleviate them.

Where to stay, 1812

JOHN GALT

There was no tolerable hotel in Malta while I happened to be there; but one, sufficiently spacious, was preparing, and has since, I understand, been opened. The house, in which I obtained lodgings had formerly been a tavern; but the owner was induced to give it up for a singular reason.

"When it was an inn," said the waiter, a Sicilian who spoke English, "it was so full of noises, that there was no living in it. The officers of the men of war came making noises. They went to the play, and came back making noises. Then there were the stranger gentlemen, all English, making noises – sitting up in the night, singing, roaring, jumping on the tables, breaking glasses. O, my God! What terrible noises! So we put down the sign from the wall; and, if there be less money now, we have no noises."

First impressions from his notebook, 1804

SAMUEL TAYLOR COLERIDGE

Saturday, April 19th [in fact it was May]. One's first feeling is that all is strange, very strange; & when you being to understand a little of the meaning and uses of the massy endless walls and defiles, then you feel & perceive that it is very wonderful. – A city all of freestone, all the houses looking new, like Bath; all with flat roofs, the Streets all strait & at right angles to each other; but many of them exceedingly steep, none quite level; of the steep Streets some all stepped with a smooth artificial Stone, some having the footpath on each side of stone steps, the middle left for carriages; lines of fortification, fosses, Bastions, Curtains, &c &c endless, endless – with gardens or Bowling Grounds below the high ones; for it is all height and depth – you can walk no where without having whispers of Suicide, toy of desperation. Explosive Cries of the Maltese venders [sic] – shot up, and bulky noises, sudden and violent. The inhabitants very dark, some almost black, but straight clean limbed lively active – cannot speak in praise of their cleanliness – Children very fair. Women from the use of the Faldettoe or cloak hooding their Heads as Women in England in a shower throw over their aprons, & from the use of always holding it down to one side of the face, all have a permanent languishing way of holding their heads one way – picturesque enough, as expressive of a transient emotion; but shockingly insipid, all & always. –

All the mystery and glamour of the East, 1917

VERA BRITTAIN

Vera Brittain came to Malta as a nurse during the First World War. She had been ill on the journey but recovered before she landed.

At first I thought I should hate Malta, as, when I came in feeling so ill, I thought I had never in the world heard so many bells clanging (afterwards it turned out to be a special feast day) or seen such a glare. But its attraction grows, especially at sunset & sunrise, when the domes & towers are violet-grey & softened with mist, & the skies more wonderful than anything I have ever seen. The tiring glare all day is due to the extreme whiteness of the soil, of roads & cliffs. There are of course no trees here to provide shade, – only clumps of tropical shrubs such as cactus, prickly pear, palms and eucalyptus. As soon as the swift night has fallen, this wonderful place seems to hold all the mystery & glamour of the East, though really it is only the fringe of it.

The Great Britain Hotel, 1929

EVELYN WAUGH

Evelyn Waugh, returning from a pleasure cruise of the Eastern Mediterranean, had picked up ship in Egypt with passengers returning on leave from India.

Just before lunch on the third morning, we came in sight of Malta. There was some delay about landing because one of the passengers had developed chicken-pox. There was only one other passenger disembarking... We went ashore in a lighter and landed at the Custom House. Here I was met by two young men, both short, swarthy, and vivacious, and each wearing a peaked cap above a shiny English suit. [*These were the representatives of two hotels; both were eager for his business. Waugh chose the Great Britain.*]

The porter of the Great Britain chartered two little horse-carriages, conducted me to one, and sat with the luggage in the other. There were low, fringed canopies over our heads so it was impossible to see out very much. I was aware of a long and precipitous ascent, with many corners to turn. At some of these I got a glimpse of a baroque shrine, at others a sudden bird's-eye view of the Grand Harbour, full of shipping, with fortifications beyond. We went up and round, along a broad street of shops and more important doorways... We turned off down a narrow side street and stopped at the little iron and glass porch of the Great Britain Hotel. A little dark passage led into a little dark lounge, furnished like an English saloon bar, with imitation leather arm-chairs, bowls of aspidistra on fumed oak stands, metal-topped tables, and tables with plush coverings, Benares brass work, framed photographs, and ashtrays stamped with the trade-marks of various brands of whisky and gin... I ascended, storey by storey, to my bedroom... The food at the Great Britain was good; the servants particularly willing and engaging. One evening being tired and busy, I decided to dine in my room. At Mena House [*by the Pyramids, near Cairo*], where there were hosts of servants and a lift, the dinner was brought up in one load and left outside the door; at the Great Britain every course was carried separately up three flights of stairs by the panting but smiling valet de chambre.

SOME HISTORY

To understand the Malta of today one needs at least an overview of her past, and particularly of her period as host to the Knights Hospitaller of St. John—the Knights of Malta—that marks the land and particularly the historic towns. Reverend William Loftie gave a quick glimpse of the impact of this long occupation.

Malta's history is far more significant than its tiny size might lead one to suppose. It attracted invader-occupiers over the centuries from at first the Phoenician colonies from about 1500 BC, with the Romans taking possession from the second Punic War in 218 BC. Then in the sixth century the Byzantines moved in, but made little impact. In AD 870 the Arabs conquered the islands. They brought Islam, technology, culture and an impact on the language. The Normans, under Roger of Sicily, came in 1091 and gained ownership of a kind; they were happy to live alongside Islam until all Muslims were expelled from the island in 1224.

But, as Henry James Forman commented in 1927, the Phoenicians in 1500 BC were 'mere parvenus'. The temples of Tarxien, then newly discovered, pre-dated them by more than 1,500 years—and are perhaps the oldest stone built buildings in the world. Malta is an archaeologist's dream with human habitation resting upon human habitation. Elliot Warburton in 1831 descended into the Catacombs at Rabat and believed them to be of Phoenician origin—and found them grim. But they were still in use up to the fourth century AD.

The coming of the Knights Hospitallers—the last Crusaders—to Malta, when they fled Rhodes in 1530, linked the island to the greatest families and powers in Europe for the next 370 years. Malcolm Billings describes the impact of their building tradition on the face of Malta, leaving a wonderful sixteenth-century Renaissance city and palaces and forts across the island.

In 1565 Islam came to punish the Knights for their continuous harrying of the seas and Suleiman the Magnificent's empire. The Cross and the Koran again tangled in war. Francisco Balbi di Correggio, a foot soldier in the Knights' army, recorded each day of the siege in his journal, from the landing in May until their departure in September. Vainly Malta looked for external support, for none came, and in their triumph the Knights and the people of Malta could claim victory as their own.

But the Knights of Malta, as their title of Hospitaller suggests, were not only fighting men. From their original foundation they were Hospitallers: devoted to the care of pilgrims and the sick and poor. Their regulations defined this work, and the prison reformer John Howard saw the continuing evidence of their care in 1786.

Once the siege was over, the Knights set to creating the proudest surviving Renaissance city in the world, named in honour of their leader, La Valette. But without a real cause, the Knights foundered, as the artist W.H. Bartlett described, and fell prey to the needs of Napoleon for a staging post to Egypt in 1798. Vivant Denon, who had been an apparent 'tourist' in Malta two years earlier, watched as the Knights surrendered.

Louis de Boisgelin looked on with some dismay as the Knights were overrun by the revolutionary French—"these new Goths and Vandals" —and their treasures were carried off into apparent oblivion. In 1800 a British officer described the island prize, and Sir Ralph Abercromby, who would lead the British expeditionary force that ousted Napoleon from Egypt, spoke of the island as a valuable potential possession for Britain.

And so British occupation began, and lasted for a century and a half until independence in 1804. Samuel Taylor Coleridge, in Malta as secretary to the first British Governor, Sir Alexander Ball, and Admiral Horatio Nelson all summed up the importance of Malta in the Mediterranean of their day. Douglas Austin described the special relationship which Malta had to Britain – having become, in effect, a colony by choice, and thus an extension of Britain as a great naval base in the Mediterranean. As W.H. Bartlett commented in 1851, "even the most unmilitary eye" can recognise the obstacle that Malta presents to potential enemies.

Mrs. Elwood saw the relics of the Knights in 1826, and the Reverend William Loftie saw the first growth of democracy in 1879.

The impregnability of Malta was proved by its brave people through the second terrible siege, from the air, for three years from 1940: heroism recognised by the award of the George Cross to honour the island and her people. In 1965 independence came to the Maltese for almost the first time in history. It was not until 1979 that the last British military left, which, despite the substitution of the tourist industry, still shook the Maltese economy. Nowadays Malta enjoys a relatively high standard of living, due in large part to tourism (over a million visitors arrive each year), manufacturing and limestone extraction.

✳ MALTA UP TO THE SIEGE OF 1565 ✳

So much of interest, 1879

REVEREND WILLIAM LOFTIE

Now, Malta is a place full of interest for many different kinds of travellers. Soldiers may want to see the forts, artists to sketch the up and down stairs streets. The ordinary tourist even may have many things to see in the three little islands that form the group. He has read St. Paul and Josephus, and would visit the scene of the wreck of 'a certain ship of Alexandria'. He may have an interest in the history of orders and chivalry, and desire to examine St. Elmo, and fight over on the spot the famous siege of 1565. He has studied architecture, and would verify Mr. Ferguson's account of the wonderful dome of Mosta. If he is a botanist he may propose to judge for himself as to the genus of a so-called *Centaurea*, about which Linneans are in doubt. The language of the natives has not yet been successfully reduced to writing. The statistical problems offered by the thickly-populated islets are but half worked out. There are in short, few places of the same size in Europe – for the Maltese reckon themselves Europeans – in which so many objects of interest, social, political, geographical, or only picturesque, may be found; and the traveller easily makes up his mind to land...

Malta's military past, 1994

PETER DIETZ

The whole of urban Malta is a memorial to Malta's military past. The two most stirring events in Maltese history, the defeat of the Turkish Siege in 1565 and the resistance to the Italian and German attempts to bomb Malta into a state of helplessness in 1940–3, rank equally in the heroic story of the islands. The town of Valletta, built by the Knights of St. John after the siege of 1565, contains most of the important buildings and monuments of the period, including the Grand Master's Palace ... The Palace Armoury, where Thackeray's 'truculent little scimitar' is housed, the principal Auberges, the museums of the Cathedral, of Archaeology and of War, and the Manoel Theatre and the Malta Library, are all within easy walking distance of central Valetta. ... Although most of the buildings in the town were completed well after the Siege, they convey an impression, situated as they are within the massive fortifications designed to dissuade the Turks from another attack, of a city and a people continually at war or risk of war.

Malta powerless, 1789

VIVANT DENON

Malta became the emporium, and place of refreshment, for all European vessels trading in the Mediterranean, and fell successively under the power of every invader.

The new Neolithic, 1927

HENRY JAMES FORMAN

Forman and his companion were newly come from Sicily and found 'the whole island is literally a museum of antiquity and every step a classic memory. We were face to face with some of the earliest known beginnings of civilisation, and we adored the Neolithic!'

Hagiar Kim and Gigantia, remains of Phoenician temples vaguely reminiscent of Stonehenge, with immense upright slabs and monoliths, I am obliged to pass over. For what, after all, were the Phoenicians? Mere parvenus and upstarts. In Malta they date only to 1500 BC. But the newly discovered Stone Age temple in the suburb of Hal Tarxien (pronounced Tarsheen) is dated to at least 3000 BC, and is probably older.

The excavation was made during the war, when Malta was hermetically sealed. The world has scarcely heard of it as yet because archaeologists are still busy studying it. The excavation is barely finished. And the discovery is a romance of science.

In 1913, just before the war broke out, a peasant, digging his field, found some well-squared blocks of stone beneath the surface, only about two feet below. In July, 1915, when the war seemed to have settled down to a normal condition of existence, Professor Zammit of the Valletta Museum began digging, and to make the story brief, found, as he says, "three pairs of symmetrical apses, connected with each other by means of narrow passages, formed by large slabs placed on end." The floors of the ellipsoid rooms, which seemed to grow like leaves from the stem of the passageway, are paved with enormous flag-stones. All, all stone, everything in stone, cut with implements of stone and flint, chert and obsidian.

An altar stone in one of the largest of these rooms is elaborately carved with spiral ornaments, such as we often made on a pad absently while waiting for a telephone connection, or such as are familiar to keepers of lunatic asylums.

The altar stone is hollow, and the sacrificial knife of flint found there, the bones and skulls in the niches, and the cleverly concealed oracle room behind the sanctuary, dimly show the processes of religion in those distant days, when humanity was cave-dwelling and when even the celebrated 'vamp' Calypso inhabited a grotto de luxe, so different from her modern sisters in the films.

Into the Catacombs
and a city embalmed, 1831

ELLIOT WARBURTON

In the suburbs of Citta Vecchia, we entered a church where about a score of priests were chanting mass. At a beckon from our Maltese guide, one of them instantly abandoned his occupation, doffed his surplice, and accompanied us to the Catacombs: these are of considerable extent, and probably of Phoenician origin.

We groped our way with torches through long narrow passages, from which, on each side, opened crypts, hollowed out for the reception of the corpses. Some were made double, as if for the convenience of those who, even in death, would not be divided; some were cut into little cradles for dead children. Here and there were larger chambers with altars, and blood channels for sacrifice, or perhaps for washing the corpse. These corpses must have been embalmed, by-the-bye, or it would have been impossible for the living to enter this stifling labyrinth with their dead.

These Catacombs scarcely repay the trouble and the disagreeability of their examination, particularly to those who have seen the Catacombs of Rome and Syracuse. The deserted city of Citta Vecchia is much more interesting, and is indeed, as far as I know, unique.

You pass along unguarded fortifications of great strength, and enter, by a broken drawbridge, into a stately but profoundly silent city. The houses are handsome, and in good repair; they seem to want only inhabitants to be homes once more. The palaces are magnificent, and appear the more imposing from the deep silence that invests their mysterious-looking walls. Grass and rank weeds are growing in the streets that echo to your horse's tread; and the wind sighs among the lonely pillars and porticoes, with that wailing sound so peculiar to deserted places.

A gallop through history, 1879

REVEREND WILLIAM LOFTIE

Few countries have undergone so many changes of rulers. Phoenicians, Greeks, Carthaginians, Romans, Goths, and Arabs, all held it in turn before the close of the ninth century of our era. Since Roger the Norman in 1090 drove out the Moslems, the series of Christian dynasties has included German emperors, Aragonese kings, French princes, and Spanish dons. History records few stranger transactions than that by which in 1350 the islanders freed themselves from the grasp of Don Gonsalvo Monroi, to whom they had been pledged by King Martin of Sicily for 30,000 florins; but even by buying their own freedom and taking themselves out of pawn did they secure independence; and when in 1530 the Knights of Rhodes were seeking a new habitation, Malta was given up to them by Charles V, at the peppercorn rent of a falcon to the King or the Viceroy of Sicily.

For the first time in their existence, perhaps, the Maltese enjoyed the blessings of home rule under the sovereignty of the Grand Master, but we have no reason to suppose that they were satisfied with what was only a tyranny tempered by the Inquisition. Even Roger the Norman had respected the conscientious scruples of such Mohammedans as remained after his conquest; but the order of St. John enforced the strictest orthodoxy, and before the French expelled the Knights and the Inquisition with them, Malta had become what she is still, more completely Romish than Rome itself. Even the Grand Master fell under the terrible rule of the Dominicans, and a window is pointed out at a street close to St. John's Church, where executions took place, in sight of the crowd assembled in the adjacent square.

The French abolished the Inquisition as well as the Knights, but with that strangely short-sighted policy which has made them hated wherever they have come, in Egypt, in Syria, in Germany, as in Malta, they plundered the unhappy people and their churches to an incredible extent...

The English are not, however, very popular...

The Hospitallers before Malta, 1565

FRANCISCO BALBI DI CORREGGIO

For the purpose of this book, I have both condensed and built upon Francisco Balbi's account, but it can be read in its full original from the translation provided by his descendant and translated by Ernle Bradford in 1965.

After the kingdom of Jerusalem, Syria and Egypt fell into the hands of the enemy of our faith (that is the Muslims), it was made difficult for Christian pilgrims to visit the Holy Sepulchre in Jerusalem freely and, once inside the walls of the city, no one would give them food, drink or shelter. Traders from Amalfi in Italy, seeing their plight, petitioned to erect a hospice where Christian pilgrims could be received. Thus was created a body that became the Hospitallers and protectors of ill-treated Christians.

Linked to the hospice was a monastery dedicated to the Virgin, Sancta Maria Latina, and friars from the Order of St. Benedict of Monte Cassino (near Naples) were invited to minister to the church and hospice. The brotherhood persevered in this good work until it pleased God to deliver Jerusalem to the Crusader Godfrey of Bouillon in 1099.

On the death of the Custodian of the hospice in 1115, he was succeeded by Raymond of Puy, and he founded the Order of St. John according to the Augustinian canon, and became the first Grand Master. He introduced the black mantle with a white eight-pointed cross which the monks wore – and which would become the Maltese cross. The members of the Order were knights because they carried arms; they were brothers because of their love and charity and their holding of property in common.

Men of many nations enrolled in the Order to protect Christian pilgrims and escorted pilgrims in increasing numbers from the ports to Jerusalem. For this work they were granted the title of Knights of Jerusalem.

Hospitallers extended their caring role – though never abandoning it – to join in the defence of the "Kingdom". They were an elite corps, drawn from the noble families of Europe, who took religious vows. They were supported by more lowly serving brethren and mercenaries. Across Europe they had a network of religious houses to raise funds and recruits for their work in the East. Wealth flowed in... The Hospitallers were great builders. They, like the Knights Templar, built strings of castles to guard the routes to Palestine. Among the greatest were the huge castle at Marqab in Syria, which could accommodate thousands; the almost unaltered twelfth century Belvoir Castle on the edge of the Jordan valley, and, most famed of all, Crac des Chevallier, controlling access to the Orontes valley and the hinterland of Syria – possibly still the most impressive fortress in the world.

In 1187 Jerusalem was won again by Islam, ultimately by negotiation under the leadership of Saladin, and the Master of the Order of St. John was taken prisoner. The holy city was won back again with great loss of life, but finally lost in 1217 and "destroyed completely". However, through the following years of turmoil, the Hospitallers were both flourishing and powerful, until, in 1291, the Christians were driven out of Syria. The Order retired to Margat (one of their greatest castles) but had to retreat to Acre on the coast and from there, "unable to resist alone the onslaughts of the enemy", withdrew to Cyprus.

Grand Master Foulques de Villaret petitioned the Emperor of Constantinople for a base. He granted them the outlaws' island of Rhodes. They took it with difficulty in 1309 and held it, as the Knights of Rhodes. Over the years they were threatened and molested and in return attacked and molested from Rhodes and their one remaining castle near Boudrum. In 1480 a powerful attack and a three month siege of Rhodes by the Turks was abandoned. Later the Knights fought a great battle against the Sultan's fleet and scored a great victory.

The Order continued to grow richer. To strengthen and extend itself, it was divided into eight national-based *langues* or "tongues". In order of seniority they were Provence, Auvergne, France, Italy, Aragon, England, Germany and Castile with Portugal.

In 1453 Constantinople fell to the Turks. But the life of the Knights on Rhodes continued until 1522. At this time Philip Villiers de L'Isle-Adam was Grand Master; Suleiman the Magnificent was Sultan of the Turks. Suleiman sent a powerful force against Rhodes and, hearing of its imminent defeat, went to Rhodes himself. It took six months to overcome the Knights, but at last Suleiman succeeded.

The numbers of the Order had dwindled, but the remaining Knights and any Rhodians who wished to accompany them embarked and sailed for Crete, and then on to Sicily. Pope Clement VII, who had himself been a Hospitaller, granted them temporary residence at Viterbo. From there Grand Master de L'Isle-Adam went out to the Christian Princes of Europe to seek a new home. Emperor Charles V, moved by the plight of this Order, granted it the islands of Malta and Gozo, together with Tripolo (Barbary), "as the most suitable places whence to carry on their perpetual warfare against the Infidels". Their homage fee was to be a falcon which was to be presented annually to the Vice-Roy of Sicily.

In December 1522 Sultan Suleiman, "the Magnificent, the Law Giver", accepted the surrender of Rhodes from the Grand Master, Philip Villiers de L'Isle-Adam, with the comment: "It saddens me to cast this brave old man out of his home." He allowed the defeated Hospitallers to leave Rhodes with their dignity, their archive and their possessions. Among these were the bejewelled and mummified hand of St. John the Baptist, their greatest relic, acquired during their time in Rhodes. A young knight from Provence, Jean Parisot de la Valette, departed with them.

On 14 October 1530 Grand Master de L'Isle-Adam went to Malta with the whole of his Order and sent a governor to Tripoli.

The hierarchy and workings of the Order are described by Francisco Balbi in the first extract of the second half of Chapter 5. The descriptions of Malta provided by Louis de Boisgelin for the Knights are in Chapter 2.

MALTESE PROVERB

Better to rule devils than be ruled by angels.

The Knights in Malta from 1530

MALCOLM BILLINGS

In the autumn of 1530 the Knights Hospitaller of St. John set out for their new home on Malta. They settled in Birgu (now Vittoriosa) and Senglea. Vittoriosa's narrow winding streets still have some of the Order's original *auberges* or hostels for the young Knights tucked in between the houses and the shops of a typical Mediterranean town; they stand out, however, because of the typical Rhodian architectural details of the facades. The English *auberge* is one of those still standing. Built soon after 1530 out of the warm yellowish local stone, it has a balcony over the street, a circular window over the door and its distinctive heavy stone moulding around the windows survives as an architectural echo of Rhodes. In one small square, not far from the *auberges* of France and England, a convent of Benedictine nuns occupies the site of the Order's Hospital…

Walking around Vittoriosa and Senglea today, traces of sixteenth-century Malta are everywhere. The Knight's first conventual church of St. Lawrence has relics brought from Rhodes in its treasury, and on display in the oratory of St. Joseph are a hat and sword that were once worn by La Valette. The quays where the war galleys tied up in

Dockyard Creek are still there, and, overlooking the Grand Harbour, the fortress of St. Angelo, a round, flat-topped castle of enormous strength it squats like a heavyweight boxer on the end of the Vittoriosa peninsula. That was where the galley slaves were quartered at one time, in tunnels under the Fort. Looking across the water to the northern shore of the Grand Harbour, you can see the battlements of Fort St. Elmo – the scene of the Knight's heroic defence in the 1565 siege of Malta.

MALTESE PROVERBS

The greatest curse is to need help from others.

The new building should be rented to your enemy.

An English Knight, 1531

F.N. WESTON

The district around the Plain of Curmi has its place in Maltese history. In 1531 a Turkish force under the famous Corsair Dragut, landed at Marsamuscetto and swept inland, plundering and burning. An English Knight, Nicholas Upton, who was Turcopolier, or leader of the cavalry, collected 30 Knights and 400 Maltese horsemen and fell upon the Turks, who rallied on this plain; but he drove them back with great slaughter through Birchireara to their ships. This worthy Nicholas, however, though a gallant knight was very corpulent, and a day in the saddle under a tropical July sun combined with the weight of his armour was too much for him. As soon as the fighting was over he completely collapsed and died a few hours later. A suit of armour in the Palace Armoury (No. 11) dates from about this period, and from the girth might be that of Sir Nicholas.

Preparing for Siege, 1565

MALCOLM BILLINGS

Sultan Suleiman the Magnificent, master of an empire spreading from the Persian Gulf north to the Danube, sent his fleet against Malta in the spring of 1565. He was by then 71 years old, the same age as his opponent, Grand Master La Valette, whom he had chased from Rhodes 43 years before.

The Grand Master made sure that the forts of the Order and the main settlement on the shores of the Grand Harbour were packed with supplies and the necessities of war: water was carried and stored; the countryside was stripped of its produce; the wells polluted, and many old people, women and children were evacuated. Malta had battened down.

In mid-May, when invasion seemed hourly imminent, the 48th Grand Master of the Noble Order of the Knights of St. John of Jerusalem called together all his Brethren. It was the last opportunity that he would have to speak to them in general assembly. No one knew better than he that there were many present whom he would never address again.

La Valette speaks to the Knights, 1565

GRAND MASTER JEAN PARISOT DE LA VALETTE

"It is the great battle of the Cross and the Koran, which is now to be fought. A formidable army of infidels are on the point of investing our island. We, for our part, are the chosen soldiers of the Cross, and if Heaven requires the sacrifice of our lives, there can be no better occasion than this. Let us hasten then, my brothers, to the sacred altar. There we will renew our vows and obtain, by our Faith in the Sacred Sacrament, that contempt for death which alone can render us invincible."

✵

The call to arms, 1565

DUN KARM

The Maltese poet brought a terrifying vision of the attack to his readers.

The Turkish fleet, the most powerful of those times, charged with that army whose very name made monarchs tremble, armed with the most recent instruments of war and with all that the art of warfare demanded, besides whatever was required by the evil desires and powerful mind of Sultan Suleiman, who had sworn that he would sweep the Knights of St. John out of Malta, had appeared in unending columns on the pale horizon, advancing with billowing sails, towards this dear little island which is our homeland.

The summons worked like magic. Inside the cities the knights made themselves ready in a flash. In the country Maltese of every class to every part of the island looked once about them; they understood; they left their work just as it was, let go of these tools and an hour later appeared in bands with weapons in their hands marching towards the city to see what was afoot and to receive their due orders.

The forces of Suleiman, 1565

FRANCISCO BALBI DI CORREGGIO

Balbi recorded the number of troops who sailed for Malta:

6,000 Spahis, alle archers, commanded by a Sanjaz-Bey and his two lieutenants who are called Alabeys. Many more had reported for service but only the best were retained.

500 Spahis from Caramania under a Sanjaz-Bey.

6,000 Janizaries of the Sultan's bodyguard under a Janizar Aga, a lieutenant of the General of the Janizaries who never leaves the Sultan. They all carried firearms (arquebuses).

400 Adventures from Mytheline under a Sanjaz-Bey.

2,500 Spahis and

3,500 Adventurers form Rouania under a Sanjaz-Bey and a Alaybey.

4,000   Adventurers, all religious fanatics, most of whom had private means and could lead an idle life in or about their Mosques. The greatest number were dressed in white, and some wore the green turban (as descendants of Mohammed). These men had implored the Sultan to allow them to go and fight for their faith, believing that they would gain salvation if they die fighting.

6,000   Volunteers, seamen and corsairs, all differently armed. Many Jewish merchants joined the expedition with their goods and with money with which to buy Christian slaves.

The military force which sailed from the East to attack Malta consisted of 28,000 fighting men.

The Admiral too mustered his ships and his men. It is considered a safe estimate that, including the oarsmen, the volunteers, and also the Moors of Dragut, Pasha of Tripoli and Hassan of Algiers, the total number of fighting men who went against Malta was 48,000, not counting the sailors and camp followers.

GLOSSARY

Adventurers	Meaning freelance (carrying their own lance or arms freely) or mercenaries
Alle	All
Arquebus	Muzzle-loaded firearm
Bey	Chieftain
Corsair	Pirate
Janizary	Member of an elite military unit of the Turkish army
Spahi	Title given to cavalry units

The days, weeks and months of the siege, 1565

FRANCISCO BALBI DI CORREGGIO

From Francisco Balbi's journal of the Siege, these excerpts from May to September link together some significant events.

Friday, 18th May At dawn, the 18th May 1565, our watch at Saint Angelo, and also at St. Elmo, discovered the Turkish Fleet thirty miles distance towards the South-East. As soon as the Fleet was seen, the pre-arranged signal was given for the peasantry to take shelter within the

fortified places, and two guns were fired to warn the Old City and the Island of Gozo.

At this signal the people of the Island hastened to Birgu, bringing with them their children, their cattle and their goods.

The Turkish Fleet was making for Marsaxlokk – the Grand Master sent a thousand fighting men, infantry and cavalry to stop them landing. The Turkish Fleet changed course along the shore – the men followed intent on discouraging a landing.

A Neapolitan renegade escaped from the Turkish Fleet the next day and reported on their intentions: they had 50,000 fighting men and provisions for six months, much very heavy artillery with plentiful munitions of all kinds – but the Pashas were not in harmony which was considered a bad augury.

Inevitably the Turkish forces landed, despite strong opposition.

Friday, 25th May The enemy began to transport their heavy artillery from the fleet to St. Elmo. It was no light task, for the guns were heavy...the distance they had to cover was nine miles, and the ground was very rough and full of stones. The many labourers and the beasts of burden which the Maltese had abandoned in the country helped them over with their difficulties. From the Spur of St. Michael we could see ten or twelve bullocks harnessed to each piece, with many men pulling on the ropes.

The Grand Master ordered reinforcements to St. Elmo and when the Turks came upon St. Elmo, there were eight hundred fighting men within its walls.

The Grand Master sent them biscuits, wine, cheese, lard, vegetables, oil, and vinegar. For fresh meat there was the cattle that the peasants had brought into the ditch with them, and, as they were not able to take water from a pool which was near the fort, they put salt into it. He (the Grand Master) also sent powder, rope, fire-balls, and all that was required for the defence.

Sunday, 27th May The Turkish gun platforms on the height of St. Elmo were ready in all respects, and on this same night, they mounted the pieces they intended to bombard us with. They kept up a fusillade for a very long time, and when it was over, they fired their heavy guns which had been aimed during the day.

Thus the siege continued day and night into the long hot summer months.

Wednesday, 25th July From the 22nd, which was the day when the enemy began to bombard us everywhere ... their fire never stopped by day or night...

The 25th July being the feast of St. James, we felt sure that relief would come on that day...but when both the day and the night had passed and no relief had come, at a loss what to say so as to reassure the people, the Grand Master said publicly that he expected no help except from God who was our real mainstay, and had hitherto preserved us, and who would deliver us again from the hands of the enemies of His holy faith, and that we should derive confidence from him.

The Grand Master kept all on alert both by day and by night.

Many times the Turks came silently to make an assault, and, on being discovered, our bell tolled, causing them to retire without daring to assault because they knew we were on the alert and ready to receive them.

Although the works were battered by the bombardment, they did not show any great inclination to assault, warned as they were by their past experience when they had suffered so much in their land and sea experience.

In mid-September there was real battle between the forces, each seeking the best ground. At last the Knights were gaining.

Tuesday, 11th September On seeing his troops completely broken, Mustapha jumped from his horse and killed it. He then placed himself in front of his squadron to encourage his men and try to keep them in order. He sent word to the fleet to approach the shore so as to cover them with their guns and take him on board; for which purpose their boats were ready.

At this moment our tired troops charged once more into the Turks, and with such effect that neither Mustapha nor any officer could stop them in their flight. Those who could not get into the boats, threw themselves into the sea, and as they were wounded and tired, were drowned before they could reach the galleys.

Their galleys then put their prows to the shore while their artillery opened fire to cover the retreat.

The Knights estimated that on the day the total loss must have been more than 3000 and more than 4000 barrels full of water to be taken on board were broken.

When the Turks had embarked they stood off and waited till night. They then took in all the water they could, and, after despatching the corsairs of the West, sailed Eastwards.

The church bells rang, 1565

DUN KARM

One hundred and eleven times the sun rose and set, and every day it looked sadly down out of a smoke-laden sky upon the fearful battle which went on unremittingly, without any respite, without any mercy; upon flames of fire that flashed out of the mouths of the savage cannons; upon a hail of cannon balls, of stones, of arrows; upon a network of gleaming sabres; upon terrifying scenes of hacking, cleaving, rending, groaning, of pain, sobbing, bereavement, sorrow, destruction, tears, blood, and death; while Europe looked on fearful and amazed, waiting – alas, somewhat listlessly, – to see the end of the struggle.

Our men were in the right; and hope did not deceive them. St. Elmo, St. Michael, and the Castille opened up like three fearful tombs, and numberless were the Muslims who vanished inside them.

At dawn on 8 September the church bells rang solemnly; from the shattered bastions cannon were fired; from ruined houses, from clean-swept fields issued a sigh of repose; from the crowded squares the thunderous cry of victory was heard, and from the church of St. Lawrence of Birgu, in joyous albeit tearful voices, a hymn of thanksgiving to God and to the Child Mary spread abroad through the moist morning air. From that day forward, the day of victory was linked so inseparably with the feast day commemorating the Virgin's birth that the word Vittoria in our country came to denote both the one and the other.

The army of Soliman the terror of Europe, broken, routed, with three men lost out of every four, loaded with shame and disgrace, embarked once more in the galleys, impoverished of sailors and oarsmen, and like a lean, dazed man slowly moved farther and farther away and vanished, never to reappear.

MALTESE PROVERB

Necessity makes you do everything.

The siege is lifted, 1565

FRANCISCO BALBI DI CORREGGIO

I do not believe that music ever sounded so sweet to human ears as the peal of our bells did to ours on that eighth of September – the day of the Nativity of Our Lady. For the last three months they had only been struck to give the alarm signal, but now the Grand Master ordered them to be rung at the hour when the reveille was usually sounded.

MALTESE PROVERBS

Better peace than having to make peace.

He who waits rejoices—in the end.

The word spread across the world, 1565

ERNLE BRADFORD

The news that Malta had been relieved, and the Sultan defeated, was carried all over Europe by ships, horsemen and signal fires. From Palermo, to Rome, to Paris, and even London, the bells rang in the churches and cathedrals. Although it was natural that the Pope, the protector of the Order, should command rejoicing and festivities in Rome; it is significant that the victory was not forgotten in Protestant England. Matthew Parker, Archbishop of Canterbury, (no doubt after consultation with Queen Elizabeth) appointed a Form of Thanksgiving to be used thrice weekly for six weeks after the event. Malta "that obscure island", "that rock of soft sandstone", became known as "the island of heroes" and the Bulwark of the Faith."

The Great Victory, 1565

DUN KARM

The Great Siege! I suppose there is not one of the historians who have written on the sixteenth century who does not place the great siege of Malta among the fairest and greatest events of those hundred years.

Bosio, the historian of the Order who wrote down the history of the Siege in all its details, and in his writings prepared the material for all subsequent historians, becoming the most reliable authority on the subject, never tires of showering praises upon Malta's defence during the four months of the Siege.

Scipione Ammitrato, put by Samminiatelli Zabarella in the very forefront of his book on our Siege, has this to say in his *Stories of*

Florence: "If, when weighing the facts according to their worth, we do not allow ourselves to be blinded by deceptive appearances, we are able to retain with all right and truth that the famous battles of Salamis and Marathon – the finest and greatest passages in Greek history – may well pale into insignificance before the defence of Malta."

✳ MALTA SINCE THE SIEGE OF 1565 ✳

A second great phase of Maltese history began when the forces of Suleiman withdrew. The Knights turned their attention to rebuilding and reinforcing the island and making it into the city and the island that we know today.

The Knights as Hospitallers, 1565

REGULATIONS TRANSLATED BY W.K.R. BEDFORD

In order that the sick poor living in the four towns, Valetta, Borgo, Isola, and Burmola, and in the island of Malta, should receive proper assistance, two professed knights of different nationality are nominated by the Most Eminent the Grand Master, who are called Commissioners of the sick poor. They take it in turns by the month, and are entrusted with making a list, at the beginning of each week, of the sick poor in the four towns, in order to give them the proper assistance. They superintend the doctors, to see they perform their duty and visit each day the poor whose names are down on the list, noting the remedies for those who require them, with due charity. To effect this, they are accustomed frequently to visit the above-mentioned poor at their homes, to relieve the wants of each, with the assistance of supernumeraries, and to see that they are given the portions allowed them from the *Pitansiera*, and also that the surgeons attend to the abscesses, wounds, etc properly.

The commissioners of the poor must examine one by one the prescriptions written by the doctors, and sign them with their own hand, that they may be given out from the dispensary of the Holy Religion.

~

They take every precaution that the poor who apply for relief are leading a respectable life, according to their praiseworthy regulations; and to effect this, all the cases from the country must be accompanied by the recommendation of the parish priest as to poverty and respectability of the sick.

Malta after the Siege, 1565

BRIAN BLOUET

After the Siege the Order of St. John had complex problems. The fortifications were in ruins and the cost of the Siege had been high. There was speculation that the Turks might return. In these conditions the old dissensions broke out and many Knights were in favour of abandoning Malta. Even Grand Master Valette had doubts about remaining, or was not fully in control of the situation. As soon as the Siege was lifted the Grand Master had asked the Pope to provide a military engineer capable of planning a new town for Scenerras peninsula. By the time the man chosen for the job, Francesco Laparelli, reached Malta in December, 1565, he found that many of the possessions of the Order were packed and ready for removal. As the Knights were in an uncertain and disorganised condition, Laparelli worked quickly. Within the space of a few days he placed the plans of the new city of Valletta before the Council of the Order. Although the Knights vacillated, Laparelli assembled workmen and materials and traced out the line of the fortifications for the new town. Laparelli's initiative was effective and on 28 March, 1566, Grand Master Valette laid the foundation stone of the city which bears his name. Valletta gave the Maltese work and helped the community recover from the losses it had suffered in the war.

Welcome, Valetta! 1566

ANONYMOUS BRITISH OFFICER

The Grand Master La Valette after having sustained against the Turks a Siege, which the multitude of the assailants, the small number of the besieged, the daring valour of the Knights, the prudence and heroic courage of their Chief, the vivacity of the attack, and the almost incredible efforts made use of in defence, having rendered for ever memorable; fearing another descent from the Ottoman troops again preparing to fall upon the Island, and despairing of the succours so often promised from Spain, pretended himself about to abandon its possession, hoping that from the importance of the Order to Christianity, particularly as its late establishment had rendered it the bulwark of Sicily, and the protector of commerce for all the nations of Europe in the Mediterranean, His Catholic Majesty would be induced to grant him the supplies which he had demanded. Having by this means obtained them, he instantly in concert with the Council of the Order, caused the walls of the new City to be traced, according to a plan at that time believed of Captain Francesco Laparelli, but which was in reality conceived and laid down by himself.

The Hospital of St. John of Jerusalem, 1786

JOHN HOWARD

The hospital for men is situated near the water. The three principal wards are in the form of a T, which communicate one with another, having an altar in the centre. By additional buildings the ward on one side is made longer than that on the other. Their breadth is 34½ feet, but the cross ward is only 29 feet 4 inches. These three wards, connected, are called the hall. The pavement is of neat marble (or stone) squares. The ceiling is lofty, but, being wood, now turned black; the windows being small, and the walls hung round with dusty pictures, this noble hall makes but a gloomy appearance. All the patients lie single. One ward is for patients dangerously sick or dying, another for patients of the middle rank of life, and the third for the lower or poorer sort of patients... The wards were all so dirty and offensive as to create the necessity of perfuming them; and yet, I observed the physician, in going his rounds, was obliged to keep his handkerchief to his face... There are several other wards, and some single rooms for each of the knights as choose to come here when sick.

The patients are twice a day, at eight and four, served with provisions; one of the knights and the under-physician constantly attending in the two halls, and seeing the distribution. From the kitchen (which is darker and more offensive than even the lower hall, to which it adjoins) the broth, rice, soup and vermicelli are brought in dirty kettles first to the upper hall and then poured into three silver bowls, out of which the patients are served. Those who are in the ward for the very sick, and those of the middle rank of life, are served in plates, dishes, and spoons of silver; but the other patients (who are far the most numerous) and served on pewter. I objected to the sweet-cakes and two sorts of clammy sweetmeats which were given to the patients.

The number of patients in the hospital during the time I was at Malta was from 510 to 532. Those were served by (32 of) the most dirty, ragged, unfeeling, and inhuman persons I ever saw... At the same time I observed that near 40 attendants were kept to take charge of about 26 horses and the same number of mules in the Grand Master's stables, and that there all was clean. I cannot help adding that in the centre of each of those stables there was a fountain out of which water constantly running into a stone basin; but that in the hospital, though there was indeed a place for a fountain, there was no water.

Topography of the Great Harbour, 1851

W.H. BARTLETT

Bartlett probably stood on the promenade of the Upper Barracca Gardens to describe this scene.

The Great Harbour, capable of holding a thousand ships of the line, is everywhere defended by lines of impregnable bulwarks. First on the left appears Fort Ricasoli, erected in 1670, under the Grand Mastership of Nicholas Cottonera, principally from the funds of the Italian knight whose name it bears. Behind it on a projecting precipice is the Naval Hospital, a magnificent retreat, capable of containing about three hundred patients, erected by order of His Majesty, William IV, and built under the superintendence of Admiral Sir Poulteney Malcolm, upon the site of a palace and gardens belonging to the knight named Boghy, the centre of this edifice being incorporated in the modern structure. Prominent beyond this advance, two long parallel tongues of land, the nearer being the ancient 'Borgo', and at its extreme point the formidable Fort St. Angelo, the only one existing when the knights took possession of the island – and the more distant, the quarter called Senglea… Joining these, around the head of the deep cove they enclose (the secure seat of the Dockyard and Arsenal) is the quarter of Burmola, and, forming the immense defensive curve, extend the Cottonera Lines, thrown out by Grand Master Cottonera in 1670, to cover this important portion of the city, and afford a retreat for the country people during a siege. Beyond Senglea again is another cove, called French Creek, where a great number of fine merchant vessels are built; and rising above it, marked by an obelisk in memory of the Hon. Sir R. Cavendish Spenser, is Mt. Corradino, whence the Turks erected their batteries against Senglea. These are the prominent points on the left or eastern side of the Great Harbour.

The long tongue of land extending from the Great Harbour to that of Marsa Muscet is now entirely covered by the city of Valetta.

~

The entrance of the second, or Quarantine, Harbour, is defended by Fort Tigne, erected near Point Dragout, so called from its being the position whence that corsair directed his batteries against Fort St. Elmo. Beyond this is the more extensive Fort Manoel, and the buildings appropriated to the quarantine.

The dockyards, 1800

BRIAN BLOUET

When the Order was expelled from Malta in 1798, the navy consisted of four galleys, one sailing vessel, three frigates and a number of smaller vessels. Such a force was technically and numerically insignificant in terms of the great European navies of the day.

In 1800 Captain Ball R.N. could describe the island as possessing "a small but complete shipyard". The yard proved to be important for it gave the Royal Navy and initial repair base in Malta. Gradually the facilities were extended under British rule until, in the mid-twentieth century, over 12, 000 people were employed in the yard.

✳

La Valette's tomb

This is the inscription on La Valette's tomb in the great crypt of the Cathedral of St. John's. Beside him lies Sir Oliver Starkey, an Englishman, his secretary and faithful friend. The inscription was composed in Latin by Starkey. It reads in translation:

Here lies La Valette, worthy of eternal honour. He who was once the scourge of Africa and Asia, and the shield of Europe, whence he was expelled by his holy arms, is the first to be buried in this beloved city, whose founder he was.

The Castle of St. Elmo, the Citadel of the city, 1840

MALTA PENNY MAGAZINE

This fortress is built on the extremity of the peninsula of land which separates the two chief harbours of the island. The present site of St. Elmo was anciently called *Della Guardia;* as here the watch was constantly kept to notice the entrance of all vessels into both harbours.

Here also was a small chapel dedicated to Sr. Erasmus or St. Elmo, the tutelary saint of seamen; from which the fort derives its name.

The fort was first erected by order of the viceroy of Sicily, on an occasion of an attack of the Turks in 1488. When the Knights of Rhodes took possession of Malta, they soon saw the importance of having this point well-fortified, and after an invasion of the Turks, when it was first projected to build a new city on Mount Shaab-er-Ras, by order of the Grand Master Jean D'Oriedes, in the year 1552, this fortress was much enlarged, and destined to form the citadel of the town.

~

After the defeat of the Turkish expedition when the first stone of the city of Valetta was laid, the Fort of St. Elmo was repaired and fortified, and built in more regular form than it was before. ... On the angles of the ramparts which commanded the entrance into both harbours are two turrets, formerly intended for the purpose of watching the vessels that entered and left the harbour. At present, the entrances of these are closed up with two marble slabs, one bearing an inscription to the memory of Admiral Sir A. Ball, once governor of Malta, below which are interred his remains surrounded by an iron railing; and the other in memory of Sir Ralph Abercrombie, whose embalmed body is enclosed in a barrel within the turret, just as it was brought from Aboukir (in Egypt where he had died in battle against the French).

Nowadays, at weekends, Fort St. Elmo is taken over by 'soldiers' dressed in the costume of the sixteenth century, who perform the routines of a guard. The fort is transformed into a scene from the past...

✳

The Knights of Malta and the Knights in Malta, 1858

WHITWORTH PORTER

The Maltese, as such, were not admitted into the highest class of the Order. Such of them as could bring forward the necessary proofs of nobility, and were otherwise eligible, could, it is true, become received as members of the Italian *langue*, and in a few cases even after marriage, on the condition that their wives should retire into Italy when about to become mothers; still the number who had entered the fraternity was but trifling, and even they were not ranked in the same position as the other members of the langue, being incapable of occupying the post either of Grand Master or of Conventual Bailiff. The Order was consequently always regarded as foreigners by the natives, and but little friendship or cordiality was to be traced in their social intercourse. It must not, however, be inferred from this that the Maltese were dissatisfied with the rule of the Knights over them. That government was certainly a despotism, and one of the strongest nature, still it was well suited to the habits of the people, and usually wielded with equity and moderation. Those cravings for liberty and personal action which characterise the Anglo-Saxon temperament are not so strongly felt in southern latitudes, and the decrees of the Grand Master and his council met with a ready and cheerful obedience from those who felt no very urgent desire to undertake the responsible duty of governing themselves.)

The Order in retreat

BRIAN BLOUET

During the eighteenth century, the military power of the Order became insignificant. In the late Middle Ages the Order had been a very useful ally, but by the end of the eighteenth century its fleet was comparatively small and obsolete.

The Order's crusading role became outmoded and it was difficult for the Knights to develop new functions or to maintain their position in relation to other European powers. During the sixteenth, seventeenth and eighteenth centuries, as more powerful European states emerged, the Order was placed at increasing disadvantage by its lack of size. The Knights did attempt to acquire additional territories, but expansion was never seriously pursued. In 1653 the order bought a number of small West Indian islands. However, the distance between the Caribbean and Malta was too great and, in 1665, the investment was sold for about four times the original outlay. In the first half of the eighteenth century there was talk of the Order stationing a naval squadron on the Red Sea, to clear the area of slave traders and to establish a foothold in the spice and precious materials trade. Once again the problems of communication and capital outlay were great. The scheme came to nought.

~

The Order's fate depended principally upon France. Any other power could display hostility to the Knights and not do terrible damage, but if the French turned against them then the Order would fail financially. However, the French, throughout the greater part of the eighteenth century, assumed a tolerant attitude, in spite of the cost. The moneys transmitted out of France by the commanderies cannot have been approved of in a mercantile nation. But the Order did keep Malta out of the grasp of rival powers, and French shipping made use of the harbour facilities.

The downfall of the Order, 1851

W.H. BARTLETT

Secure in their impregnable bulwarks, and covered with the *prestige* of former exploits, the Knights of Malta became rather a corporation of wealthy princes than a body of hardy warriors. Their luxurious habits and their scandalous dissensions rapidly undermined their power, and paved the way for a downfall as ignominious as their rise was full of glory. The island, however, has much to thank them for. They applied themselves to the development of its resources, and carefully fostered the cotton manufacture, which greatly enriched the population, increased nearly tenfold under their flourish rule. Those stupendous fortifications which attract the wonder of the stranger, were, under the rule of the successive Grand Masters, also carried to completion; but the heroic spirit that should have defended them had gone.

The property of the Knighthood in France was confiscated in the French Revolution in France, and later their Spanish and Italian revenues followed. The next object of the Republic was Malta itself. [*Bartlett's description of the Knights departure is coloured by his British background, but appears largely to reflect the facts.*] Emissaries were accordingly sent to the island, who secretly fomented the divisions already existing among the knights, and also successfully laboured to form a party favourable to the pretensions of the French. Bonaparte also despatched a ship of war, which, under the pretence of repairs, was permitted to enter the port for the purpose of refitting, but, in reality, to take such observations as might facilitate a conquest; a measure soon followed by the sudden appearance of a French fleet, having on board the grand army destined for the reduction of Egypt.

Bonaparte immediately sent a summons to the Grand Master, Hompesch,* to demand the free entry of all ports for the whole of his fleet and convoy; a proposal equivalent to a surrender... The preparations for defence had been neglected; and in the midst of panic and confusion the terms of capitulation were hurriedly arranged. Thus ignominiously came to a close on 12 June, 1798, the once illustrious Order of St. John of Jerusalem, having subsisted for more than seven hundred years.

Britain comes to Malta, 1802

BRIAN BLOUET

The idea that the British might leave Malta, particularly if it involved the return of the Order, was not acceptable to those Maltese who were politically active. In a statement to Commissioner Cameron, dated 19 October, 1801, drafted by representatives from the villages and other interested parties, request was made that Malta remain attached to Britain. If this course of action was not followed then the islanders should be "permitted to conduct their own affairs." By now, however, it must have been clear to politically perceptive inhabitants

---

* Hompesch was secured a large pension for life in Germany; the French knights were pensioned off; the inhabitants were promised that their property would not be invaded, nor their religion disturbed. 'The members of the Order consisted of 200 French knights, 90 Italian, 25 Spanish, 8 Portuguese, and 5 Anglo-Bavarian—in all 328, of whom 50 were disabled by age and infirmities; and the force under arms amounted to 7,100 men, which might easily have been increased to 10,000.'

that their room for manoeuvre was limited. Obviously Malta would not be left to the Maltese, for all the interested external powers feared that the others would try to occupy the islands. A strong effort was made to persuade the British to stay. In February 1802 a deputation, consisting of Philip Castaagna representing Birgu-Senglea; Michele Cacchia, an engineer from Zajtun who constructed artillery batteries for the siege of Valletta; Don Pietro Mallia, a theologian; Antonio Mallia, reprsenting Gozo; and Don Emanuel Riccaud, arrived in London to put the Maltese point of view and seek the protection of His Britannic Majesty.

After a long period of disagreement and negotiation, eventually Malta and Britain settled down together, in a relationship which continued for more than a century ... and a friendship which continues today.

The new Goths and Vandals, 1798

LOUIS DE BOISGELIN

No sooner were the French become masters, than they established all the laws of the Directory, and formed a municipality and a provisional government. The commander de Ransijat was appointed president of the new administration, under the command, however, of the commissary (St. Jean d'Angeli); whom he servilely obeyed, and whose yoke was very different and much heavier to bear, than the one this perjured knight had so lately thrown off. Everything in the public buildings which bore the stamp of nobility, or recalled to mind the celebrated exploits performed by illustrious chiefs was broken or destroyed. These new Goths and Vandals likewise threw down with impious hands the busts of those heroes who had graced the annals of chivalry and which were placed on different elevated spots. It will appear scarcely credible to posterity, that such ravages should take place in the presence of an army which contained more than two hundred literati and artists;* and whose principal object,

---

* Attached to the French army were some two hundred savants or scholars who would study every facet of Egyptian history, geography and knowledge and document this knowledge in great illustrated works.

according to all appearance, was to make (and that in most solemn name) a kind of honourable amends to the arts and sciences, by going into a country where they formally flourished, and by endeavouring to draw forth from obscurity those precious monuments of antiquity which an ignorant and superstitious people had permitted to remain concealed from the public eye... In a very few days, the arms of the Order, together with those of the principal chiefs, were defaced not only in all the different inns, but in the palace of the Grand Master, himself being present on the occasion. Such an outrage as this, was not even committed by the Mussulmen of Rhodes, where marks still remain of the residence of the Knights of St. John of Jerusalem in that island.

When Napoleon was in Malta, 1839

THOMAS MACGILL

A large portion of the people found occupation under the Knights; and through their protection and influence, the cotton yarns and stuffs of the Islands (which could only be exported in a manufactured state) became a mine of wealth to the inhabitants. The knights had now become impotent through their dissolute lives, and loss of revenue from continental revolutions; and in a most dastardly and treacherous manner, without firing a gun yielded up their invulnerable island fortifications in 1798, to a republican armament under the command of General Bonaparte, who, on his way to Egypt, thought it advisable to hold Malta as an intermediate post.

On the evening of his arrival Bonaparte, with one of his generals, walked round the bastions, at one he stopped and exclaimed "What sublime fortifications!" his companion answered "It was fortunate we had good friends within, or you never would have got possession of them." Leaving a garrison of 5,000 men, carrying off an equal number of natives, after three days Bonaparte proceeded to his destination.

The republicans through their acts of spoliation and loose conduct, so irritated the natives, that after an occupation of only two months, the whole country rose against them, and shut them and shut them up within Valletta and the surrounding fortifications. – The English came to the assistance of the patriots, and after a siege and blockade of two years, the French were obliged to capitulate.

The patriot chiefs, and national representatives in 1799, proposed that their islands should become an integral part of the British Empire, which proposal being accepted of, from that period the Union Jack became the national flag.

MALTESE PROVERB

Whenever the band plays there is always someone stealing the prickly pears.

Grand Master Hompesch and Napoleon Bonaparte, 1797

SIR THEMISTOCLES ZAMMIT

Napoleon, en route to Egypt, asked for agreement for his fleet to enter the Grand Harbour. The Council of the Knights met and agreed to send an ambiguous reply to gain time. Bonaparte announced that he was resolved to obtain by force what he had asked for, and advised the Knights and the people to find some means of coming to terms with him.

The same night the French troops were landed at four different points: at Gozo under Reynier, at St. Paul's Bay under Baragnet d'Hilliers, at St. Julian's Bay under Vaubois, and at Marsacirocco Bay under Desaix. Early on the 10th the forward movement was started and the principal forts were invested.

The landing at Gozo was effected at Ramla Bay. The French troops cleared the heights and occupied the plateau and the small tower and, after the complete landing of the force, a rapid advance was made towards Rabat and Ghain Sielem. Fort Chambrai, in which all the people of the neighbouring villages had taken refuge, was invested and forced to surrender early in the afternoon, and the citadel of Rabat was occupied at nightfall.

The fleet in the meantime was slowly entering the Grand Harbour and the gates of the city were thrown open to admit the conqueror. Bonaparte himself landed at the Old Barriera and walked up through Strada Levante and Strada Cristoforo, surrounded by a dense crowd of officers.

The account of the next few days in Malta, described by Sir Themistocles Zammit, should be read in full; here, we can only add a final sentence of the account:

On the 13th June, the Grand Master (Hompesch) visited Bonaparte, who paid but little respect to his dignity and his age. During the brief interview, Hompesch was asked to leave the island within three days. The Grand Master returned crestfallen to the Palace and prepared to leave the island with his Knights.

The island prize, 1800

ANONYMOUS BRITISH OFFICER

Malta, 30th December, 1800
The position of this Island in the centre of the Mediterranean, the convenience and security of its ports, with the almost impregnable fortifications which secure the town of Valetta, evidently point out the importance of such a capture to a commercial people, independent of the beneficial consequence before stated.

Situated nearly at an equal distance from the entrance of the Straits (Gibraltar) and the coasts of Syria, the whole trade of the Mediterranean and Levant in time of war, must be at the mercy of its possessors. With these advantages should the nature of circumstances admit of its being retained, the decided superiority of our marine, will most probably render it by far the most valuable possession that could have been acquired by the British Nation in the Mediterranean.

MALTESE PROVERBS

The man with wheat has no sacks; the man with sacks has no wheat.

The man to make you laugh is the man to make you cry.

The man to make you cry, 1798

WHITWORTH PORTER

On 12th June, 1798 General Bonaparte entered the town, and took up his residence in the house of the Baron Paulo Parisio, a noble Maltese, who lived near the Auberge de Castile; and here he established his headquarters. As he entered within the stupendous fortifications of Valetta and witnessed their great strength, he exclaimed: "Well was it for us that we had friends within to open the gates for us, for had this place been empty we should have had far more difficulty in obtaining an entrance." Bonaparte had good reason for self-congratulation; his proverbial good fortune had not deserted him. Had he been detained for a very short time before Valetta, the fleet under Nelson would have been upon him, and the glorious victory of the Nile would have been anticipated, and have been fought beneath the ramparts of Malta.

The departure of Napoleon (for Egypt on 21 June 1798) caused no relaxation in the rigour and despotism of the French policy, and it gradually dawned on the unfortunate inhabitants that the liberty, the equality, and the fraternity for which they had so fervently prayed were practical nonentities, and that these high-sounding titles of philanthropy were but the cloaks to a tyranny, compared with which the rule of the Grand Masters was mild indeed.

Among the grievances under which the Maltese laboured were: no promised subsistence was paid to the families of soldiers from Malta who sailed with Napoleon; the debts of the Grand Master were never paid as promised; all pensions were stopped; no interest was paid on loans from the Maltese to the Treasury; quartering of officers in Maltese families and taxing the population to pay for barracks was a great burden.

These were some of the principal grievances of which the inhabitants complained. Still, although thus rendered discontented, the French might have succeeded in maintaining their sway over the island had they not insulted the feelings of the people on a point where they were most sensitive. Had the French refrained from interference with the religion of Malta, and left their churches intact, they might possibly have carried their other acts of spoliation with a high hand: but they committed a grave error of policy when they commenced to plunder the churches of the costly offerings and decorations in which the inhabitants took so great a pride. From the moment that they commenced these sacrilegious depredations, all sympathy between them and the Maltese was at an end. These latter regarded with a sense of horror and detestation a nation who, openly regardless of all religion themselves, could be guilty of such acts of wanton desecration; and the spirit of discontent, which had hitherto found vent in idle murmurs, was now aroused to such an extent that ere long it broke out into open revolt.

French rule, 1798–1800; British rule, 1800

SIR THEMISTOCLES ZAMMIT

The well-known Maltese historian describes the experience of French rule, which led to Britain being invited to take responsibility for Malta.

The Maltese revolted against French misrule and a reign of terror then ensued: Valletta, despoiled and democratized, saw its strong gates barred in the face of her citizens, and its cannons posted to keep away the infidels, trained against the Maltese themselves. The treasures brought together by the princely knights were plundered, the palaces thrown open to the soldiery, the churches despoiled and profaned, and the citizens who had nothing to give to the besieged French were thrown out in batches from the gates as an encumbrance.

For the two years during which they were besieged in Valletta, the French soldiers made free use of the buildings, but beyond removing most of the coats-of-arms, they did no material damage. Then followed the hauling down of the French colours from the flagstaff on the Palace, and the hoisting of the Union Jack, and contemporary history was ushered in. The British sovereignty over the Maltese islands is set forth in a concise, but pithy, inscription over the gateway out of the main guard in the Palace square:

MAGNAE ET INVICTAE BRITANNIAE
MELITENSIUM AMOR ET EUROPAE VOX
HAS INSULAS CONFIRMANT.

(The affection of the Maltese people and the voice of Europe confirm these islands as belonging to unconquered Great Britain.)

The advantages for Britain, 1800

SIR RALPH ABERCROMBY TO
THE RIGHT HONOURABLE HENRY DUNDAS

General Sir Ralph Abercromby was in Malta at the end of 1799 and the start of 1800 as head of the military expedition sent to force the French out of Egypt. The British forces went into Egypt at Aboukir Bay and, in the fullness of time, defeated the French. Abercromby was wounded leading the first assault and died from his wounds. His body was brought back to Malta and his memorial can be seen in the Abercromby Bastion of Fort St. Elmo.

Malta, in point of situation, does not possess the advantages of Minorca, and is not so convenient a station for a fleet in time of war, yet possessing so many other advantages, it may almost, on a comparison, be equal, if not superior; and if it were to fall into the hands of a powerful enemy, we should severely feel the consequence of it. To France, it would afford an opportunity of again attempting an establishment in Egypt, and to Russia, it would become a depot of naval for the powers in the Mediterranean who are hostile to us, and might give to either of these powers a preponderance in the Mediterranean, and the means of weakening the Turkish empire.

Britain or the Knights? 1801

SIR THEMISTOCLES ZAMMIT

When the Knights had been expelled by the French, there came the question of under which nation Malta should be placed for protection.

In Malta, meanwhile, a strong feeling had grown up in favour of the islands remaining under British rule. Only a very small party desired the restoration of the Knights, and the partisans of the King of Naples were thwarted by the armistice forced upon Naples by France in February 1801. Those who favoured British rule had been encouraged by the action of Sir Ralph Abercromby who, on his return to Malta in November 1800, had instructed General Pigot to consider the Maltese as being under the protection of Great Britain, and not to allow the pretensions of any other sovereign, or body of men, to be brought forward or discussed. He had, moreover, directed Captain Ball to take over the Civil Government and to hoist the British flag in all places in Malta and Gozo where colours were usually displayed.

To the Right Honourable William Pitt, 14 November, 1796

SIR MARK WOOD

Mark Wood travelled east to India where he worked as Chief Engineer in Bengal. He calculated that the journey to Alexandria in Egypt through France and Malta was faster and easier than the route he had taken himself through Italy. He argued strongly for taking Malta for Britain for this purpose and thus securing the route to India.

Were Providence to give us the power to place an impregnable fortress and harbour on any spot in the Mediterranean, most suitable to the views of our country, it would hardly be possibly to select one preferable to Malta. It would give us completely the command of the Levant; not one ship from thence could sail to or from any port in Europe, unless by our permission, or under the convoy of a superior fleet; the coasts of Spain, France, Italy and Africa must be subject to our control, and whilst at war with this country, be kept under necessary subjection; from Africa and Sicily we could have ample supplies for our fleets and garrisons, and, by the Dardanelles, from the Euxine and Caspian Seas, inexhaustible supplies of various naval stores, which, if not secured to ourselves, must inevitably find their way to the arsenals of France.

Double benefits to Britain, July 1804

SAMUEL TAYLOR COLERIDGE

First, we exclude the French and deprive them of a Port, which would furnish such facility to their Enterprises in the Levant, of whatever nature they might be and against whatever countries they might be directed as no maritime superiority might be sufficient to counteract; while the presence of our troops & Squadrons in that most commanding position not only deprives them of their advantage, but opposes a positive obstacle, wholly insurmountable to any considerable Expedition from the French or Spanish Ports in that direction.

Malta's importance, 1805

ADMIRAL HORATIO NELSON

I now declare that I consider Malta as a most important outwork of India, and that it will give us great influence in the Levant, and indeed in all the southern and northern parts of Italy. In this view, I hope, we shall never give it up.

A taste of democracy, 1879

REVEREND WILLIAM LOFTIE

William Loftie attended a sitting of Malta's 'miniature parliament' in the former palace of the Grand Master. The Council sat in the Tapestry Hall, with its walls hung with Gobelin tapestries, 'of good design and in brilliant preservation, though (then) a hundred and fifty years had passed since they left the loom'. 'The eye,' he noted, 'seeks in vain for signs of the English domination... Even the carpet, where one might expect Axminster or Glasgow, is apparently contemporary with the tapestry, and bears the golden fleur de lis of old France. The most English feature in the room is a set of desks for the deputies, of new varnished yellow oak, which must at some not very remote period have left their native Tottenham Court Road.'

Loftie wrote of the parliament:

The experiment, first tried in 1849, of calling together a local legislative body, would be more interesting from a political point of view if free discussion involved equal freedom in decision. But the members of the Government are always ranged on one side and the elected members of the Assembly on the other, and the Government, having the majority of votes, can always carry its measures. It may be questioned whether the existence of a permanent Opposition is to be attributed to the importance of the local vote, or whether it is not rather to be accounted for by the religious and social condition of the native electors. When education has reached the lowest classes we may hope for clearer political views among them...

The debates of the local Parliament are carried on, however, either in Italian or English; and the stranger present at a sitting has often the gratification of hearing Southern eloquence in his own Northern tongue, and of listening to English spoken with a grammatical correctness and distinctness of utterance which he might miss in the House of Commons at home.

The "Council of Government", as it is called, assembles daily between November and June, in the Governor's palace of Valetta. It is composed of eighteen members, of whom ten are appointed by the Crown, being the holder of such offices as that of Crown Advocate, Collector of Customs, or Treasurer, and including the Governor himself, who is thus at once Sovereign, Speaker, and Prime Minister. All the Government offices are open to natives, except those of Chief Secretary and of Auditor; and of the nine members of the Council sitting on the official side, only two others besides the general commanding are English. They include on Roman Catholic priest, two ecclesiastics only being allowed to sit at the same time, together with three lawyers, and several members of the old Maltese nobility.

A special relationship, 1927

DOUGLAS AUSTIN

Malta became an island like no other colony of the British Crown. The title of Great Britain in the islands was neither that of colonisation nor of conquest; for since the British occupation no immigrants from the old country had settled there in any numbers, and the islanders made it quite clear in their dealings with (the first Governor) Sir Alexander Ball after the expulsion of the French, that they ceded their territory to the British Crown upon the express conditions that their laws, privileges and customs, both civil and religious, should be safeguarded. The laws of Malta, when the English came, presented certainly a curious mixture, consisting in part of the Roman and the Sicilian Codes, and the ancient Canon Law of the Church, all modified by the 'Bandi', Notices, Ordinances, and Pragmatics of successive Grand Masters. These things, the growth of time, would not be swept way at once, nor would it have been politic to impose English laws and customs upon a people not understanding English, and clinging on closely to their traditions. Indeed, as a matter of fact, the Civil Code of the Grand Master de Rohan remained in force in the islands long after the British occupation: the greater part has been gradually repealed though certain sections are still in force.

A lingering relic of history, 1825

ANNE KATHERINE ELWOOD

But for the poor knights where are they? Alas for them! Well might Burke exclaim, "The days of chivalry are over." Of them whose deeds "once kept the world alive with lustre and with noise", nought remains but splendid tombs and stupendous fortifications to tell us such men as were... Occasionally may be seen wandering forth, like a ghost, an old-fashioned figure, clad in habits formed a century ago, with an enormous Maltese cross, the only token by which may be recognised a lingering relic of the illustrious Order of the Knights of Malta, looking, however, like a burlesque upon that glorious, that chivalrous race of men, whose prowess and whose exploits once filled all Europe with their renown.

An impregnable place, 1851

W.H. BARTLETT

It may be doubted whether the world can show within the same compass so stupendous a series of fortifications. Even the most unmilitary eye cannot fail to perceive that from whatever point an enemy can direct his attack he is met with some insuperable obstacle, and that, even could this be surmounted, he has yet to commence the herculean labour anew, – that from all quarters a cross fire can be directed upon approaching fleets or squadrons, – that, in short, a blockade is the only means of reducing such a place – a means which, provisioned as the city is for several years, and relieved as it would be by an English fleet, is entirely out of the question; so that, in short, in its present hands, Malta may justly be considered a stronghold and influence of Great Britain in the Mediterranean, and by far the most important of the links of that chain which unites her to her distant empire in the East.

Malta in World War II

NATIONAL WAR MUSEUM ASSOCIATION, MALTA

In the event, and in circumstances unimaginable to earlier writers, a century later Malta was to face again bombardment and a blockade—and survive both.

When Italy declared war on Britain and France on 10th June, 1940, Malta found itself in the front-line. France's collapse soon after worsened the situation as the air and naval base at Bizerta could not provide the planned protection to the island, which, as a result, became an isolated outpost, 60 miles from the nearest Italian airfields and nearly 1000 miles from the closest Allied bases at Gibraltar and Alexandria. Although strategists held out little hope for Malta, history was to prove them wrong as it records the island's stand as one of the epics of the Second World War.

At 6:55a.m. on 11th June, 1940, the sirens heralded the first air raid as ten Italian bombers, with a heavy fighter escort, approached the island and branched into two formations. One group attacked the Marsamxett and the Grand Harbour, while the other raided the Hal Far and the Dolimara area. The island, unprepared for such an early start to hostile activity, witnessed scenes of desolation as buildings crashed into dust. Mothers huddled their children under tables and beds and in cellars. The anti-aircraft batteries were joined by heavy guns from H.M. ships *Terror* and *Aphis*, berthed in Marsamxett Harbour.

⁓

As the enemy realised that Malta could not be subdued by bombs, the siege was tightened further. Convoys to Malta were subjected to intensive attacks and many ships were sunk or had to turn back. In early 1942, the Maltese faced heavy bombing, starvation and the threat of invasion. Food, ammunition and fuel were running out. There was an acute shortage of everything except courage and the determination to win.

✳

Gozo in wartime, 1941–2

MICHAEL GALEA

The writer recalls real events in his story 'The Captain'.

As time passed the enemy attacks became much heavier. The air-raids went on without intermission; there was hardly time to breathe between one attack and the next. Everyone took cover as best he could, and did his work in the shortest possible time so as to avoid remaining long in the open, as enemy aircraft hovered overhead continually, often diving down to sow destruction with their fire.

The crews of the Gozo boats were in great danger. The enemy planes had taken to hunting these craft as they plied between the two islands, and shut them up until they made them look like sieves with their machine-gun bullets. Many sailors were killed, many others were gravely wounded, and so many of the boats were sunk that hardly any more remained to sail between Malta and Gozo. Although most of the sailors had been wiped out, the few who remained did not neglect their duty, and with amazing courage continued to transport the produce, goods and harvest from Gozo to Malta.

In Malta itself there was great misery, and many people suffered from hunger; thus the cargoes of the Gozo boats were of no small value for keeping up the morale of the Maltese and encouraging them to hold out. But in the end the attacks became so fierce and the destruction of the craft so thorough, that there were hardly any boats or sailors left to carry on the service between Malta and Gozo.

The second Great Siege, 1942

PHILIP VELLA

In compliance with Hitler's directives, aerial pressure over Malta gained momentum. Most attacks were directed against military objectives, but populated areas did not escape unscathed. Extensive areas in the Three Cities (around the Grand Harbour), Luqa and other parts of the island were wiped out. Valletta suffered the destruction of a number of historic buildings, including several of the Auberges built by the Knights of Malta. St. John's Co-Cathedral escaped with light damage to the Chapel of the German Langue, the vestry, the belfries and the main portico.

~

The Maltese on the whole accepted the loss of their homes and belongings with composure. The unlucky ones, surveying the desolate scene, searched amid the rubble for items of utility. This was a heart-and-back-breaking operation in which neighbours and strangers lent a hand. The Demolition and Clearance Squads, numerous as they were, could not cope with the demands made upon them. The local stone resisted fire, blast and nearby explosions but could not withstand direct hits. Crumbling buildings collapsed into heaps of masonry which was very heavy to remove by hand. There was no other means of doing the job, as the limited mechanical equipment available had priority at the airfields and the dockyard. It was inspiring to see men, women and children removing debris.

True Christian charity helped to mitigate the burden of loss; the bombed-out found moral support and material help from more fortunate neighbours. Their comradeship and generosity were spontaneous; people realised they could find themselves in the same desperate situation the next day, or after the next raid.

~

Although practically every day had its own story, the 15th of February, 1942 stands out in particular, as on that day the Island was under alert for 19 hours and 59 minutes. There were four raids lasting respectively from 2:00 a.m. to 7:35 a.m., 7:59 a.m. to 6:36 p.m., 7:25 p.m. to 7:34 p.m., and 7:57 p.m. to 11:35 p.m. During the second raid, at 5:54 p.m., a solitary German aircraft flying over Valletta dropped a stick of three bombs along Kingsway (now Republic Street); one got the Palace, the other the Casino Maltese (now Casino 1952), killing six members and two of the staff besides passers-by, while the third landed squarely on the Regent Cinema (now Regency House), where "The North-West Mounted Police" starring Nelson Eddy and Jeanette MacDonald was being screened.

Malta's finest hour, June 1942

PETER ELLIOTT

This year – 1942 – was to be the greatest test of all, for the brave people of Malta and for their defenders. The assault of the Germans, and especially of the expert bombing force brought specially from Russia, had one objective only – to subdue the island by breaking the will of its people, and by starving them of supplies of food and ammunition to keep the fortress in being, and for its striking force of submarines and bombers.

Despite all the gloomy predictions of the British Army and Air Force, Malta had been proved to be just that vital island for which the Royal Navy had always argued. The only real threat to the Axis convoys running from Italy to North Africa bearing the arms and men to conquer Egypt, lay in this little island and its striking forces. The Mediterranean Fleet was starved of aircraft carriers and could not strike at long distance from Alexandria in face of the German dive bombers; but that unsinkable aircraft carrier, Malta, could and did in a neat reversal of their pre-war policy, the combined chiefs of staff in London expressed their view to Churchill that Malta was so important as a staging post for aircraft being ferried east, and as a striking base, that the most drastic steps were justifiable to sustain it.

The horribleness of war, 1942

ALEC GUINNESS

It was late in the afternoon of a hot sultry day when we arrived in Malta. I hadn't seen the Grand Harbour, Valletta, since the Old Vic (theatre) tour to the island in the spring of 1939. Then all had been sparkling, with great battleships and cruisers, very spick-and-span, at their huge moorings, brass-funnelled Admiralty barges speedily chugging their way to the Customs House steps hooting shrilly, Liberty Boats full of raucous sailors, dghaisas – gaily painted red, green and white – plying for trade, bugle calls echoing from Fort St. Angelo and flags flying everywhere. Now all looked dilapidated and sulky. The Navy was there in force but grim and unlit.

Valletta had suffered terribly from bombing, its honey-coloured houses sliced in half like pieces of cheese, the streets chocked with rubble and the inhabitants, many living a troglodyte existence in caves, seemed scarce and very war-weary. I was to find when I got ashore, that the splendid Opera House, where the Vic Company had played, no longer existed.* The sadness and horribleness of war was self-evident. My immediate task, however, was to berth where instructed, which proved an impossibility. I was required to squeeze my craft between two others, bow on to the quay, which meant slewing my stern within about four feet of my favourite ship, the crack minelayer, *HMS Manxman.* She was beautiful, swift, and with a first class, hand-picked crew, most of whom lined their gunwale to watch, with concern, my cautious and useless endeavours. There was a rather unpleasant snapping sound. I had managed to crack the *Manxman's* gangway. I promptly sent a signal of apology to the Captain, who replied immediately. "Whoever told you to berth in that position is a fool. Stop. You did very well considering. Stop. Good luck. Stop. End of message. Stop."

Interview with Miss Strickland, 1970

STEWART PEROWNE

In 1970 BBC journalist Stewart Perowne interviewed a British resident of Malta about her experiences of the siege, for his book The Siege Within the Walls.

MISS STRICKLAND: I was born in Malta and resident there.
INTERVIEWER: Including the siege?
MISS STRICKLAND: Yes, right through from the beginning to the end.
... Malta's war struggle for survival began with Italy's entry into the war. Britain reinforced the island with troops, both infantry and gunners, and the Maltese Territorial Regiment was embodied.
INTERVIEWER: And the R.A.F.?
MISS STRICKLAND: Well, they fought their first air battles over Malta by manning four naval Gladiator planes. But in August 1940, Britain reinforced us with twelve Hurricanes which she could ill spare. And it fought the Italians at odds of twenty to one.

---

* The Opera House has not been rebuilt—unlike the rest of the city.

Malta survived but at great cost:

MISS STRICKLAND: Malta won that battle but three of her cities, Vittoriosa, Senglea and Cospicua lay in ruins by the time the *Illustrious* (under repair in Malta) was ready. The dockyard grimly moved underground into the living rock, soft yellow limestone rock that trembles and vibrates under direct hits but does not yield. "Just like a thousand snakes running round my stomach" was how a dockyard foreman summed up his experience. "Full fifteen minutes of direct hits and all Senglea down on top of us."

And through those terrible days and weeks and months, the Maltese and the British worked side by side.

MISS STRICKLAND: Infantry from the United Kingdom and Maltese soldiers who mended the craters and fought for the aerodromes and serviced the planes and unloaded the ships along with Maltese workmen. Infantry filled in the craters for months on end, often surrounded by unexploded bombs, subject to continual attack – and it's no fun just shovelling earth into craters in the target area. As a soldier once said to me, "They may have a war in England, but it can't be just like ours."

Deep in those 'living rocks' there is today a museum of the Siege, run by volunteers. To visit it gives one a real sense of those hard war-torn days, weeks, months and years. On one visit to Malta, a few years ago, I was sitting with a Maltese friend drinking coffee. I asked him about his memories of the Siege. One bomb, he remembered, had seriously damaged the Knights' Palace and brought down the café at whose tables we were sitting. 'I still have nightmares about it,' he said. 'More than half a century later.' For a moment he was thoughtful. 'In fact,' he added, 'I had such a nightmare only last night...'

✷

The terror of the Siege, 1941

JOANNA TROLLOPE

In her novel The Brass Dolphin, *Joanna Trollope (under her pen-name Caroline Harvey) wrote of the experiences and destruction of the second great siege of Malta. It is astonishing here, as across Europe, how little the scars remain.*

I don't quite know where to start. It is like some kind of hell to the Three Cities (around the Great Harbour). The streets are full of rubble, everything is burned and broken, there is the stench of TNT. When I went down to Kalkara after the first raid, I was so shocked I could hardly breathe. There wasn't anything that wasn't violently damaged and there were people everywhere in tears because they are now beggars. And, if they aren't beggars, they're dead or wounded, and the refugees are pitiful, struggling out of the city with their children and their sad bundles. You wouldn't recognise the Three Cities. I wonder if you'd recognize Malta. And there are more raids to come, we're promised another big one tomorrow. Sometimes it's so frightening you feel you'll go mad. But you can't because people need help, all the time, so you have to fight down everything you're feeling and do what you can.

~

Every day, whatever happened, a newsboy came panting round with a canvas satchel of copies of the *Times of Malta* and at midday a group of orderlies (in the hospital) were dispatched to the nearest victory kitchen, set up by the government to provide one hot meal a day, to collect the hospital's ration of bread and goat stew, cooked sometimes on wood from bombed-out buildings, but invariably tasting strongly of paraffin.

The George Cross, 1942

KING GEORGE VI

On 15 April 1942, the following message was sent from His Majesty King George VI to the people of Malta:

"To honour her brave people I award the George Cross to the Island Fortress of Malta to bear witness to a heroism and devotion that will long be famous in history."

The Siege Bell War Memorial

Independence and after, 1974

BRIAN BLOUET

On 13 December 1974, Malta became a republic, Repubblika Ta' Malta, within the Commonwealth after the House of Representatives passed, by the necessary two-thirds majority, acts which amended the 1964 constitution. The head of state ceased to be the British sovereign and became a President of Maltese nationality, appointed by the House of Representatives for a five-year term. The first President was Sir Anthony Mamo (1974–6), who had previously served as Governor General (1971–4).

The last British forces left Malta in 1979 and the islands came to enjoy not only independence but freedom from military involvement in the affairs of external powers. Perhaps such a condition has not existed since prehistoric times for, from the Phoenician period on, Malta has been, to a degree, a base for important Mediterranean powers. Long may independence and neutrality be preserved.

Modern Maltese Politics

WIKIPEDIA

The politics of Malta take place in a framework of a parliamentary representative democratic republic, whereby the President of Malta is the constitutional head of state with executive powers remaining with the Prime Minister of Malta who is the head of government and the cabinet. Legislative power is vested in the Parliament of Malta which consists of the President of Malta and the unicameral House of Representatives of Malta with the Speaker presiding officer of the legislative body. Judicial power remains with the Chief Justice and the Judiciary of Malta. Since Independence, the party electoral system has been dominated by the Christian democratic Nationalist Party (*Partit Nazzjonalista*) and the social democratic Malta Labour Party (*Partit Laburista*).

Since independence, general elections have been held in 1966, 1971, 1976, 1981, 1987, 1992, 1996, 1998, 2003 and 2008. Two parties have dominated Malta's polarized and evenly-divided politics during this period: the Partit Nazzjonalista and the Partit Laburista. Third parties have failed to score any electoral success: in the 2008 election the Democratic Alternative (a Green Party established in 1989) managed to secure only 1.31% of the first preference votes nationwide. Elections have invariably generated a widespread voter turnout exceeding 90% of registered voters.

The 1996 elections resulted in the election of the Labour Party, by 8,000 votes, to replace the Nationalists who had won in 1987 and 1992. Voter turnout was characteristically high at 96%, with the Labour

Party receiving 50.72%, the Nationalist Party 47.8%, the Democratic Alternative 1.46%, and independent candidates 0.02%. In 1998, the Labour Party's loss in a parliamentary vote led the Prime Minister to call an early election. The Nationalist Party was returned to office in September 1998 by a majority of 13,000 votes, holding a five-seat majority in Parliament. Voter turnout was 95%, with the Nationalist Party receiving 51.81%, the Labour Party 46.97%, the Democratic Alternative 1.21%, and independent candidates 0.01%.

The Nationalist government wrapped up negotiations for European Union membership by the end of 2002. A referendum on the issue was called in March 2003 for which the Nationalists and the Democratic Alternative campaigned for a "yes" vote while Labour campaigned heavily for "no" vote, invalidate their vote or abstain. Turnout was 91%, with more than 53% voting "yes".

The Labour Party argued that the "yes" votes amounted to less than 50% of the overall votes, hence, and citing the Integration referendum as an example, they claimed that the "yes" had not in fact won the referendum. The then MLP Leader Alfred Sant said that the General Elections that was to be held within a month would settle the affair. In the General Elections the Nationalists were returned to office with 51.79% of the vote to Labour's 47.51%. The Democratic Alternative managed 0.68%. The Nationalists were thus able to form a government and sign and ratify the EU Accession Treaty on 16 April 2003.

On 1 May 2004 Malta joined the EU and on 1 January 2008, the Eurozone with the euro as the national currency. The first elections after membership were held in March 2008 resulting in a narrow victory for the Nationalist Party with 49.34% of first preference votes.

5

THE PEOPLE

Travellers and Maltese authors have written about the people of the islands and their language over the centuries. They found the people solid, active and orderly, with a love of fun and of festas and an ease with the sea and their boats.

The women, as Elliot Warburton recorded in 1842, were beautiful with a mix of the East and the North. In the warmth of Malta people spent much time outside, whether in the towns or in the country. Reverend Charles Swan in 1824 and many others thereafter admired how the people struggled to make a living from the difficult terrain. Over the centuries travellers have enjoyed the pleasure the Maltese take in their celebrations, as did Anne Katherine Elwood in 1825. They also recognised the deep religious commitment of the people.

Foreigners in Malta have also been closely observed over the centuries. Francisco Balbi di Correggio described the roles of the Knights in 1568, but by 1804 the young poet Samuel Taylor Coleridge reported sadly on how the Order had deteriorated. David Niven's adventure in the 1930s gives a vision of the life of young British army officers serving in Malta.

✳ THE MALTESE ✳

The people long, long ago, 1972

NIGEL DENNIS

Nigel Dennis considered the evidence of Maltese people in pre-historical times.

The pre-historical remains of Malta have only two things to tell us about how the Maltese figure fared in the olden days and what the people looked like. Two sorts of statues, statuettes and figurines are found, and although both may be found together, each entirely contradicts the other. One sort would seem to be entirely representational pressed out in clay, often very crudely, or cut out of stone, it represents a figure of ordinary proportions with nothing very interesting about it. Such figures are usually classed as votives, some of them showing signs of serious illness and swollen or wasted parts. They are only a few inches high.

The other sort is not only interesting but includes the greatest triumphs of Maltese sculpture. They are exercises in obesity, and the degree to which they represent exaggeratedly a living figure cannot be ascertained at all. Classed recklessly as 'priestesses' and 'goddesses', they do not, in fact, even deign to state whether they are men or women. The great Maltese scholar, Sir Themistocles Zammit, judging by the relative fatness or rotundity of the chest and the absence or presence of nipples, decided that most of them are men. But the general observer takes for granted that all of them are women, their crossed or tucked up legs suggesting immediately to the modern eye a serene femininity of posture.

Valletta: a thronging city, 1844

WILLIAM MAKEPEACE THACKERAY

Valletta does not disappoint you on a closer inspection, as many a foreign town does. The streets are thronged with a comfortable-looking population; the poor seem to inhabit handsome stone palaces with balconies and projecting windows of heavy carved stone. The lights and shadows, the cries and stenches, the fruit shops and the fish stalls, the dresses and clatter of all nations; the soldiers in scarlet; and women in black mantillas; the beggars, boatmen, barrels of pickled herrings and macaroni; the shovel-hatted priests and bearded capuchins; the tobacco, grapes, onions and sunshine; the sign-boards; bottle-porter stores; the statues of saints and little chapels which jostle the strangers' eyes as he goes up the famous stairs from the water-gate, make a scene of such pleasant confusion and liveliness as I have never witnessed before. And the effect of the groups of multitudinous actors in this busy, cheerful drama is heightened, as it were, by the decoration of the stage. The sky is delightfully brilliant; all the houses and ornaments are stately, castles and palaces rising all around; and the flag, towers and walls of Fort St. Elmo look as fresh and magnificent as if they had only been erected yesterday.

The Scala Reale (now Republic Street) has a much more courtly appearance than that described. Here are palaces, churches, courthouses and libraries, the genteel London shops, and the latest articles of perfumery. Gay young officers are strolling about in shell jackets much too small for them; midshipmen are clattering by on hired horses, squads of priests, habited after the fashion of Don Basilio in the opera, are demurely pacing to and fro, professional beggars run shrieking after the stranger; and agents for horses, for inns, and for worse places still, follow him and indicate the excellence of their goods. The houses where they are selling carpet-bags and pomatum were the places of the successors of the goodliest company of gallant knights the world ever heard tell of. It seems unromantic, for *these* were not the romantic knights of St John. The heroic days of the order ended as the last Turkish galley lifted anchor after the memorable siege. The present stately houses were built in times of peace, splendour and decay. I doubt whether the 'Auberge de Provence' has ever seen anything more romantic than the pleasant balls held in the great room there.

The Maltese language, 1815

CLAUDIUS SHAW

The language chiefly spoken (in Valletta) is Italian. Maltese is a kind of Arabic.

They have also a third, which they call English, it is a strange mixture: all Englishmen and all male animals they call "John", all females "Maryanne". In the market you may buy John fowls or Maryanne fowls. John horses and Maryanne horses are constantly for hire at the corner of Strada San Giovanni and Strade Reale.

The Maltese and their language, 1926

SIR THEMISTOCLES ZAMMIT

Malta presents the peculiar feature of an island people that, talking a Semitic language, was cut off from the active influence of its parent tongue. The lack of a Semitic literature to nourish it left the primitive language of the Maltese stunted and meagre. Ingrained in the mind of the people, the syntax and the mechanism of the primitive language was retained, but as time went on, the vocabulary distorted here and there for the want of a written literature, was constantly fed from foreign sources, mostly through mariners and merchants who had to tarry on the island, once a great commercial centre. It was thus that Sicilian, Genoese, Spanish and Portuguese words were added from time to time to the Maltese language which, though devoid of Semitic feeders, still managed to remain Semitic. "Remove a language from its native soil," says Max Muller, "tear it away from the dialects which act as feeders and you can arrest its natural growth. There will still be the progress of phonetic corruption, but no longer the restoring influence of dialectic regeneration." But the grammar resists all corruption and is always there to tell the tale, for though language may get mixed in their vocabulary they never can be mixed in their grammar.

The Maltese language, 1930

SIR HARRY LUKE

When the Arabs came to Malta in 870 they found, so the philologists hold, the rank and file of the population speaking an old Semitic (namely Punic) dialect, and on this stock grafted, during the two hundred years of their occupation, a vocabulary of contemporary Arabic which did not entirely oust words of the older and kindred stratum. The dialect received, in point of fact, a second, fresher infusion from the same reservoir, and the resulting blend is the Maltese language of today.

Inevitably, in the course of ages, this language has borrowed words from the languages and dialects of the other countries with which Malta has been connected – from Sicilian, from Aragonese, from Italian, from French, even from English – but it has always fitted such words into its own Semitic framework, has governed them accordingly to the rules of its Semitic grammar. Thus the Maltese who have emigrated to Syria and to the north coast of Africa have no difficulty in making themselves understood by their Arabic-speaking neighbours, who for their part can make themselves readily understood in Malta.

MALTESE PROVERBS

The word of a Maltese is more reliable than the oath of a king.

I likened you to those I saw you with.

Your soul goes to God, your body to the dust,
your belongings to your people, for so things happen.

Guard well your house and don't make your neighbour a thief.

Where the heart yearns the feet will go.

Who are they? 1972

NIGEL DENNIS

Where is Malta? is a question that can be answered. Who are the Maltese? is quite unanswerable. We read in the old histories of pirate raids in which virtually all the inhabitants of Gozo were carried off into slavery: by whom were they replaced? We read of the planting of Italian colonies, we know that large numbers of Sicilian workmen were imported by the Knights. No less than 4,000 Rhodians – surely an exaggerated number – are said to have been imported by the Knights. No less than 4,000 accompanied the Knights to their new home. And yet, it would be wrong to conclude that the result is a Mediterranean hybrid of no recognisable stock. A distinct population is not made only by the mixed stocks of a people; it is made by inherited habits, language, and traditional beliefs.

The indefatigable Maltese, 1789

VIVANT DENON

No spot on earth can be more fortunate and more fertile than Sicily *[from whence Denon had just come]*; none can be more ungrateful, more barren, or more wretchedly situated than the Isle of Malta, if what the indefatigable Maltese attempt to cultivate, deserves the name of earth. In Sicily crops of every kind are to be produced, and though they rapidly succeed, and as I may say press upon each other, the peasant there is poor, languid, and disgustingly dirty: at Malta the farmer can only force from the soil a little corn and cotton; yet poverty there is so active, so industrious and so neat, that it has the air only of abstinence. Large breeches, a shirt of blue linen, a broad sash, and the arms and feet left naked, form the whole description of the light dress and ornament of the Maltese. Their features and complexion are as Arabian as their language; interested and artful in all their bargains, they are scrupulously faithful in fulfilling every contract, which renders all commercial intercourse with them safe and easy.

The people as seen by a Viscount, 1809

GEORGE, VISCOUNT VALENTIA

The Maltese are frugal, temperate and industrious. They proved themselves brave soldiers during the blockade of La Valletta, when about three thousand of them were under the command of Sir Alexander Ball. They are as good seamen as any in the Mediterranean, and are rapidly improving their connections with the English. During the voyage I found them lively and good-humoured and was frequently entertained by the different games with which they occupied themselves in moderate weather; they did not often quarrel, and when they did their shirts suffered more than their bodies...

The ordinary people of Valletta, 1815

CLAUDIUS SHAW

The lower classes are a fine, active sort of men, capable of enduring great fatigue; they make good sailors, being brought up principally about the harbour and among boats. They can swim almost as soon as they can walk, as you often see the smallest *skikens* (boys) swimming about – many of those who gain their living about the marina have not any houses to live in; they are found at night during the summer months, sleeping on the stones in corners of the streets. In wet weather they get into the porches and stairs of the houses, they have not any beds of bedding.

A people so comfortable and orderly, 1812

JOHN GALT

The Maltese, in their figure, are rather sinewy than muscular. They are, uniformly, more slenderly made than the English, and have a certain columnar appearance in the body, which I have never observed in any other people. Their national features are rather regular than pleasant, and their complexion is much darker than that of the Sicilians. In their habits, they are singularly frugal: a little garlic, or fruit, with a small piece of bread, is their common repast. Butcher-meat is a luxury of which they seldom partake. Their language is a dialect of the Arabic; but many speak Italian, and French. In Valletta, the young men, generally, understand English, of which the sounds accord, in some degree, with those of their native language.

The great amusement of the Maltese is the enjoyment of conversation, sitting, in family parties, at their doors, after sunset. In speaking of national peculiarities, my observations chiefly refer to the practices and customs of the common people. There is but little difference between the genteel manners of one Christian nation and those of another; all educated Europeans having now a great similarity in their domestic habits.

When the magnitude of the Maltese public works, and the general character of the people, are considered, it is impossible not to draw a conclusion favourable to the government of the Knights; who, whatever may have been the extent of their alleged licentiousness as individuals, must have ruled with wisdom, to form a people so comfortable and orderly, and, with their comparatively limited means, to construct works which rival the greatest monuments of the Roman empire.

The population of the island, when the Knights arrived, was reckoned only at twelve thousand; when it fell into the hands of the French, it exceeded a hundred thousand. I have been told that the Maltese speak with regret of the reign of the Knights, or, as they call it, of the time of the Religion. This I was sorry to hear. The British have much difficulty in familiarising themselves to foreigners. The contempt with which they are accustomed to regard every other nation, enables the French, by the practice of their habitual politeness, often to acquire a superior influence, even in those countries which are the pensioners of Great Britain. There is no doubt that the French are, individually, a more accommodating and agreeable people than the British, who, instead of condescending to imitate their rivals in those little arts of address that win the affections, only the more vehemently despise such arts, for the sake of those by whom they are practised. The common consent with which the British undervalue the character and institutions of other nations, is strikingly exemplified in their mode of speaking of the Maltese; and a considerable degree of jealousy seems to be entertained, because the government endeavours to conciliate the native inhabitants... Whatever may be the prejudices of the Maltese, we can have no right to bend them in conformity to ours. We may endeavour, by the fairness, justice, and temperance of our conduct, to awaken their respect, and to excite them to imitation; but I know not what tyranny can be, if it do not consist in compelling men to act against the convictions of their understanding.

The past is always rosy, 1843

ELLIOT WARBURTON

A little beyond Citta Vecchia in St. Paul's Bay... conversing with the people as he rode shipwards, Elliot Warburton found that they, like other people, had their good old times ('all times when old are good'), and these they considered to have been when the Order possessed the island.

Being a mere populace, they would of course willingly exchange their present for their ancient, or for any other, government. They are fain to forget their degraded condition under the Knights, who prevented any native from entering the Order (or even the city, without permission); – who, being disdainful as incapable of a lawful connexion, took their daughters to be concubines, and exercised arbitrary powers as mournfully as oppressively. If there is less foreign money spent among the Maltese now, their taxation is far lighter. They have all the advantages of English laws as well as of their own; they sit on juries; are capable of serving in any department, and have a native regiment paid by the British government. Important as this island now is to us, it was perhaps fortunate for England that a less scrupulous nation took that advantage of the degeneracy of the Order and the imbecility of (Grand Master) Hompech which our ideas of justice might have forbidden.

They are sailors, 1810

DR. CHARLES MERYON

The Maltese are very expert and daring seamen. In their *speronaras*, which are boats without a deck, about thirty foot long, they are seen in all parts of the Mediterranean, and, like all sailors of the Kentish and Sussex coast, as their principal occupation is smuggling, they cannot always wait to choose their weather to put to sea in.

... and anglers, 1834

GEORGE WARING

The Maltese are great anglers, and on Sundays and holydays we see numbers of men and boys, and sometimes women, on the rocks with their immensely long cane-rods, but I have not yet had the pleasure of seeing a fish caught by any of them. They make excellent horse-hair lines, and I have bought one thirty or forty yards in length for sixpence. When we are outside the harbour in the packet, we heard a noise on the water like the ringing of a small bell, and on examination we found it to proceed from a cork buoy placed there to mark the situation of some lines. On this buoy two little pieces of metalware suspended from a short upright stick, and as the motion of the waves kept them continually striking against each other, when the owner of the lines had occasion to examine them in the night, he was directed to the spot by the sound.

... and shipwrights, 1839

THOMAS MACGILL

We ought not to overlook the shipwrights of the Island; they are by all esteemed excellent workmen, and build good ships of fine model, both for the merchants of the Island, and by commission from other parts. If the Island possessed a dry dock (too great an undertaking for a private individual), this branch would become one of the most extensive and important on the Island. The dry docks at Toulon are the only ones in this part of the world; did Malta possess a dry dock she would become the resort of all steamers and other vessels wanting repair in the Mediterranean.

The people and their boats, 1840

GEORGE ANGAS

The Maltese boats are very different to ours, and always attract the attention of a stranger.

They are flat-bottomed, and both the stem and stern have an appendage of an upright piece of wood which projects about a foot above the level of the boat. They are painted with all the colours of the rainbow, and as they are exceedingly numerous, they present a very gay appearance, skimming in all directions over the water of the Grand Harbour.

The pleasure boats *(caico)* have a canopy over them, which can be taken down at pleasure, and is generally a most necessary appendage to protect and screen the traveller from the great heat of the sun.

Ferry boats *(barrea del passo)* are constantly crossing over to the town of Vittoriosa, on the opposite side of the harbour; the proper fare for these boats is one penny, though the boatmen are always ready to impose upon foreigners.

The fishing boats are out every morning before sunrise, and generally return laden with excellent fish, which is sold directly it is brought on shore. The Maltese boatmen always row standing, and are remarkably expert in avoiding the waves which often threaten to swamp their little boats.

The dress of the males, 1838

GEORGE PERCY BADGER

In regard to the male population, the Maltese have in general adopted the Frank (European) costume; but the native dress, which is still worn to some extent by the lower class of people in the town, is somewhat dissimilar, though not very peculiar. The chief difference is in the cap, which resembles a long bag made of wool, hanging down behind, and dyed with various colours. This article often forms a receptacle for small articles which the wearer wishes to carry about with him, and sometimes serves all the purposes of a purse.

The girdle around the loins is still in use among the Maltese of the lower order; that made of cotton is called a *terha*, that of silk is a *bushakka*. With this the pantaloons are confined round the waist, and is generally three or four yards in length. There can be no doubt that this is a relic of the oriental costume, introduced into Malta by the Arabs.

... and the women, 1843

ELLIOT WARBURTON

Many of the women were very beautiful, combining the gazelle eye of the East with the rich tresses of the North, and the statuesque profile of Greece and Italy. Their peculiar head-dress, the *onella*, contributes not a little to the effect of their beauty. This is a black silk scarf, worn over the head like a veil, but gathered in one side so as not to eclipse the starry eyes which it seems always endeavouring to cloud over.

The old aristocracy, proud and poor, form a society among themselves, to which the English are seldom admitted. Nothing can be more melancholy-looking than their high-walled enclosures scattered over the island; in these, nevertheless, they maintain their exclusiveness and *morgue* in not undignified poverty.

A simple life, 1839

THOMAS MACGILL

The wants of the peasantry are few and easily supplied. Their clothing is the produce of their own fields, spun, and often wove in their own families; their living is of the most simple kind: bread made at home forming the predominant part; the other parts may be called a *companatic,* or relish composed of cheese, olives, onions, garlick, dried fruit, salt-fish, oil, etc; in their season, they eat freely of melons, prickly pears, and vegetables in a crude state; they drink wine in moderation. Their evening's repast, after returning home from the fatigues of the day is generally hot, consisting of a *minestra* of cooked vegetables, strengthened with a little oil or grated cheese – this may be called low living, by those who are accustomed to higher fare; but they through life have been used to it, and are contented, robust and healthy.

Through all eastern countries the peasantry live on a similar fare; many worse but few better than those of this island – butcher meat they rarely taste. It is considered as holiday food; but when they have their *caulata* the most dainty palate wants to join in.

The *caulata* of the Maltese is an appetite stirring dish, composed of all sorts of vegetables, boiled together with little water, and a piece of pork to give it a relish. Their *raviola* is even reckoned a dainty dish by the high fed: it is composed of fresh cheese, *ricotta,* beat eggs and chopped parsley enveloped in a thin paste, first boiled, then stewqed in a savoury sauce, with the juice of the love apple.

The in-side comes out, 1840

MALTA PENNY MAGAZINE

First we were saluted, as we pushed our way up the steep sides of the hill, through narrow and winding streets, by a crowd of most importunate beggars, who seemed to increase upon us every step we advanced. As we passed on, there seemed to be around us the stir and hum of great activity. One thing, however, struck us as very peculiar. It seemed as though all the in-door work of Valetta had come out into the streets this morning to take an airing. The tailors, the shoemakers, the carpenters, with the numberless chairs etc, and all the various mechanics, sat out of doors in front of their business with great apparent industry.

This, I afterwards learned, was the common custom of the place. On our way to the lodgings we passed St George's Square, in the Strada Reale, in front of the governor's palace, where we saw crowds of Roman Catholic priests, with their three-cornered hats, tight small clothes, and loose outward robe – a multitude of gaily-dressed English officers – large groups of Scottish Highlanders, kilted, and in their usual military dress – numbers of native Maltese, the men wearing a blue checked shirt, with a red or purple knit worsted cap, the top folding

Gold and silver, 1927

F.N. WESTON

Filigree work in both gold and silver has long been a staple craft of the Maltese, which they probably learnt from contact with the Levant, whence also it came to the southern cities of Italy. The metal workers in Strada Irlandaise – as in other old towns, certain streets in Valetta were assigned to particular trades – formerly also made massive brass knockers in the shape of dolphins, realistic reproductions of the fish, which still adorn the doors of the better houses in the island. Souvenirs for tourists, too, are cleverly made by embellishing all sorts of articles with the coins of the departed Order – huge thick silver pieces, flamboyantly emblazoned with the arms of the Grand Masters in direct violation of the Rule of Raymond, which forbade such worldly vanities. This coinage was accepted currency for many years under British rule.

Doorstep delivery, 1930

S.E.G. PONDER

In the past goats were very much a part of the Maltese scene and often appear in scenes of both town and country.

Goats are milk-providers in most parts of the East and Near East, and nowhere more so than in Malta. At all hours of the day, at some corner, not on a main road, or being led down one of the side-roads, are the goats, about a dozen in number, in charge of the goat-herd, who might be a man or a woman.

They are all females and are animated dairies, for the Maltese housewife demands that her milk shall be delivered fresh and undiluted direct from the factory. The animals are large, hairy creatures, of all shades of white, brown and black. They are always in excellent condition and do not smell offensively... Their long ears flap and they gaze out on the world with silly, vacant stares, whilst the udders are often so dreadfully distended that they make it very difficult for the animal to walk.

Maltese matrons have no illusions where milk-men are concerned, and when requiring their daily supply of milk they come to their doors and signal to the nearest goat herd. He selects one of his animals, takes it by one of its ears, and leads it to the customer, who hands him a glass or jug. The goat is then milked under the eye of the consumer, when it is not easy to dilute the milk whilst watched by a highly suspicious matron, – and yet it is sometimes done.

The Maltese goats, 1839

THOMAS MACGILL

But where is there anything to match the intelligent looking goat of Malta: the assistant nurse to the ladies of the island. The Malta goat is taught to suckle children, they soon acquire the art, and appear to like it, it is truly astonishing with what intelligence they do their work. They leave their pasture when they think the child requires a suck, bleat at the door until admitted, scamper to the nursery where the little urchin is placed on a pillow on the floor, the goat lies down beside it, a tit is placed in its mouth, and then it sucks its fill, or, when Nanny is of the opinion it has had enough, she rises, goes through her gambols, then bounds off to feed. We have known families where the same goat has suckled five or six children; the children, become attached to their quadruped nurse, smile at her gambols, and cry when they think she is neglecting them.

Domestic animals of Malta, 1926

SIR THEMISTOCLES ZAMMIT

The husbandman is always a lover of animals, and in Malta every tenant of a good-sized field owns a mule, one or more cows, a few sheep and a donkey besides pigs and poultry.

The local cattle, large animals of a fawn colour, are extensively used for agricultural work. Cow's milk is not much in demand as goat's milk is generally preferred, but its use is increasing.

The Maltese goat is of the best variety in the world; it has a dainty head, a clean glossy coat, either white, red or black. The amount of milk yielded is rarely below nine pints a day and at times is much greater. The number of goats in the island is reckoned at about 20,000.

Sheep are also numerous, but their milk does not find its way to market as it is mostly turned into cheese. The most common form of cheese is a small disc, about three inches in diameter, which is sold either fresh or half dried. The latter is extensively exported to the East, pickled in brine. The fleece of our sheep is not very thick, and the wool is rarely sold, as it is the custom of the farmers to turn it into homespun for their own use.

The island was for a time famous for its breed of mules and donkeys, but nowadays, unfortunately, they are growing very scarce. The local donkey is as tall as a horse and is a hardy animal which does the work of a mule. The mule is very graceful, powerful and impervious to fatigue.

The Maltese and their education, 1840

GEORGE ANGAS

The Maltese are generally of an ordinary stature, strong, robust, and of a sallow complexion; the country people are very tawny, and are said to bear extreme heat better than any other nation. They have large black eyes, and those you see in the towns are occasionally handsome; they are full of fire, and endowed with a warm and lively imagination, and in their love and hatred, as well as in their general opinions, they are tenacious and affectionate. Notwithstanding the natural fertility of the island beneath a sky of almost continued serenity, the population is so dense that a large portion of the supplies of grain, fruit, vegetables, etc., on which most of the inhabitants subsist, is constantly brought over in boats from Sicily. Many of the over-plus population find an asylum in the Barbary states, in Egypt, Syria and Turkey.

The language is certainly a dialect of Arabic; and in many of the villages, and particularly in Gozo, the original is preserved almost pure. In Valetta most of the better classes understand Italian, and some few speak English, though not nearly as many as I should have supposed.

In the town, there is a normal school, attended by about 500 children, as well as several private schools for the children of the better classes. Education is, however, chiefly in the hands of the priests. The Government University is a large building, and is attended by about 90 students; in the Lyceum, there are nearly 100. It is governed by a rector, and has professors in the four faculties of arts, theology, law and medicine. There is a confessor appointed by the youthful pupils who pay 2s 6d per month each; those of the Lyceum pay one shilling per month, and both later have the use of the extensive library belonging to Government.

The Maltese stand straight, 1851

NASSAU WILLIAM SENIOR

Nassau William Senior, a British civil servant, came to Malta to advise his government back home on the future development of the island. He talked with Mr. Inglett, a Maltese who had passed some years in England, and reported Inglett's view of his fellow countrymen, who had lived for centuries with ruling 'outsiders'.

I remember Malta before the Commissioners came. Seldom has such a change been produced in twenty years. At that time no Maltese stood straight before an Englishman. They were almost on all fours. Now, for the first time in their history, they feel themselves really free men. Labour, food, houses, everything of which the high price denotes prosperity, has doubled in value. Emigration has ceased; the demand for labour is such that it is difficult to get servants. One symptom of improvement is the prevalence of complaint and criticism. When I was young, no one complained of misgovernment, that is to say, to see our welfare sacrificed to the convenience or the caprice of our rulers, seemed to me to be the natural state of subordinate people.

No one complained that the Maltese were not regarded by the dominant stranger as fellow-creatures, because no-one recollected a time when they had been so regarded. The English treated them merely with contempt. The interests of the Maltese were never thought of when those of the garrison were in question, but there was no active oppression. Under the Knights they had to suffer not only contempt, but every sort of injustice and wrong when a dissolute debauched aristocracy could inflict on subjects with whom it had no community of race or language or feelings.

The struggle with the land, 1824

REVEREND CHARLES SWAN

Reverend Charles Swan, chaplain to the Royal Naval ship Cumbrian *during a tour of duty in the Mediterranean, visited Malta three times, had friends there and learned more than most seamen about the place.*

The *carruba*, which is the only tree in Malta that appears to flourish, affords the chief part of the subsistence of the islanders. It yields a kind of bean which is also given to cattle; and indeed the food of their masters is seldom other, or better. This fruit, with a little fish, satisfies them; but the latter is scarce. This easiness of obtaining a bare existence, if it has not rendered them indolent, has probably contributed to making them appear so. Being content with little, and the produce which their country supplies being attainable by creating, not tilling, a soil; by communicating verdure to the rock, not by directing or assisting a natural fertility; no wonder if they should look with despair upon a labour so unpromising, and turn with disgust from hardships for which they can expect so slight a remuneration.

Yet wherever industry would be available, they appear readily to have exercised it. The valley in which we rode bears ample testimony to this truth. The smallest space, whether upon the summit or upon the sides of the rock, has had the stone broken and cultivated; walls are raised for enclosures; and steps, constructed with much neatness and skill, afford a passage upward from one field or compartment to another. These places are open to every inclemency of the weather;

and though its mutations are rare, yet in the rainy season, the water rushes down with tremendous force, and, in a single night, sweeps away the whole expected harvest of the husbandman. But his perseverance is greater than his loss; he resumes his laborious occupation beneath a burning sun, and gathers, at last, the very limited recompense which nature's parsimony admits.

Agriculture, 1839

THOMAS MACGILL

The system of agriculture pursued at Malta is patriarchal, and from the particular nature of the soil cannot be conveniently changed; the soil is turned up with a large hoe, and where it is argilious it is broken with the pick-axe. A primitive looking plough, which a man can carry on his shoulder, is also used, drawn by a cow and an ass, some times a mule or old mare, this plough does not penetrate into the ground, we would say it was more for mollifying the soil, which is apt to cake and indurate, than for any other purpose. The harrow used is also simple and original; not seldom have we seen the seed harrowed in, by branches of trees drawn by the yoke mentioned.

Some of the early English brought ploughs from home, but it was soon found they would not answer, as they brought up the small stones, on which the soil reposes, spades were also attempted but with the same effect, nature and practice has pointed out to the natives, that which is best adapted to the nature of the ground they have to work on. It is truly wonderful how they get on in their own way, and how productive the soil becomes under their management.

Dyers in Gozo, 1839

THOMAS MACGILL

It may be said that there are no regular trades carried on at Gozo, except such as are connected with agricultural pursuits. Many of the females how ever employ themselves in the spinning and weaving of native cotton.

There are several dyers, on different parts of the Island, who dye the Tyrian Purple from the Orchilla weed, which they found on their rocks; this we presume to call a gift, left to them by their ancient friends and masters.

A religious people, 1802

AENEAS ANDERSON

To relate the proceedings of their religious solemnities, the processions by day and the illuminations by night, with the splendid fire-works that enliven the pious joy of their sacred anniversaries, to describe their fastings and acts of penitence, and represent the groups of devotees who, at certain seasons, were seen dragging their voluntary chains, and inflicting voluntary punishments in order to obtain remission of their sins, would be little more than a history of those superstitions which Popery, in its present and enlightened state, has ceased to encourage...

...The Maltese are industrious people, being educated to labour and active employment from their cradles; nor are they ever seen in a state of inactivity, but when they are engaged in the duties of their religion, which, however, must appear to the more enlightened professors of Christianity to occupy to large a proportion of their time.

Lapsi, *c.*1920

SIR THEMISTOCLES ZAMMIT

Lapsi is the celebration of the Ascension of Jesus Christ to heaven. The Maltese say that at midnight on that blessed day the sea loses its salt which makes it bitter and unpalatable and becomes sweet.

I remember the time when at the approach of Lapsi, in all the creeks around the island – San Pawl il-Bahar, Ban Giljan, Tas-Sliema, I-Imsida, il-Fossa, the shores at I-Isla, il-Karkara, Wird il-Ghajn, Birzebugga, – wherever "walnut-shells" (small boats) were to be found tied up, there you would see its owner unfurling the sails and lifting the anchor to catch the morning breeze that had just begun to be felt, and seeking to set forth into the open to glide the surface of the water, happy as a bird, with his flag fluttering at the mast-head, the sun hot as fire on his face and the bells ringing out around him from all the churches in the land... Luff now and take the wind and fill the sails: it's daybreak.

The people living by the sea, after church was over, used to scatter in search of some sheltered corner on the rocks where they could be near the sweet coolness of the water, for the heat of the atmosphere now began to be felt in earnest. All along the beaches you could see, behind some great rock at the entrance of a grotto or under some brink of shore, blankets, flags dangling and hanging down, anything that might cast a bit of shade which at midday might extinguish the heat of the sun. And so all through all that festival holiday the people amused themselves and rested from their daily labours.

The women went round with pots and pans and built fireplaces with stones and pebbles from the beach, and lighted fires to cook what they had brought with them in bags, baskets, panniers, bundles. The men with rolled-up sleeves looked to see if they could catch anything from the sea: "ringing" for octopus, casting a line for young rock-cod, hanging down fishing cords for sargus or gudgeon, throwing bait for black-tail, while others stooped after limpets, snails, sea-anemones, and if they could lay hands on a grab, after any sea urchins in the vicinity.

MALTESE PROVERB

Give me my luck, and throw me to the sea.

Fond of fun, 1828

PRIVATE WILLIAMS

Before we left Malta the Carnival commenced on Saturday 17th February. It continued three days. To anyone fond of fun this was the time to enjoy it. I had never witnessed anything of the sort before. I took good care to be over to Valetta each day before it began. By a general order the British residents and troops are not allowed to mask. About 12 o'clock each day a corps of drums beat through the streets to summon the people, the streets soon became crowded by people of both sex, dressed in every possibly way one can imagine. Angles

[sic], Devils, wild beast, Old men and women, young lads and buxom lasses. In short here was as the song has it "Old and young, grave and sad, deaf and dumb, dull and mad etc."

Every street was so thronged that we were *obliged* to elbow our way through the crowd, every now and then saluted by a volley of sugar plumbs, everything that ran on wheels were in requisition, the middle of the streets were crowded with carriages, gigs, cars, etc, all were masked except the British. This fun continues until sun set, when the drums again beat and the people disappear for the night. In the midst of all this merriment there did not happen one single misunderstanding, for foreigners are not like the English who generally get drunk and fight before their feast or revels are half over. Foreigners drink sparingly and always keep in their senses, thus the three days passed over without rows of any kind. Every face seemed to smile, with content, until about half an hour after the Carnival had closed, when the whole city, I might say Island, was thrown into the deepest sorrow and anguish of mind imaginable.

The cause of this sorrow was a terrible accident involving children sent to a convent during the day who were suffocated as they tried to leave through a door that had been left locked.

Celebrations, 1792

LOUIS DE BOISGELIN

The festival of St. John draws a great concourse of people to the city of Valetta, and on this day the church of St John is thronged; all the troops are under arms and line the streets during the general procession, in which the Grand Master, the Council and the whole body of Knights bear a part. Discharges of Artillery from the fort are made during the ceremony.

In the afternoon the people are amused with races, in the prizes for which are some yards of cloth of gold and silver embroidery.

The race track extended from Fort St. Elmo to the Porte Reale. The first race is performed by men on foot; the second, "which affords the most diversion", by asses of a very fine breed, called the Maltese janetta, the third of mares and the fourth of horses. The asses and the horses are without saddles or bridles, and mounted by boys of twelve or fifteen years old, who manage them with thronged whips. At night a general illumination took place in the city. The Harbour is covered on those days by a multitude of boats, ornamented with colours and streamers, and filled with singers and musicians, making a gay appearance and continuing all night ...

Festas and customs, 1927

F.N. WESTON

Not only does a visitor to Malta find himself in the midst of buildings and ruins reminding him at each step of a great historical past, but he is at the same time surrounded by phases of life which, viewed aright, are full of interest, and also, like the buildings, carry the mind back to days of old. Brought up, as many of us have been, in a creed comparatively undemonstrative and lacking in colour, to come to Malta, where, it is said, there is more public expression of religion than in Rome itself, is much like stepping into a medieval city. This is the effect of the ceremonial, of the religious processions with their rich vestments, emblems and banners, and of the picturesque garb of the members of the various mendicant orders that one meets at every turn. We are not called upon to agree with all we see, but we should at least strive first to understand. In so doing we shall learn to appreciate better the Middle Ages, the ages of faith, in which Malta is nearer than we are. Our spiritual development bears the imprint of the period of Puritanism and the Industrial Revolution, which, whatever good they have left behind them, certainly did much to destroy the poetry and colour of life. We are apt to forget that our forefathers, after all, passed through an age of faith; that they too rejoiced in religious processions, pictures and ceremonial; and that their only holidays were "holy days" or festas. In fact, a complaint was made in Parliament in 1532 that the number of holy-days, especially in harvest time, was excessive.

Good Friday, 1927

F.N. WESTON

There are still today many festas in Malta, when the churches are lit up both in their interiors and exteriors, and the people join the traditional celebrations, as Mr. Weston observed several decades ago.

On the evening of Good Friday most parishes have a procession of 'mysteries', or groups presenting various episodes of the Passion, with symbolical emblems, and in some cases, such as Rabat, people dressed in character. Among those taking part are generally some performing penance in fulfilment of a vow, dragging a heavy chain by the ankle, carrying a large cross, or walking bare-footed. Such have their face covered by a masked hood. There are also at different times processions of certain of the religious lay confraternities, which are attached to all the parishes and many of the other churches, and which are the direct descendants of the religious guilds of the Middle Ages. Most of the altars in the aisles are allocated to them, and it is possible to gauge the wealth of the various brotherhoods by the richness of the frontals and other altar ornaments displayed during the festa. They have, of course, their peculiar duties and privileges. Some, for instance, are entitled to hold services in a special chapel of the church; the Society of Our Lady of Senglea parish church is responsible for the care of the much-prized image of the Madonna, "Our Lady of Victory"; the Confraternity of the Blessed Sacrament carries the Host to the dying; and the Confraternity of the Holy Rosary, attached to the Dominican Order, among other services, collects offerings for masses for the soul of any criminal condemned to death. Such occasions are rare, as in Malta conviction for murder is not necessarily followed by the extreme penalty.

~

Associated with certain festas are various special forms of recreation. On St. Julian's festival (25th August) there are aquatic sports at St. Julian's Bay; Ascension Day is celebrated by parties and picnics on the water; on 29th June the festa of St. Peter and St. Paul, after the procession has returned to the cathedral at Citta Vecchia, crowds proceed to Boschetto for a picnic, and in the evening there are horse races up the hill by Notabile Station. Similar races take place at Sliema about 5 p.m. on 11th July, two days before the festa of Our Lady of

Mount Carmel, and at Pieta on 16th August, the festival of St. Roch, or on the following Monday if that day falls on a Sunday.

These last races were instituted in 1593 to celebrate the cessation of the plague which had raged for eighteen months, and as St. Roch is the patron saint for the cure of the dread disease, the races are naturally associated with his anniversary.

Celebration of the anniversary of the great victory, 1789

VIVANT DENON

We had arrived on the eve of the anniversary of the raising of the siege of 1565, which is always celebrated as a publick festival. It commences with a mortuary service at the church of St. John, for the gallant knights who lost their lives at the siege, and whose names are commemorated with an eulogium on the heroick deeds by which they have been immortalized. The next day all the troops being under arms, the Grand Master is saluted when the Gospel is read, by the grand standard of the order, which is displayed by his seat under a canopy; and a page brings him a sword and poniard sent by Philip II, on the occasion, to the Grand Master, La Valette. The whole concludes with a long procession; during which, salvoes of cannons are fired from the batteries of all the forts.

Celebration of the anniversary of the great victory, 1927

F.N. WESTON

On September 8th in celebration of victory over the Turks (in 1565), and associated with the festa of the Nativity of Our Lady, boat races are held in the Grand Harbour at 4 p.m. Much money is staked on them, and the rivalry between the Marsammuscetto and Grand Harbour partisans is so great that the spectators from the two districts are made to take up their positions on opposite sides of the Harbour.

The races are best seen from a boat looking up the course from near the finishing point off Senglea, although there is often much excitement at the start owing to attempts to foul. The police, however, are gradually stamping this out, and follow the races closely in motor boats to ensure fair play, and to prevent fights at the finish…

…The places associated with that historic event are decked with evergreens, red and white flags, and streamers bearing the names of Knights who distinguished themselves in the year 1565. Formerly some of the identical suits of armour worn by the Knights in the defence, with the rents and holes made by the Turkish sabre and shot, were placed during the day for the public to view in St George's Square, at which awestruck peasants came to gaze from the ends of the island.

The crypt, with the tomb of La Valette in St. John's, is thrown open to the public, who visit it, and the Column of Victory at Vittoriosa, in great numbers.

The women in Rabat who were unable to leave their homes for the commemoration in Valletta used to climb out upon the roofs, and keep up in chorus with one another across the housetops a sort of paean of victory, in memory, no doubt, of the honourable part their sex played in the siege, when they helped to repulse the Turks by carrying the ammunition to the guns.

The horse races, 1765

PATRICK BRYDONE

The horse-races of Malta are of a very uncommon kind. They are performed without either saddle, bridle, whip, or spur; and yet the horses are said to run full speed, and to afford a great deal of diversion. They are accustomed to the ground for some weeks before; and although it is entirely over rock and pavement, there are very seldom any accidents. They have races of asses and mules performed in the same manner four times every year. The rider is only furnished with a machine like a shoe-maker's awl, to prick on his courser if he is lazy.

The Maltese terrier, 1840

GEORGE ANGAS

The race of Maltese dogs, so renowned for their scarcity and singular appearance, is now nearly extinct, though they may still be obtained at an exceedingly high price.

They are very small, with long glistening hair reaching down to the feet, and a turned-up nose. Buffon terms them 'Bichen' in his Natural History. Her Majesty Queen Adelaide procured one of these little creatures during her residence in Malta. It was carried to England, where it was greatly admired as being the only one of its race in the whole country.

What the guidebook said, 1873

MURRAY'S HANDBOOK

The higher classes of native Maltese are not surpassed by those of any country in general intelligence, in highly cultivated tastes, or in the accomplishment or personal character of individuals. But for many years it had been so much the practice of English residents to treat the Maltese with indifferent or contempt, that there is very little opportunity for a stranger to form any opinion except from such examples as may be found in most places where a large fleet and garrison are stationed.

How many people? The 1851 census

NASSAU WILLIAM SENIOR

Monday, March 17, 1855: I have been examining the Census of Malta and its dependency Gozo. Malta contains ninety-five square miles, Gozo twenty. On the 31st March, 1851, the population of Malta was 108,883, that of Gozo 14,663; in all 123,546, giving 1,146 to the square mile in Malta and 753 in Gozo. The population to a square mile in England is 360, so that Malta is almost four times as populous as England, and Gozo is more than twice so. Those 123,546 persons are divided into 29,400 families, or hearths, giving about four to a family. The number of inhabited dwellings in Malta is 21,483, giving about five to a house, and in Gozo 3628, giving about four to a house. For a town population, which that of Malta is, this is an unusually favourable proportion. I do not believe that there is a town in England in which there is a house to every five persons.

Of the professional classes, Senior found:

The advocates are 160; the physicians are 106; the Catholic clergy are 1022; of whom 750 are secular, 257 are regulars, and 15 are Jesuits. The persons employed in the government offices form the largest among the professional classes. They are 745, of whom only 30 are females... The persons returned as attending schools and other places of instruction are returned as 5681, of whom 3181 are males and 2500 are females... The whole number of children between the ages of four and fifteen is 25,083, so that of those who require education only one-sixth receives it.

✳ THE FOREIGNERS ✳

Throughout Malta's long history—as we have seen—there have been foreigners influencing the nation and its history. Now, perhaps, the dominant foreigners are the tourists who have found this place in the sun, with its extraordinary history—and its easy use of English and other languages...

The Knights in their roles, 1568

FRANCISCO BALBI DI CORREGGIO

The Knights of St. John held Malta for over two and a half centuries from 1530 to 1799, and the influence of their way of life was important both then and thereafter. A military-religious order, committed to both fighting 'the infidel' and caring for the poor and sick, their aims influenced the structure of the Order, the roles of the Knights and the buildings and architecture of Malta...

So as to develop and extend its organisation the Order was divided into eight *langues*, or tongues, which embraced all the nations of Christendom, and knights of all nationalities were comprised in its several divisions. The *langues* of the Order of St. John, in order of seniority, were Provence, Auvergne, France, Italy, Aragon, England,* Germany, and Castile with Portugal.

In church matters a *Prior of the Church* was appointed who had authority from the Pope to celebrate pontifical mass with mitre and crook, power to excommunicate and absolve, and to take precedence of all the Bailiffs and "Grand Crosses".

---

* At the Reformation Henry VIII withdrew support from the Order and after this date English knights served as individuals, not as a *langue* or group speaking one tongue.

Each *langue* was placed under one of its own knights who was called a *Pillier*, and each of the Pilliers held one of the principal offices of the Order, the office being allotted to the Pillier of each Langue and always held by it. The Pillier of Provence holds the dignity of Grand Commander. He supervises the finances of the whole Order, and, together with other elected members, is one of the Commissioners of the Treasury. The Pillier of Auvergne is the Marshal and principal arbiter of all disputes which may arise between the knights. He is the Captain General of the land forces and he entrusts the standard of the Order as he thinks fit. The Pillier of France is the Hospitaller. He has full authority over the hospital and is responsible for the provision of doctors and medicines, and all that is required for its maintenance. The Pillier of Italy is the Admiral. He has authority over the officers and crews of the ships of the Order and over the mercenaries, and is responsible for their payment. Together with the Grand Commander he has control over all the stores in the arsenal. The Pillier of Aragon is the Grand Conservator and superintends the distribution of the annual amount that is made to each knight for his maintenance. The Pillier of England [was] the Turcopolier and had charge of all the guards and authority over all dependents of the Order. The Pillier of Germany is the Grand Bailiff and has the supervision of the defences of the Order and is responsible for their munitions, victuals and all their requirements. The Pillier of Castile and Portugal is the Grand Chancellor and has charge of all the documents. He signs all bulls before the Grand Master... To these chiefs of the several *langues* was given the title of Conventual Bailiffs...

Each knight was required to take his meals at the Auberge of his own *langue*, but all expenses were paid by the Treasury.

The Knights: men of the world, 1765

PATRICK BRYDONE

All the knights and commanders have much the appearance of gentlemen, and men of the world. We met with no character in extreme. The ridicules and prejudices of every particular nation are, by degrees, softened and wore off, by the familiar intercourse and collision with each other. It is curious to observe the effect it produces upon the various people that compose this little medley.

The French skip, the German strut, and the Spanish stalk, are all mingled together in such small proportions, that none of them are striking, yet every one of these nations still retain something of their original characteristic: It is only the exuberance of it that is wore off; and it is still easy to distinguish the inhabitants of the south and north side of the Pyrenees, as well as those of the east and west side of the Rhine; for though the Parisian has, in a great measure, lost his assuming air, the Spaniard his taciturnity and solemnity, the German his formality and his pride; yet still you see the German, the Frenchman, and the Spaniard. It is only the caricature, that formerly made them ridiculous, and that has disappeared.

Presentation to Grand Master Pinto, 1765

PATRICK BRYDONE

I forgot to say anything of our presentation to the Grand Master, for which I ask pardon of both you and him. – His name is Pinto, and of a Portuguese family.

He has now been at the head of this singular little state for upwards of thirty years. He received us with great politeness, and was highly pleased to find that some of us had been in Portugal. He mentioned the intimate commercial connections that had so long subsisted betwixt our nations, and expressed his desire of being of service to us, and of rendering our stay in his island as agreeable as possible.

He is a clear-headed, sensible, little old man; which, at so advanced a period of life, is very uncommon. Although he is considerably upwards of ninety, he retains all the faculties of his mind in perfection. He has no minister, but manages everything himself; and has immediate information of the most minute occurrences. He walks up and down stairs, and even to church, without assistance; and has the appearance as if he would still live for many years.

His household attendance and court are all very princely; and as Grand Master of Malta, he is more absolute, and possesses more power, than most sovereign princes. His titles are Serene Highness and Eminence; and as he has the disposal of all lucrative offices, he makes of his councils what he pleases; besides, in all the councils that compose the jurisdiction of this little nation, he himself presides, and has two votes. Since he was chosen Grand Master he has already given away 126 commanderies,* some of them worth upwards of £2000 a year; besides priorities and other offices of profit. – He has the disposal of twenty-one commanderies and one priory every five years; and as there are always a number of expectants, he is very much courted.

He is chosen by a committee of twenty-one; which committee is nominated by the seven nations, three out of each nation. The election must be over within three days after the death of the former grand master; and during these three days, there is scarce a soul that sleeps at Malta: all is cabal and intrigue; and most of the knights are masked, to prevent their particular attachments and connections from being known: the moment the election is over, every thing returns again to its former channel.

The galleys of the Knights, 1790

CHARLES SONNINI

The French naturalist and naval officer, Charles Sonnini, wrote of the Knights' naval power with little enthusiasm.

They are defended, or rather embarrassed, by an incredible number of hands; the flagship had eight hundred men on board. They were superbly ornamented, gold blazed on their numerous bas-reliefs and carvings on the stern; enormous sails, striped blue and red, carried in the centre a great cross of Malta painted red. Their gorgeous flags floated majestically, in a word, everything concurred to render them a magnificent spectacle.

Their construction, however, was little adapted either for fighting or for standing foul weather. The Order kept them rather as an emblem of their ancient splendour than for practical purposes. The navy was one of those ancient institutions which had once swerved to render the brotherhood illustrious but which now only attested its selfishness and decay.

---

* Districts under the control of a commander of an order of knights.

The Knights near the end of their rule, 1789

VIVANT DENON

*Vivant Denon came from France in the very last year of the rule of the
Knights in Malta.*

There are two inns at Malta, the *Falcon* and the *Three Kings*. We put
up at the latter, where we were exceedingly well treated and lodged
for three livres (half-a-crown) a day. I was recommended to the French
resident, who is always one of the Knights. He presented me to the
Grand Master, formerly Prior of the Convent, then Chief of the Order,
and now Sovereign; a situation the most eminent a private individual
can attain, except the Papacy.

He is accordingly distinguished by the title of Your Eminence. Yes,
notwithstanding this, it is very possible that he may be the happiest
of men. Surrounded by ambitious pretenders, his court, like that of
the most powerful monarchs, is a prey to intrigue, and his states are
so limited that he can never move any great distance from his tomb,
towards which he well knows that a thousand of the brotherhood regret

that his approaches are so slow. Notwithstanding their submission, they seem to reproach him with every moment he steals from their ambition, by continuing too long to occupy a place, they all aspire to in their turns.

Manners and actions, 1765

PATRICK BRYDONE

As Malta is an epitome of all Europe, and an assemblage of the younger brothers, who are commonly the best, of its first families, it is probably one of the best academies for politeness in this part of the globe; besides, where everyone is entitled by law as well as custom, to demand satisfaction for the least breach of it, people are under a necessity of being exact and circumspect, both with regard to their words and their actions.

The Knights' last years: a collective influenza, 1804

SAMUEL TAYLOR COLERIDGE

The poet Coleridge came to Malta as a young man to work as secretary to the first British Governor of the islands, Sir Alexander Ball.

The very existence, for so many generations, of an Order of Lay Celibates in that island, who abandoned even the outward shows of an adherence to their vow of chastity, must have had pernicious effects on the morals of the inhabitants. But when it is considered too that the Knights of Malta had been for the last fifty years or more a set of useless idlers, generally illiterate, for they thought literature no part of a soldier's excellence [*Coleridge based this comment on his assessment of the books given to the library on the death of each knight*], and yet effeminate, for they were soldiers in name only: when it is considered, that they were, moreover, all of them *aliens*, who look upon themselves not merely as of a superior rank to the native nobles, but as beings of a different race (I had almost said *species*), from the Maltese collectively; and finally that these men possessed exclusively the government of the Island; it may be safely concluded that they were little better than a collective influenza, relaxing and diseasing the hearts of all the families within their sphere of influence. Hence the peasantry, who fortunately were below their reach, notwithstanding the more than childish ignorance in which they were kept by their priests, yet compared with the middle and higher classes, were both in mind and body, as ordinary men compared to dwarfs. Every respectable family had some one knight for their patron, as a matter of course; and to him to honour of a sister or a daughter was sacrificed, equally as a matter of course.

Dining with a Knight, 1811

CLAUDIUS SHAW

There were three or four Knights who returned to Malta when things got quiet there under the British rule; they were often invited to the Governor's tables, balls, etc.

The first time I dined at the palace, I was seated next to one of these old gentlemen. He was dressed in a full suit of black, wore his cross, a well-powdered wig, black buckles and his knees and on his shoes. We were very friendly, considering that I did not speak Italian, nor he English. Yet we contrived to say *"Poco vino"* frequently, and my worthy old friend got quite gay when the party broke up. Whenever we met we always shook hands, and he seemed much pleased when I was able to converse with him in Italian

Wanted, January 1827

MALTA GOVERNMENT GAZETTE

A GRAND PIANOFORTE of good quality and tone. An English one will be preferred. Any person having such to dispose of is requested to leave his address at the Office of the Gazette, which will be duly attended to.

✳

Some singular figures, 1832

H.J. ROSS

When I was about twelve, Disraeli, accompanied by Mr. N. Willis, the American author, came from Alexandria to Malta with letters of credit to my father, and presented himself at the office dressed in a silk dressing-gown with a guitar suspended with a broad riband round his neck. My father asked him to dine and to go to the opera afterwards, and we boys were allowed to come down to dessert and to accompany the party to the theatre. Disraeli wore lace ruffles on his shirt-front and his wrist-bands, and his fingers were covered with jewelled rings; so we looked much more at him than at the scene on the stage.

Another quaint figure that I well remember was one of the Knights of Malta, an old man who always dressed in breeches and silk stockings, a green coat, a wig, and a three-cornered hat. He was the last of the Knights of the Order who remained in Malta.

Everyone joins in, 1825

ANNE KATHERINE ELWOOD

We came in for all "the fun, frolic and foolery" of the Carnival. There were masked and fancy balls, musical parties and dances innumerable. During the last two or three days, the natives paraded the streets in masks, and the English entered into it *con amore*, pelting each other with sugar plums in a most determined manner.

The social life of the establishment, 1930

SIR HARRY LUKE

To say that Malta was a social place would be a notable under-statement, particularly between the Wars, when it was the base of the greatest single naval force then in existence, The British Mediterranean Fleet. Parties (except in the hot summer months, when they took the form of bathing picnics) had to be arranged weeks in advance, while minor entertaining was continuous. The Opera season in the early spring was a characteristic feature of Malta life before the impressive Opera House was destroyed in the last War. It was to the best of my belief the only Opera House in the world where the men invariably wore mess dress or, if civilians, tails and decorations. The ever hospitable Navy was assiduous in giving dances on board ship, while children's Christmas parties in large aircraft carriers such as the *Glorious* were Christmas parties of almost unbelievable resources and a joy to the not so young as well as the young. A highlight of summer parties was to dine in a battleship anchored in the Grand Harbour, then adjourn to the quarter-deck and from a comfortable armchair enjoy a good film to the accompaniment of a Havana cigar.

The fancy dress ball, 1930

DAVID NIVEN

Actor Niven was an army officer before the war and served in Malta. It was a small station for a young man to stretch his wings to the full without boredom setting in—and mischief breaking out.

The other boredom reliever of those last twelve months was the fancy dress ball in the Opera House. It was a predictable show – admirals dressed as pierrots, their wives as columbines. Bo-peeps were plentiful and there was a sprinkling of Old Bills and Felix the Cats among the military. Parties took boxes in the lovely tiered building and everyone tried hard to pretend that it was every bit as gay and abandoned as the Chelsea Arts Ball.

Trubshawe and I went as goats.

First we put noisome rugs on our backs. Then horns on bands were fixed to our heads and finally, between our legs, for the goat fittings, football swung with rubber gloves sewn on to them by the regimental cobbler. Half a pint of dry martinis apiece and we were ready for the fray.

We arrived just in time for the Grand March for the prize-giving. The judges for the best costumes were on the stage and round and round in front of them, two by two, like the animals going into the Ark, went the clowns with their red hot pokers, the ballet dancers and the Mickey Mice. Rumblings of disapproval arose from the boxes as the two drunken goats joined in at the back of the parade.

"I'm getting dizzy, old man," said the goat behind me after we had completed several circuits.

"Left wheel!"

Obediently I turned out of the parade towards the empty centre of the floor.

"Now squat!" commanded Trubshawe.

"What?" I asked, apprehensively.

"Squat, you bloody fool!"

So there are the very hub of the wheel with a kaleidoscope of colour circling round us and the focus of hundreds of disapproving eyes. I squatted. Trubshawe produced a brown paper bag from the folds of his smelly rug and sprinkled back olives on the floor directly behind me.

MALTESE PROVERB

When I saw you I knew half of you; when we spoke I knew everything.

6

VALLETTA

The first part of this chapter tells of the creation of Valletta; the second gives travellers' responses to this extraordinary creation. Valletta is almost unique in Europe—a city founded only five centuries ago and built as a planned whole.

The Great Siege ended in September 1565, and the Turkish forces disappeared over the horizon (out of sight but not out of mind for generations). Within three months, Francesco Laparelli, once pupil of Michelangelo, now middle-aged, was sent by Pope Pius V to place his military engineering skills at the service of the Knights. He was to create a wholly fortified new city—a planned city. And it is his city that we see today, and that travellers have seen since 1600. There have been few, very few, later invasions, and the strength of Laparelli's city is so powerful that it has withstood even twentieth-century invasions—and now it is a United Nations World Heritage site.

Peter McGregor Eadie introduces the city's extraordinary position on a rocky outcrop jutting into the sea. Francesco Laparelli's own diary tells of the laying of the foundation stone. Nearly 300 years later Benjamin Disraeli praised Valletta to the heavens. Malcolm Billings in his *The Cross and the Crescent*, which accompanied a BBC radio series in 1987, reported on the impact of the Knights as builders. Only five decades after the foundation stone was laid, George Sandys, a British antiquarian, on his Mediterranean travels in 1610, visited and admired.

Water on Malta is—and always will be—a problem: the problem was resolved and Grand Master Wignacourt's aqueduct secured the supply, as Vivant Denon and Louis de Boisgelin described at the end of the eighteenth century.

Another problem Laparelli faced was the slope of the land—so steep that only stairs mount in its place. Today this makes parts of Valletta more car-free than most similar Mediterranean cities. W.H. Bartlett, topographical artist, observed these stairs with interest. Valletta was created as a fortress for the Knights and the people of Malta, threatened not only by the formal Muslim world but also by corsairs from the Barbary coast. In 1804 Samuel Taylor Coleridge commented on these fortifications. The lifting of the two sieges of Malta—by Suleiman in

1565 and by Germany in 1940–3—is celebrated on 8 September. Lady Grosvenor had a splendid view of the first in 1842.

The travellers through time have been stunned by the architecture of the city—by the grand buildings of the Knights and their fortifications, and beyond the buildings to the glinting sea.

Valletta, 1926

SIR THEMISTOCLES ZAMMIT

Valletta, the miniature capital of the Maltese isles, is a quaint, fascinating city, oriental in its colouring and in its crowds, occidental in the severity of its buildings, its regular straight-cut streets and its tidiness. It vies with Genoa in its seventeenth century palaces, with Naples in the blueness of its harbours. When approached for the first time it appears haughty and imperious, girded by its high bastions and isolated by ramparts, moats and redoubts. It is built upon a narrow peninsula, the sides of which, rising sharply from the sea, slope inwards to form a steep plateau known to the old inhabitants as "the mount".

~

Deep, sinuous harbours extend on either side of the peninsula. To the eastward lies the blue Mediterranean and to the westward the suburbs and open country. The town stands compact, as a single block of buildings, closely encircled by solid bastions, for the primary purpose for which it was built was purely military. The streets, judged by modern standards, are narrow, but the Middle Ages seldom used carts and carriages and there were no problems of traffic congestion to be faced ; moreover, as a well known writer says, the narrow streets shaded the burgesses from the sun and protected them from cold winds, and for this reason the side streets are mere lanes. The sanitary outlook of the time was very limited and it was no small advance that the town planners provided gutters to carry away the rain water, and prohibited pigs from haunting the public ways.

The chief aim was to provide straight streets and regular blocks of buildings, and a town as rectangular as the irregularity of the ground allowed.

First impressions, 1843

WILLIAM MAKEPEACE THACKERAY

Valletta is one of the very few places in any country which have more than equalled his expectations. In general, the imagination is so vivid, that anticipation has small chance of being realised. But here it was not so. Valletta has all the poetry of an Italian city, divested of its disagreeable prose. It reminds you of a scene in a drama, in which everything wears a holiday garb. All that you see and hear accords well with an old romance, while the conscious possession of substantial comforts enhance instead of diminishing the charm.

Valletta, however, is but one of the four quarters of the Maltese capital; the others are Vittoriosa, Senglea and Cospicua. These, altogether, encircle the great harbour, and are called the Cottoniers district. Valletta, the principal section, occupies the whole of the rocky ridge which separates the port from the quarantine harbour. Its streets, solidly built of stone, and often connected by long flights of steps, cross each other at right angles, and, from their elevated position, frequently end in views of the open sea – *"Nil nisi ponts et aer."* The aspect of the city from the harbour, with its numerous batteries, breastworks, bastions, forts, and glacis, is that of one vast fortress, rising in successive stages from then water, and bristling with cannon; here and there surmounted with open colonnades, called *baraccas,* which look like hypaethral temples, and which, besides enclosing parterres and military promenades, are decorated with monuments in memory of distinguished officers. Yet even these formidable works were not deemed complete; and various new defences were in progress at all assailable places.

From his novel *Venetia*, 1837

BENJAMIN DISRAELI

If that fair Valletta with its streets of palaces, its picturesque forts, and magnificent church, only crowned some green and azure island of the Ionian Sea – Corfu, for instance – I really think the ideal of landscape would be realised.

From the guidebook, 1965

PETER MCGREGOR EADIE

Valletta occupies the seaward half of Mount Sceberras (43 m), the long rocky promontory which divides the Grand Harbour from the harbour of Marsamexett. Founded by Grand Master La Valette on 28 March 1566 on virgin rock, the city was designed by Francesco Laparelli and completed in 1571 by his assistant Gerolamo Cassar. Its plan comprises a rectangular grid of streets, twelve along and nine across the peninsula, with a perimeter road inside the fortifications. The streets follow the natural terrain with the result that many are steep and rise in steps, Byron's cursed streets of stairs.

'Every span of ground', 1566

SIR THEMISTOCLES ZAMMIT

The site chosen for the construction of the new city was the tongue of land which from the Marsa valley extends to form the Grand Harbour on the south and the Marsamuscetto Harbour on the north. This strip of land was known to the Maltese as *Xaghriet Mewwija* and its extreme point as *Scebb-ir-ras*. The meaning of these names is not very clear but the best interpretation of *Xaghriel Mewwija* seems to be the 'inhabited plain' and of *Scebb-ir-ras*, "the light of the point" suggests that a beacon was kept burning by the first inhabitants on the extreme point of the land to guide their ships into harbour. The modern *Scebb-ir-ras* would therefore be St. Elmo lighthouse, used for this purpose.

An old Maltese saying is that: *F'Xaghriet Mewwija ghad kull xiber jiswa mija* which means "A time will come when at Xaghriet Mewwija every span of ground will be worth a hundred" – a prediction that came to be true – as we all know.

Valletta and its harbours, 1765

PATRICK BRYDONE

To understand Valletta one needs to understand the rocky peninsula on which it stands and the harbours that surround it. There are harbour tours by boat which help give an appreciation of the city as one walks its streets and squares.

We have been admiring the wonderful strength of this place, both by nature and art.

It is certainly the happiest situation that can be imagined. The city stands upon a peninsula, betwixt two of the finest ports in the world, which are defended by almost impregnable fortifications that on the south-east side of the city is the largest. It runs about two miles into the heart of the island, and is so very deep, and surrounded by such high grounds and fortifications that, they assured us, the largest ships of war might ride here in the most stormy weather, almost without a cable.

This beautiful basin is divided into distinct harbours, all equally safe, and each capable of containing an immense number of shipping. The mouth of the harbour is scarcely a quarter of a mile broad, and is commanded on each side by batteries that would tear the strongest ships to pieces before they could enter. Besides this, it is fronted by a quadruple battery, one above the other, the largest of which is a *fleur d'eau*, or on a level with the water. These are mounted with about 80 of their heaviest artillery; so that this harbour, I think, may really be considered as impregnable; and indeed the Turks have ever found it so, and I believe ever will.

The harbour on the north side of the city, although they only use it for fishing, and as a place or quarantine, would, in any other part of the world, be considered as inestimable. It is likewise defended by very strong works; and in the centre of the bastion there is an island on which they have built a castle and a lazaret.

The fortifications of Malta are indeed a most stupendous work. All the boasted catacombs of Rome and Naples are a trifle compared to the immense excavations that have been made in this little island. The ditches, of a vast size, are all cut out of the solid rock. These extend for a great many miles; and raise our astonishment to think that so small a state has been able to make them.

Marsa Macetta Harbour, 1815

CLAUDIUS SHAW

On the west side of Valletta is the Marsa Macetta harbour, the entrance to which is between Fort St. Elmo on the east, and Fort Tigne on the west side – with Fort Manoel higher up the bay, so as to have a full front command of the entrance.

Fort Tigne is on the point, and the ground round it is mined in the most effective and correct manner, so that any force landing there could be blown up in an instant.

The Lazaretto is upon a small island, the same on which Fort Manoel is built. Fort Manoel is a correct square and has excellent accommodation for 1,000 men. These two works, especially Tigne, serve to corroborate what may be said about the ability of the Knights as engineers, most of them having been constructed under their supervision.

The city from the water, 1840

GEORGE ANGAS

The castle and fortress of St. Elmo stand on the right shore of the Grand Harbour as you enter it. It is surmounted by a lighthouse; and beyond, in a southerly direction, lies the city of Valletta. The Marina, lined with stores and crowded with vessels from all parts of the world, extends along the water's side for about a mile. The houses rise one above another, so that almost the whole city can be seen from the water, interspersed with churches and gardens, which have a remarkably pleasing appearance. At the extremity of the harbour lie the British men-of-war. The *Howe*, the *Indus*, and the *Vanguard* were there on my arrival. On the left side of the harbour lie the towns of Borgo (Vittoriosa), Birmula and Senglea ... guarded at the entrance by the towers of Fort Riccasoli, and, further in, the tremendous fortifications of St. Angelo.

Seen from the shore, 1817

JOHN LEWIS BURCKHARDT AND KATHERINE SIM

Katherine Sim wrote a biography of John Lewis Burkhardt called Desert Traveller, *and used his manuscripts to inform her descriptions of his experience of Malta, his first stopping place on his journey to the East, and his dream of returning with the Mecca caravan to West Africa—a dream ambition from which he would never return.*

Here in Malta, Africa was close, the very smell of it was on the seaborne wind, and his thoughts must have turned more and more to the vast little-known continent.

The sun was setting in gold and flame, gilding churches and bastions with fire, the room glowed blood-red and then grew dark. Suddenly from the Moorish ship below a haunting falsetto cry floated up to arouse him from reverie. It was the *mahgrib* call to prayer. He got to his feet, pushing away the writing table, stretched his strong arms, straightened his robes about him, and went to fling wide the half-closed shutter. Small lamps were lit on the decks below, dark-faced figures dressed in white flung themselves down prostrate, stood, bowed and fell forwards again *kibleh*-wards – in the direction of the holy city – engrossed in their evening oblations. For some time he watched intently; when they had finished their prayers he turned to go out. There might be news that evening from the Greek sea-captain – the news he awaited of a passage to Syria.

Approached from the land, 1805

GEORGE, VISCOUNT VALENTIA

Towards the land, La Valletta is perfectly impregnable, and justifies the observation of Bonaparte, when he entered it: "…that it was fortunate there was someone within to open the gates for him."

In the hands of the masters of the sea, it is an invaluable possession. Its harbours afford protection from every wind, and its dockyards furnish supplies for a fleet, at a smaller expense than they can frequently be procured in England, while its fresh provisions, fruit and vegetables, insure health to the seamen. As a naval station, it protects the trade of the Levant, and rendered the secret approach of a hostile squadron towards any part of the Turkish dominions, nearly impracticable; and so long as Great Britain preserves it, the gigantic plans of Bonaparte in the Mediterranean can never be carried into effect, nor can he impress, on the Barbary powers, that ideas of his importance, which is necessary to induce them to abandon all connection with us. As trade increases, the island will become a depot for the woollens, cottons, and hardware of England, which will thence be carried away, to all the surrounding coasts, by the vessels of the inhabitants. This will greatly increase the revenue, and soon render Malta a profit instead of an expense ...

Do not build here, 1927

F.N. WESTON

When the Knights first came to Malta in 1530 the rocky promontory of Mt. Scaberras, "the most difficult place of access in the whole island", was waste ground, with perhaps some Neolithic remains upon it. The Knights built Fort St. Elmo at its point, and the Turks at the siege occupied the rest, eventually storming the fort itself. After the departure of the Turks the Grand Master La Vallette determined, in spite of opposition to build there what should be the chief town of the Order, and, being a man of character, had his way.

One of the great sights of Malta is the spectacle of the performance at Fort St. Elmo with volunteer 'soldiers' parading in historic dress in the fort, firing cannons and mingling with the crowd.

At the laying of the foundation stone, 1566

FRANCESCO LAPARELLI

Francesco Laparelli, planner of the new city on Malta, recorded in his diary the day of the laying of the foundation stone.

On 28th March 1566 began the New City on the island of Malta. It is begun on the hill which is isolated except from the one side and has all those good qualities which we have always stated. The land front is formed at a distance of five hundred *canne* from Fort St. Elmo. There is no habitation, ancient or modern, on that hill. (I think no city was founded where there was no habitation.) St. Spirito Mass has been sung under a canopy planted near the position of the front line. After singing the mass, Father spoke. After the sermon a procession sang the Litany, another oration saying the name of the new city, which is Valletta, and passed towards the middle of the front where the main gate must be put and called the gate of St George. Then it passed to the four bulwarks.

After this the foundation stone was laid, sculptured with the Holy Cross of the Order with its eight angles. And the Grand Master gave me a chain of gold.

Valletta's foundation stone, 1566

SIR THEMISTOCLES ZAMMIT

As the Grand Master was impatient to lay the foundation stone of the City, the fortifications were marked all round by trenches and rubble walls, which showed the outline of the fortress, and the ceremony was performed with great pomp on the 28th March 1566. The rocky ground was crowded with people from the early hours of the morning. An ample pavilion was erected, under which was placed an altar, and all knights, fully equipped, and headed by their chief, attended the High Mass sung by the Prior of the Order, and heard with reverence the long sermon preached by Father Spirito Pelo Angosciola, an Austin Friar.

Amidst great rejoicings and firing of petards and guns, the Prior blessed the Stone, and the Chief of the Order placed a number of coins and medals under it.

The Knights as builders, 1566

MALCOLM BILLINGS

The Knights Hospitallers were builders. Across Europe and Asia Minor they had left proof of their skills. The Siege of 1565 had left their defences and their quarters shattered. Within six months they had founded a new city for themselves.

They chose a site across the harbour on the wide promontory where Fort St. Elmo had so valiantly held out against the Turks. That virgin site of Mount Sciberras was turned into an impregnable fortress city and was to become a byword for outstanding renaissance military architecture. Within five years, work was so advanced that the Grand Master was able to move his headquarters to this new city of Valletta, marking that moment, perhaps, when the Knights finally turned their back on Rhodes and any thought of reconquest. Money poured from a Europe that was both conscience-stricken at failure to go to the Hospitallers' aid, and enormously proud of the Order's performance during the siege. Prayers were said in English churches, and with an enhanced reputation and full coffers, the Knights were able to construct Valletta on a grand scale.

Valletta's streets that cover the rocky peninsula were laid out on a rectangular grid system and it was here that the Knights built their churches, *auberges*, hospital, schools, palace and, of course, conventual church of St John. The enclosed convent, the feature of Rhodes, was abandoned for an 'open plan' monastic city ringed by mighty fortifications.

Valletta today is virtually unchanged – a superb example of a living renaissance city in the middle of the Mediterranean. The Grand Master's palace was built as the centre piece, a home fit for a prince of the Holy Roman Empire. The Grand Masters had sovereign rights, they exchanged ambassadors with Vienna, Paris, Madrid and Moscow, and enjoyed all the trappings of a senior monarch of the day.

A city aloft, 1610

GEORGE SANDYS

Valletta ... not great, but fair, exactly contrived and strong above all others, mounted aloft, and nowhere assailable by Land, but at the South end. The Walls of the rest do join to the upright Rock as if one piece, and are beaten upon by the Sea. That toward the Land is but a narrow Isthmus, where the Rock doth naturally rise; the Ditch without hewn down exceeding broad; and of an incredible profundity, strongly flanked and not wanting what fortification can do. This way openeth the only Gate of the City...

The Buildings are for the most part uniform; all free-stone, two stories [sic] high and flat at the top; the upper Rooms of most having Out-Terraces. The Grand Master's Palace is a Princely Structure, having a Tower which overlooketh the whole Island. The Chamber where they sit in Council is curiously painted with their fights by Sea and Land, both foreign and defensive.

The seven Auberges of the Knights being of no mean building, amongst whom the City is quartered. Magnificent is the Church of St Paul and that of St John; the one the Seat of a Bishop, the other of a Prior. And St John's Hospital doth merit regard, not only for the building but for the entertainment there given; for all that fall sick are admitted thereunto. The Knights themselves there lodge, when hurt or diseased; where they have Physick for the body, and for the soul also (such as they give).

The fortifications, 1804

SAMUEL TAYLOR COLERIDGE

The fortifications of Valletta are endless – when I first walked about them, I was struck all of a heap with their strangeness, and when I came to understand a little of their purpose, I was overwhelmed with wonder. Such *vast masses* – bulky mountain-breasted Heights – gardens with pomegranate Trees & the prickly Pear in the Fosses – & the Caper (the most beautiful of Flowers) growing profusely in the interstices of the high walls & on the battlements.

The fortifications, 16th–19th centuries

DAVID TRUMP

The main inland defences of La Valette's city are the great walls and dry moat originally pierced only at Kingsgate and at the two ends. Besides the additional entrance at the Castille, Kingsgate itself has recently been substantially enlarged. Notice below the bridge to the south where the Malta Railway crossed the moat to its underground Valletta terminus, a precious fragment of industrial archaeology. The towers of Cavaliers of St. James and St. John added further to the strength of the defence. Outside the walls, a broad strip of land was kept bare as a field of fire.

In the later 17th century, an outer defence was built to take in the growing suburb of Floriana, together with the granary pits in front of the church of St. Publius. These walls too had a main central entrance at the Porte des Bombes. The gate itself originally spanned the gap in the wall near the present roundabout, and was moved a hundred metres or so downhill to ease the traffic congestion at this point. The approach was further overlooked by the Horn Work, which projects from the Floriana walls to the south of the main road. The whole of the area now covered by gardens, cemeteries, petrol stations, and the like was kept as another open glacis before the walls. Below ground, a maze of tunnels was cut to protect the walls from hostile mining.

The defences of the Three Cities, east of the Grand Harbour, have a similar history. The nucleus of the defence is Fort St. Angelo, dating from the period before the Knights came to Malta. It was Vallette's headquarters through the Siege. The walls of Vittoriosa and Senglea were the ones which withstood the Turks in 1565, though they needed very substantial rebuilding after the rough treatment they received that summer. In 1638 the Margherita Lines were thrown round the developing suburb of Cospicua. Later still, the Cottonera brothers, successive Grand Masters of the Order, began the Cottonera Lines in 1670 to take in a wider area. Finally, the wall enclosing the military area in the Corradino Heights was added, not being completed until after the British came to Malta.

The Knights' hold on the harbour area was completed by Forts Ricasoli, Manoel and Tigne on the promontories around it in the later 17th and 18th centuries.

Fort Ricasoli, 1840

MALTA PENNY MAGAZINE

The fort was founded in the year 1670 by the Cavalier Gianfrancesco Ricasoli, who contributed the sum of £3000 towards defraying the expenses of the building, and endowed it with a large portion of his income. The Grandmaster Cottonera publicly acknowledged his gratitude to the knight for so generous an action, and ordered that it should be called after his name, Ricasoli.

This fortress is built on the extreme point of an angular projection, and corresponds with St. Elmo on the opposite shore. The two forts together command the entrance into the Great Harbour. In itself it is a place of considerable strength, and is additionally guarded by the bulwarks which extend and ramify towards the Cottonera lines. From the sea, this fort, if tolerably garrisoned, would be quite impregnable. From the land side it could only be reached by surmounting a long succession of strongly defended posts, at each of which the assailants would be subject to imminent, almost insuperable, danger.

The planned city, 1792

LOUIS DE BOISGELIN

Each house is provided with a private cistern, besides which there are public ones, and a fountain supplied from an aqueduct which conveys the water from the southern part of the Island, built at a great expense by the Grand Master De Wignacourt. The length of this work from *Dier Chandal* where it commences, to the square in front of the palace where the fountain is placed, is 17,033 yards or more than 9 and a half English miles. The water is carried into every street by subterranean canals which communicate with the private and public cisterns, that in case the rains in Winter should not be sufficiently abundant, they may be supplied by the fountain.

Water, 1789

VIVANT DENON

Returning to Valletta from a tour in the countryside, Vivant Denon passed under the aqueducts by which the Grand Master de Wignacourt (1601–22) brought the water from the only fountain (spring) belonging to the city. The line of the aqueduct still runs beside the road from Mdina to Valletta.

This scarcity of water at Malta is remedied by a prodigious number of cisterns, which are easily made, as nothing more is necessary than to arch over and convert into reservoirs the excavations that serve for quarries, and the foundations of their house, so that each house has its own, and not a drop of rain water that falls upon the city is lost.

Water, 1840

GEORGE ANGAS

On my arrival, one of the first pieces of information I heard was, that there had been no rain in Malta for four years, and that water was in consequence extremely scarce. Indeed, the country in most parts resembled a barren desert, the fields being so parched up that not a single blade of grass was to be seen; and the constant glare of the burning sun upon the white rock, and the clouds of dust that arose on every breath of wind, rendered it extremely unpleasant of the eyes. There was, however, still some water in the public fountains in Valletta, and on passing any of these I was generally sure to see some twenty or thirty poor creatures gathered around with small water barrels to take home this valuable necessary to their wives and families. ... In many of the casals or villages the people are obliged to buy their water at the rate of one half-penny a gallon; this is supplied to them by water carts from the aqueduct, built by the Grand Master Wignacourt, AD 1610.

Heat and Water, 1810

DR. CHARLES MERYON

Dr. Meryon was accompanying Lady Hester Stanhope, niece of William Pitt, British Prime Minister, on her travels—and everyone was eager to be her host. She chose to stay with Mr. Fernandez who lived in the former house of the French Knights, and Dr. Meryon was able to describe it and the arrangements made in the city for water, with much interest.

The modern city, Valletta, was founded in 1566; and, by the enthusiasm of the islanders, who voluntarily aided in the works, it was finished in 1571. It is entirely built of the calcareous stone of the rock on which it stands. A piece of ground was given to each of the nations (or *languages*, as it was usual to style them) for their respective habitations or inns. The streets are built at right angles, and paved with flat square stones, and the houses are spacious, lofty, and with regular fronts, most of them having a balcony projecting over the street. The object of the architect seems to have been, besides beauty and strength, to gain shade and coolness. Hence the walls of the houses are generally from six to twelve feet thick, and the floors always of stone. The doors are folding, and the windows down to the ground. In every house of the principal inhabitants, in the summer, there is a suite of rooms thrown open. Thus, by having five or six rooms in a line, great coolness and, if required, a current of air is obtained, the value of which can be sufficiently appreciated by those only who live in very hot countries.

In most of the houses, the ground floor is used for warehouses, and shops; and the family resides on the first floor, the bed-rooms and sitting rooms being all on the same level. Every house has a cistern, into which rain-water runs from the roof. These roofs, formed of an excellent cement, are flat. Besides the private cisterns, there are public reservoirs, and also a fountain, the source of which is at the village of Diar Chandal, twelve or thirteen miles from La Valletta, whither the water is conveyed by subterranean aqueduct.

A city on a hill, 1765

PATRICK BRYDONE

As the city of Valletta is built upon a hill, none of the streets except the quay are level.

They are all paved with white free-stone, which not only creates a great dust, but from its colour is likewise so offensive to the eyes, that most of the people here are remarkably weak-sighted. The principal buildings are the palace of the Grand Master, the infirmary, the arsenal, the inns or hotels of the seven Tongues (or Langues), and the great church of St. John. The palace is a noble though a plain structure, and the Grand Master (who studies convenience more than magnificence) is more comfortably and more commodiously lodged than any prince in Europe, the king of Sardinia perhaps not excepted. The great stair is the easiest and best I ever saw.

The effect is grand, 1812

JOHN GALT

The entrance to the harbour of Valletta is truly grand. On each side, and in front, the fortifications rise in stupendous masses, with a watch-tower perched here and there in the corners. The buildings and domes above them have also a very noble appearance. Not a particle of smoke sullies the atmosphere; and every edifice looks as if it were only just finished. The internal appearance of the city corresponds to the magnificence of its exterior. The landing-place is an extensive crescent; from which a gentle ascent, partly excavated in the rock, leads towards a gate. The one side of this way is occupied with the stalls of dealers in fish, fruits, and other necessaries. Immediately in front of the drawbridge is a handsome fountain, ornamented with a bronze statue of Neptune; and, on entering the gateway, the stairs, which conduct to the upper part of the town, immediately commence, making the entrance in some respects, more like the vestibule of a great mansion, than the portal of a city. Nothing can be more striking than the streets which are first ascended passing this gateway. They are, in fact, so many vast staircases; and the buildings that rise prospectively in the ascent, are ornamented with cornices and projections, so huge, that the architecture seems to have been designed to correspond in strength and durability with the fortifications.

The domestic architecture of the Maltese cannot be considered as regulated by the established rules of good taste; nevertheless, the picturesque effect is grand; and one meets, occasionally, with vistas that seem more like the conceptions of a painter than the limited realities of an inhabited town.

Entering the city, 1840

GEORGE ANGAS

Passing through a long excavated passage called the Lascaris Gate, you enter the Strada Levante, and cross a drawbridge over a second fortification, beneath which is a small garden filled with orange, lemon and cypress trees, whose cool greenness forms an agreeable contrast to the white dusty glare of the streets on first entering the city.

Longitudinally and latitudinally, 1839

THOMAS MACGILL

The city of Valletta is divided into streets longitudinally and latitudinally, running parallel to each other, the latitudinal crossing at right angles; the principal street or *Strada* Reale, runs from the main gate Porta Reale, on the extreme south, down the hill to Castle St. Elmo; on the right or towards the east, run Strada Mercanti, St. Paolo, St. Ursula, and lastly Levante, which joins the line wall; on the left or to the west, run Strada Stretta. Forni, Zecra, Ponente, and lastly Marsamuacetta, on the line wall; latitudinally on the extreme south is Strada Merzodi, Britannica, St. Giovanni, Lucia, Teatro, Vescovo, San Cristoforo, San Domenico, San Nicola, and also some short transverse lanes.

The stranger need never lose himself in Valletta, as all the streets run parallel and cut each other at right angles: the names of the streets being on the corners, and all the houses regularly numbered.

The city of Valletta is girt round by formidable bastions and fine walls, – crowned towards the sea by castle St. Elmo, and towards the land by the Cavaliers of St. John and St. James.

The streets of stairs, 1851

W.H. BARTLETT

You arrive at the foot of one of those long flights of steps, of which Lord Byron took leave with the splendid couplet: –

> "Adieu! ye cursed streets of stairs;
> How surely he who mounts them swears!"

These stair-streets form one of the most curious features of Valletta. Troublesome as it may be to ascend them on a hot day, yet the very nature of the ground left no alternative; and to those who have made their way up the excruciating rugged alleys of a continental city, paved with sharp-pointed stones, the large, flat slabs, and easy, gradual ascent, of these of Malta, are certainly delightful by comparison.

A walk through the city, 1968

EDWARD SAMMUT

From Castile Square a wide esplanade follows the contour of the fortifications which defend Valletta on the landward side, from the embrasures and firing parapets there is a continuously changing panorama inland as far as the heights of Mdina, and across Marsamxett Harbour to the residential suburbs of Ta' Xbiex and Sliema. To the right, beyond St. James Cavalier, is the bridge crossing Kingsway, with a marvellous view down the main thoroughfare as far as Fort St. Elmo, and further on, the twin Cavalier of St. John. At this point the Bastion of St. John is laid out as a public garden, in the centre of which is a monument to Francis Rawdon, Marquis of Hastings, who was Governor General of India for ten years and Governor of Malta in 1824–26. Hastings Gardens are probably the best place from which to examine the magnificent system of fortifications, stretching from harbour to harbour, which defends Valletta on the landward side. The tremendous moat was dug, and the first line was built immediately after the Great Siege, but the outer defences, which extend as far as Pieta on the North and Marsa on the West, continued to be strengthened and increased until the middle of the 18th century.

~

... From the end of St. Michael's Bastion a few steps lead to the bottom of South Street, formerly one of the most elegant in the City, which still includes a large number of the 17th and 18th century palaces of the Knights, with their original facades. Walking towards Kingsway, the first building of importance is Admiralty House, which was the official residence of the Grand Admiral of the Order, and later British Naval Commander-in-Chief. It was built by the Bailiff Francois de la Guierche (c. 1660); and the Comte de Beaujolais, brother of King Louis Philippe, died here in 1808. In the long list of famous sailors who occupied these premises we find the names of Admiral Suffren de Tropez, Sir Edward Codrington of Navarino, Lord 'Jack' Fisher of Kilverstone, Sir Roger Keys of Zeebrugge, and Earl Cunningham of Hyndhope, and Mountbatten of Burma.

~

At the end of this walk Edward Sammut led his readers back to where he had set them off.

Leaving St. Elmo on the left, follow Irish Street, which leads between the Long Ward of the Hospital and St. Lazarus Bastion to the Lower Baracca Gardens, laid out on a three-cornered bastion rising sheer from the water's edge. In the centre is a neoclassic monument to Sir Alexander Ball, designed by Giorgio Pullicino, with statuary by Vincenzo Dimech. Just below the entrance is the new Fish Market and, standing against the bastion are the stores built by Vilhena as the *Nevaio,* a primitive cold-storage system making use of snow brought from Sicily. This part of the tour may now be concluded by proceeding up St. Christopher Street, past the National Archives, the earliest records being those of Notary Bartolomea Sillato (1485–1531), and back to the Palace Square ...

A more worldly way of life, 1994

PETER DIETZ

The Manoel Theatre, in Old Theatre Street, helps to dispel this atmosphere of living under a threat. It was built by Antonio Manoel de Vilhena in 1731 when he was Grand Master of the Order and illustrates the beginning of that decline, noted by Gibbon, into a more worldly and sophisticated way of life in the 18th century. As Gibbon said, "The Knights were more prepared to die for their God than to live for him."

The theatre has maintained its position as the artistic centre of Malta and enjoys the reputation of being the third oldest theatre in Europe. A Royal Opera House was built in the mid-19th century but was destroyed by fire in 1873, allowing the Manoel to come into its own again. The Opera House was rebuilt but it was destroyed in the Second World War. Before the war the Manoel had served intermittently as a dance hall and a cinema, and was no doubt well patronised by the Fleet. It was restored and re-opened in 1960 and has remained without a rival since then.

Life in the streets, 1850

WILLIAM MAKEPEACE THACKERAY

The streets are thronged with a lively, comfortable-looking population; the poor seem to inhabit handsome stone palaces, with balconies and projecting windows of heavy carved stone. The lights and shadows; the cries and stenches; the fruit-shops an d fish-stalls; the dresses and chatter of all nations; the soldiers in scarlet and women in black mantillas; the beggars, boatmen, barrels of pickled herrings, and macaroni; the shovel-hatted priests and bearded Capuchins; the tobacco, grapes, onions and sunshine; the signboards, bottled porter stores, the statues of saints, and little chapels, which jostle the stranger's eyes as he goes up the famous stairs from the Water-gate, make a scene of such pleasant confusion and liveliness as I have never witnessed before. And the effect of the groups of multitudinous actors in this busy, cheerful drama is heightened, as it were, by the decorations of the stage. The sky is delightfully brilliant, all the houses and ornaments are stately, castes and palaces are rising all around, and the flag, towers, and walls of Fort St. Elmo look as fresh and magnificent as if they had been erected only yesterday.

The Strada Reale has a much more courtly appearance. Here are palaces, churches, court-houses, and libraries, the genteel London shops, and the latest articles of perfumery. Gay young officers are strolling about in shell-jackets much too small for them; midshipmen are clattering by on hired horses; squads of priests, habited after the fashion of Don Basilia in the opera, are demurely pacing to and fro; professional beggars run screaming after the stranger. The houses where they are selling carpet-bags and pomatum were the palaces of the successors of the goodliest company of gallant Knights the world ever heard tell of.

The city walls, 1841

GEORGE ANGAS

The walls of the city measure about fifteen feet in width, and their entire circumference is about two miles and a half. The ditch is a stupendous work; one thousand feet in length, one hundred and twenty feet deep, and the same in width. The bottom of this ditch is cultivated, and on looking over the drawbridge of Porta Reale, I saw fig-trees and prickly pears growing in this gulf below me; whilst here and there a sportive summer butterfly could be seen wandering like some light creature of the element over the green leaves of the stunted trees.

I went through the two underground passages which lead out of the city, called St. John's and St. James's Cavaliers: they are cut out of the solid limestone, and the air strikes very cold on entering them from the sultry atmosphere without.

There are many outworks and glacis of massive stone beyond these walls, and there is a second series of fortifications outside the suburbs of Floriana, which render the city of Valletta one of the best fortified in the whole world.

I finished my survey by a walk along the walls overlooking the ditch. That part called the Baracca, surmounts a very fine view of the harbour and the surrounding country, which looks like a parched desert covered with walls and buildings, over which the eye wanders in vain in search of some spot of green to relieve and cheer the burning glare of this southern landscape. In the centre of this platform, within a grove of trees, stands the tomb of Sir Thomas Maitland, one of the late governors of Malta; and several other monuments are raised in various parts of this fortification.

The fortifications, 1994

PETER DIETZ

The best view of the peninsula of Senglea and Vittoriosa (Birgu), giving an "attacker's eye view" of the towns defended by the Knights and their Maltese soldiers, is from the Victoria Gate of Valletta, or further to the west from Magazine Bastion. Fort St. Elmo, the scene of the self-sacrificing battle to the death of its garrison, and Fort St. Angelo, across the Grand Harbour, which was vital in the defence of Vittoriosa against the first desperate attacks of the Turks, are both still standing and can be visited. St. Elmo houses the Malta War Museum.

But the best way of all to view Valletta and the fortified peninsula is by boat. There are guided tours of Marsamexett and Grand Harbours daily in winter and more frequently in summer, leaving from The Strand below Sliema. The boat trip around Valletta and into the creeks of Grand Harbour provides an excellent introduction to the architecture and layout of the towns and harbours surrounding the central urban areas of Malta.

Anniversary of the Siege, 1842

LADY GROSVENOR

We had seats in the windows of the customs house to see certain boat races and games on the water, which are held on the anniversary of the raising of the siege of La Vallette, which took place in 1565.

The boat races were succeeded by games, as follows: a long and well oiled bowsprit or pole being projected from the end of a barge, the competitors run along this to seize a flag fixed at the end, to obtain a prize of twenty dollars. The unsuccessful heroes dropped straight into the water, and swam back into the barge, which was, however, small sorrow to them, as the Maltese are mostly amphibious ... The sight was altogether pretty from the number of boats assembled, and the various colours in which it is the fashion to paint them, added to the crowds of people with which the customs house stairs were covered.

More fortifications, 1994

PETER DIETZ

The fortifications on the landward side of Valletta and another complete system of bastions, batteries and dry moats on the landward side of the suburb of Floriana were completed in the late 17th and 18th centuries according to the principal of Marshall Sebastien le Pretre de Vauban, one of Louis XIV's military advisers and the greatest military engineers of his age. Between the two lines of the fortifications on the landward side of Valletta can be found near the City Gate, the famous Triton statue, almost completely obscured by Malta's central bus terminus. From the Triton it is possible to get buses to almost every village, however, small, across the whole of the main island. Further out, but still within the fortifications is the Royal Air Force Memorial which bears the names of all the air-crew members who failed to return from missions while based on the island during the Second World War. It provides a poignant reminder of the intensity of the air battles over the island and shows in its sombre details when the crisis of the air battle came in 1942.

One can see, too, that the air battle, with all its attendant casualties, went on into 1945, well after the Mediterranean Sea was cleared of its Axis enemies, and that the island was defended by squadrons from the Commonwealth and from many of the Allied nations.

Letter home, 1830

BENJAMIN DISRAELI

The city is one of the most beautiful, for its architecture and the splendour of its streets, that I know… something between Venice and Cadiz.

The sights of Malta, 1847

JOHN GARDNER WILKINSON

Wilkinson had travelled widely in the Near East and Egypt and was invited to produce the Murray's Guide to Egypt, in which he included details of how to get there, with a stop-over at Malta before the last section of the journey. A century and a half after he wrote, sites that seemed to him almost mundane are still there and truly worthy of our attention and interest today—as to most travellers they were then...

There are few objects worthy of a visit in Malta. The principal in the town of Valletta are the palace, the government library, the cathedral church of St. John, the fortifications, the view from the two Baraccas, and the palaces of the Knights, called Auberges, particularly those of Castile and Provence.

In the palace are the armoury, a few good pictures, and some curious tapestry. Many of the apartments are good, and not less so the ballroom.

The armoury is well arranged, but the specimens of armour are not so curious, nor so varied, as might be expected in the city of the Knights. The complete suit of Vignacourt is very elegant and simple. It is the same he wore when painted by Caravaggio in a picture in the dining room, a copy of which is placed above it.

~

The Library was founded in 1790 by the Bailli de Tencin, who presented the public with 9,700 volumes. It contains many curious and old works, and is composed of the private collections of the knights, who were obliged to bequeath their books to this public institution. Here are deposited some antiques of various kinds found in Malta and Gozo, among which are a parallel Greek and Punic inscription, several strange headless figures from Crendi, two curious coffins of terra-cotta, and a few other objects of various styles and epochs.*

Of St. John's church the most curious part is the floor, where the arms of all the Grand Masters are inlaid in various coloured marbles.

---

* Such material has long been gathered in the Archaeological Museum not far from the Library.

They have been very useful for heraldry.

The tapestry of this church is also very fine. It is put up at the fete of St. John, and continues to be exposed to public view for several days, before and after the ceremony.

The silver railing of the chapel of the Madonna, at the east end is curious. It is said to have owed its preservation at the time of the French occupation of the island (1798) to the paint that then concealed the valuable quality of the material.

In the crypt below the cathedral are the tombs of some of the Grand Masters.

The different tongues, 1839

THOMAS MACGILL

We observed that in the building of the city of Valletta, the different tongues or branches of the order built for themselves stately auberges; these tongues were eight in number: France, Provence, Auvergne, Castile, Aragon, Italy, Germany and Anglo-Bavaria.

The auberge of France, in Strada Mezzodi, is an extensive building, at present the commissariat of Her Majesty (Queen Victoria).

The auberge of Castile at the eastern extremity of the same street, is a strikingly fine building, its entrance and staircase are much admired. This fine auberge is at present occupied as officers' quarters.

The auberge of Italy, near that of Castile, and in Strada Mercanti is a large building but without architectural beauty; the shield in front is sculptured on marble, once a column of the temple of Proserpine, which well have been spared in an original state; in the lower part of the auberge is the Civil Arsenal of Her Majesty; in the upper part, is the Government Printing Office.

The auberge of Provence is in Strada Reale. This is a fine building of good architecture; the upper part is devoted to the service of the Union Club, and its extensive and fine hall is a ball room, the lower part if an Auction room.

The auberge of d'Auvergne is also in Strada Reale. This is a large building but not pretty; here sit Her Majesty's courts of law.

In Strada Ponentre is the German auberge, the residence of his honour the Chief Justice, and near it is that of Aragon, where the Chief Secretary to Government resides.

At the bottom of Strada Ponente and on the line wall, facing the sea, stands that superb building, the Anglo-Bavarian auberge, isolated from all others and occupied as Officers' quarters.

From the Upper Barracca Gardens, 1927

F.N. WESTON

One of the pleasantest places in Valletta, where one can take a break from all the extraordinary history of the city, is these gardens, set high above the lower town.

The Knights were of course of different nations, so they were divided into various 'langues', or 'Languages', each of which had a definite portion of the fortifications to defend.

This part of the ramparts was allotted to the Language of Italy, who in the 17th century laid out these gardens for their own delectation, while one of their number had the arcade built and roofed at his own expense. It is said, however, that when certain of the priests and people conspired against the Knights in 1775 they assembled here, so the Grand Master ordered the roof to be removed to prevent further meetings.

Standing looking over the harbour there is a beautiful view, and one full of historical interest.

From Governor Ball's memorial, 1841

GEORGE ANGAS

Should you want a quiet place to sit and consider the past of the island and its present beauty, search out this place of memorial...

In the centre of a small square, on the most elevated part of the fort (St. Elmo), a beautiful Grecian monument has lately been erected to the memory of Governor Ball: it is built of the Malta stone, which in this fine climate retains its dazzling whiteness unsullied for many years. Around this monument is a row of shady pimento trees, and adjoining it is an arched way formerly used as a place of amusement by the

Knights, from which the distant views of land and sea are delightful, varied and extensive. The deep azure blue of the Mediterranean Sea stretched out below, till it mingles with the distant horizon, contrasts well with the snowy whiteness of the various xebecs, galliots, and other boats, which appear like specks upon the surface.

Far away to the north lay Capo Passaro, whence I could trace the shores of Sicily towards Palma and Alicata. On a very clear day at sunrise, Mount Etna, too, may be seen towering above the waters; but this is not, as many writers have supposed, an every-day occurrence.

On the outermost angle of the fort sands the lighthouse which has lately been much improved ...

A brief visit, 1839

EMMA ROBERTS

Emma Roberts was on her way to India via the overland route through Egypt. She arrived from Marseilles and very soon went on to Alexandria.

We were, of course, up by daylight, in order to lose nothing of the view. Much as I had heard of the gay singularity of Malta, I felt surprise as well as delight at the beautiful scene around; nor was I at all prepared for the extent of the city of Valletta. The excessive whiteness of the houses, built of the rock of which the island is composed, contrasted with the vivid green of their verandahs, gives to the whole landscape the air of a painting, in which the artist has employed the most brilliant colours for sea and sky, and habitations of a sort of fairy land. Nor does a nearer approach destroy this illusion; there are no prominently squalid features in Malta; the beggars, who crowd round every stranger, being the only evidence, at a cursory gaze, of its poverty.

We found a *caless* waiting for us; a very singular description of a vehicle, but one common to the island. I had seen representations of these carriages in old engravings, but had not the least idea that they were still in use. They have only two wheels, placed behind, so the horse had to bear the weight of the vehicle as well as to draw it; and there is something so inexpressibly odd in the whole arrangement, that it put me in mind of the equipages brought on the stage in a Christmas pantomime.

Our *caless* held four persons very conveniently, and was really a handsome vehicle, gaily lined with scarlet leather, and having spring seats. We saw others playing for hire, of a very inferior description; some only calculated for two persons, and of a faded and dilapidated appearance. They seem to be dangerous conveyances, especially for the poor horse; we heard of one being upset, on a steep hill, and breaking the neck of the horse that drew it.

In driving we were obliged to take rather a circuitous route to our inn, though the distance, had we walked, would have been very inconsiderable. We were glad of the opportunity of seeing a little of the suburbs, and were almost sorry to arrive at our destination.

The streets of the city of Valletta are extremely narrow, and the houses high; a great advantage in such a climate, as it ensures shade, while, as they generally run at right angles, they obtain all the breeze that is to be had.

The appearance of our hotel was prepossessing. We entered through a wide gateway into a hall opening upon a small court, in the centre of which stood a large vase, very well sculptured, from the stone of the island, filled with flowers. A wide handsome staircase, also of stone, with richly-carved balustrades, and adorned with statues and vases, conducted us to a gallery, two sides of which were open, and the other two closed, running round the courtyard, and afforded entrance to very good apartments. Everything was perfectly clean; the bedsteads of iron, furnished with mosquito curtains; and we were supplied immediately with every article that we required.

Strada Reale, 1841

GEORGE ANGAS

The principal street of Valletta is Strada Reale, which extends from the gate of the same name as far as the castle of St. Elmo, a distance of three quarters of a mile. The city is closed by three gates: Porte Reale, which is the chief entrance from the country, and the suburban town of Floriana; Porta Marssamuscetto, from the quarantine harbour and the Marina gate from the Grand Harbour.

Strada Reale, 1841

MALTA PENNY MAGAZINE

From this point at the end of the descent the pathway on either side consists of no less than 160 steps, and the road is so steep as to prevent its being passable by cart or horse. This peculiarity belongs to Valletta generally in consequence of its uneven site, which declines considerably from its centre towards the north and north east. The inconveniences of this position, however, are in some measure compensated by the facility it affords for the draining of the streets and their consequent cleanliness; nor does it detract but rather enhances the beauty of the town. The zig-zag ascent and descent, which some of the streets of Malta present to the beholder from an eminence, is very picturesque. The buildings are in general high, have many windows, and are ornamented with fantastically wrought balconies, which jut out into the street, and in the prospective appear to overtop each other. This style of architecture gives a rather sombre appearance to the streets, but renders them far less monotonous than such as are level and lined with plain-faced dwellings.

Valletta contains in all eight parallel and twelve transverse streets, which are all straight and cut into each other at right angles. Of these Strada Reale, formerly called Strada San Giorgio, is the principal, and extends the whole length of the town, from the city gates to the castle of St. Elmo, a distance of half a mile. In some parts it is paved with flint stones, in other macadamized, and measures about ten yards in breadth, including the raised pathways. In Strada Reale there are many of the principal buildings of the town, besides several small squares.

~

Many of the private dwellings, hotels and shops, in Strada Reale, are worthy of notice, and may dare with cities of far greater note in Europe; nor may an Englishman coming from London justly disparage Valletta when he compares it with the splendour and uncleanliness of Oxford or Regent Streets.

Strada Reale and sunset, 1927

F.N. WESTON

Strada Reale contains most of the important buildings in Valletta: the Governor's Palace, the Opera House. the Casino Maltese, the Union Club, the Borsa di Commercerio, one side of St. John's Church, and the Public Library, which latter is interesting as a building begun by the Knights and completed under English rule. In Strada Reale also to be found two less heroic institutions not to be omitted, however, as places to be visited: Bissazza's, where are sold, amongst other confectionary, curious Sicilian sweetmeats; and Blackley's, where a truly British "afternoon tea", including currant buns, may be obtained. In the afternoon everyone turns into St George's Square for the band, or strolls up and down Strada Reale until sunset, when, as there is scarcely any twilight, darkness falls in a few minutes upon the city, and the crowds disappear.

The sunsets in Malta are indeed magnificent, and well worth a climb into the terrazzo to witness. The east appears a rich dark purple, and the west presents "the true yellow glow of Claude Lorraine", as the observant Brydone remarked a century ago; and particularly fine is the effect, viewed on the road from Valletta, of the somewhat Oriental towers and building of Citta Vecchia in sullen silhouette against the setting sun.

Choices in the market, 1841

GEORGE ANGAS

The market in Valletta, though small, is well supplied with fruit and fish. Very little animal food is used by the natives, and owing to the heat of the climate, it is obliged to be eaten the same day that it is killed. On going through the market to purchase some fruit, I had occasion to pass by one of the butchers' stalls. The Maltese are a very shrewd people and love a joke with the English. "Any beef, John," said the butcher, with an arch smile: – this he intended, no doubt, as a hit at our national character, though it was said with that naiveté and good humour which it was impossible to be offended at.

The greatest portion of the fruit sold in the market is brought over from Sicily, and some also from Gozo. At the time of my visit the finest fruits were nearly over; grapes sold at one penny per rotolo (1 ¾ pound), and a superior kind called "ladies fingers" of a long pod-like shape, for 1 ½ pence a pound. The prickly pears were sold at four grains per rotolo; peaches fourpence per ditto; figs, of two or three kinds, a penny per rotolo; melons, one farthing per pound; of these the musk, water and winter melons were in considerable abundance. The oranges I saw were those of last year's growth; they were very scarce, owing to the want of rain.

Fish are in great abundance. They consist chiefly of mullet, whiting, tunny, sword-fish, turtles, eels, and various species of crustacea, such as lobster, crabs, prawns etc. Shell fish are much eaten by the lower classes. The men who gather them expose them for sale in the markets in small dishes upon the ground. I would frequently examine them on account of the good shells that are often found amongst them. I obtained the spondylus, two species of murex, the arca-none, the sea-date, the haliotis, and three of four kinds of Venus, in this manner. The little fish called sea-horses are common n the Maltese shores.

The public library, 1840

MALTA PENNY MAGAZINE

One of the principal buildings of the Strada Reale, set back on one side of Republic Square, is the National Library of Malta. A statue of Queen Victoria sits imperious in the square surrounded by café tables.

The Library had its own origin in the Bailiff de Tenein who in the year 1760 endowed it with 9700 of his own books, and procured for it vast legacies of literature from other sources.

At the death of the founder the Library was made over to the Order (the Knights of St John) and afterwards enriched by the private libraries of the Knights who at the decease were obliged to bequeath all their books to this institution. From the Order the Library passed into the hands of the French, and from them to the British Government. The number of volumes at present is not less than 35,000, written chiefly in Latin, French and Italian and a few books in such other languages as were included in the Order.

~

The building which encloses the National Library is one of the finest specimens of architecture in Malta. The style of the whole edifice is grand and regular, and the arcade which extends along its whole length forms a delightful portico and gives the facade a very imposing appearance. This structure was erected during the reign of the Grand Master Rohan, with the intention to serve as a Conservatory for the property of defunct Knights and others connected with the Order, and to contain at the same time the Library, Mint and Printing Office. It was begun in 1786 by the Roman architect Ittar. The shelves etc were furnished at the expense of a Bailiff, native of Alicante. In the year 1811, the British Governor, Sir H. Oakes, had all the books transported from their former incommodious rooms near the Public Treasury to the present situation.

The exterior and interior of the Library are hardly changed today, although the exterior tends to disappear behind the umbrellas of the cafés in Republic Square. Some of the furniture in the main room of the Library, which is reached by a massive staircase, appears to be that shown in the 19th century.

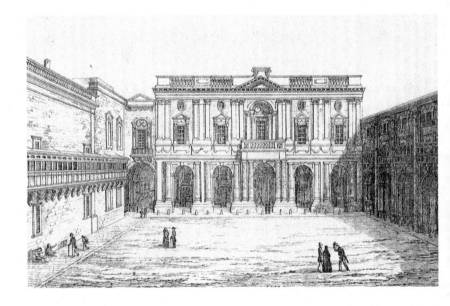

The exterior of the Palace, 1841

GEORGE ANGAS

The exterior appearance of the palace presents nothing striking, the whole forming a pile of massive building, about 300 feet square, surrounded on three sides by open balconies. It has two principal entrances in front; which open into a large central court. At the back of the palace is situated the market; and the stalls which are fixed up against the whole length of the building, tend greatly to spoil the appearance of this part of the structure.

The interior of the Palace was beautiful and adorned by Grand Master Emmanuel de Pinto. It consists of an upper and lower storey, each containing a range of noble apartments, which run round the building. The interior court is surrounded with arches, and opposite the entrance is a fountain, ornamented with a bronze statue of Neptune, fixed in the wall behind it. In a smaller court adjoining the former is a racket ground, where I observed several military officers amusing themselves with this healthy exercise.

The treasures of the Palace, 1843

WILLIAM MAKEPEACE THACKERAY

In the lofty halls and corridors of the governor's home, some portraits of the late grand masters still remain; a very fine one, by Caravaggio, of a knight in gilt armour hangs in the dining room, near a full-length of poor Louis XVI, in royal robes, the very picture of uneasy impotency, but the portrait of Vignacourt is the only one that has a respectable air; the other chiefs of the famous society are pompous old gentlemen in black, with huge periwigs, and crowns round their hats, and a couple of melancholy pages in yellow and red. But pages and wigs and grand masters have almost faded out of the canvas, and are vanishing into Hades with a most melancholy indistinctness. The names of these gentlemen, however, live as yet in the forts of the place, which all seem to have been eager to build and to christen: so that it seems as if, in the Malta mythology, they had been turned into free-stone.

In the armoury is the very suit painted by Caravaggio, beside the armour of the noble old La Valette, whose heroism saved his island from the efforts of Mustapha and Dragus, and an army quite as fierce and numerous as that which was baffled before Gibraltar, by similar courage and resolution.

Architecture with figures, 1832

ALPHONSE DE LAMARTINE

A light, golden, sweet, and serene, like that which beams from the eyes and features of a young maiden before love has engraved one wrinkle on her forehead, or cast one shade on her eyes. This light diffused equally over the sea, the earth, and the heavens, strikes the white and yellow stones of the houses, and causes all the designs of the cornices, corners of the angles, balustrades of the terraces, and carved work of the balconies, to be articulated fully and clearly on the blue horizon, without that aerial tremulousness, that uncertain and vapour undulation, out of which our western atmosphere has derived a beauty for its arts, being unable to correct this vice in its climate. This quality of the air, this white, yellow, golden colour of the stone, this vigorousness of the contours, imparts to the meanest edifice of the south a firmness and a neatness which revive and gladden the sight.

Every house has the air of not having been built, stone on stone, with sand and mortar, but of having been sculptured living and erect, out of the bright rock, and of being planted on the earth, like a block sprung out of its bosom, and as durable as the earth itself. Two large and elegant pilasters rise from the two angles of the facade, they ascent only to the height of a story and a half; there an elegant cornice, sculptured out of the shining stone, crowns them, and itself serves as a base to a rich and massive balustrade, which extends the whole length of the top, and replaces those flat, irregular, pointed and odd-looking roofs, which disgrace all architecture, which break every line harmonising with the horizon in those eccentric assemblages of houses of ours, which we call cities, in Germany, England and France. Between those two large pilasters, which project several inches from the facade, two openings only are designed by the architect – a door and two windows. The door, which is lofty, wide and arched, has not its threshold on the street; it opens on an exterior flight of steps, which encroach seven or eight feet on the quay. The stairs, surrounded by a balustrade of sculptured stone, serves for an exterior hall, as well as for an entrance to the house.

Let us describe one of these flights of steps – it will answer for them all. One or two men, in white garments, with dark visages and African eyes, having long pipes in their hands, are carelessly lounging on a couch of reeds at the side of the door: in front of them, leaning gracefully on the balustrade, three young women, in different attitudes, are viewing in silence our boat as it passes, or smiling among themselves at our foreign aspect. A black gown reaching only half way down the leg, a white corset, with wide, folded, and flowing sleeves, a head-dress of black hair, and over the head and shoulders a half mantle of black silk like the gown, covering half the face, one shoulder and the arm that holds the mantle. This mantle of light stuff, swelled out with the breeze, assumes the figure of a small boat's sail, and, through its capricious folds, now conceals, and now unveils, the mysterious countenance that it envelopes, and which seems to escape from it at pleasure. Some are raising their heads gracefully to chat with other young girls who are bending over the upper balcony, and throwing at them pomegranates and oranges; others are speaking to young men with long moustaches, dark, and bushy, hair, dressed in short tight vests, white pantaloons, and red belts.

Seated on the parapet of the steps, two young abbés in black, with silver shoe-buckles, are conversing familiarly and playing with broad green fans; while, at the foot of the last steps, a handsome mendicant monk, with naked feet, his forehead pale, bald-white, and open, his body enveloped in the heavy folds of his brown cloak, is reclining like a statue of mendacity on the threshold of the rich and happy man, and viewing with an eye of vacancy and indifference this spectacle of happiness, ease, and enjoyment.

On the upper storey are seen on a large balcony, supported by beautiful cariatides, and surmounted by an Indian veranda, adorned with curtains and fringes, a family of English, those happy and firm-minded conquerors of modern Malta.

There, some Moorish nurses, with sparkling eyes, and dark laden complexion, are holding in their arms those beauteous children of Britain, whose flaxen curly tresses, and white and rosy skin, resist the sun of Calcutta, as well as that of Malta and Corfu. On seeing these children under the black mantle and burning look of these half-African women, one might imagine them beautiful white lambs suspended at the breasts of tigresses in the desert.

On the terrace there is another scene; the English and Maltese share it together. On one side you see some young maidens of the island holding the guitar under the arm, and warbling a few notes of an old national air, mild as the climate; on the other a lovely young English-woman, leaning in a melancholy mood on her elbow, contemplating with indifference the scene of life which is pressing before her eyes, and turning over the pages of the immoral poets of her country.

MALTESE PROVERBS

The neighbour's cooking always smells best.

Ripe fruit carries its soul on its skin.

Roses are scented, but bread keeps us alive.

The hostelries of the town—and other treats, 1841

GEORGE ANGAS

The hotels of Valletta are good; Morell's is the first, where the English may find excellent accommodation; but the Minerva, where a table d'hote is daily kept, I found to be very comfortable, and the charges moderate. A person in this manner may live very cheaply in Malta. The finest Marasala wine is 10 pence per bottle, and the common Sicilian two pence. The best beef is fourpence per pound, macaroni soup, fourpence per basin, and a person may dine sumptuously for 1 shilling and 6 pence a day. Breakfast is best obtained in the cafes, which are open at a very early hour.

Travellers passing only a short time in Malta will find these places extremely convenient, as they can drop in at any hour of the day and take coffee or ice, which latter article is consumed in Malta to a very great extent. It is obtained from Mount Etna in the form of snow, and boats are constantly arriving from Catania laden with this useful and cooling substance. In the cafes, it is no uncommon thing to see them grinding up whole vats full of frozen snow, which, at first sight, appears very singular to a stranger in so warm a climate. Most of the cafes are situated in the Strada Reale, opposite the Library.

The Mediterranean Hotel is French, and the Albergo del Solo, Italian. Foreigners of these nations find good accommodation at these hotels.

Owing to its being a free port, cigars may be had at the rate of ten for a penny, and sugar from 2–4 pence per pound. The butter is bad and is chiefly imported from England. The native cheeses are made of goats' and sheeps' milk, pressed into small rush baskets; these, when fresh, are very pleasant, but are obliged to be eaten a very few hours after they are made. .... Poultry is plentiful, consisting of turkeys, fowls and ducks; quails are also every abundant in April and September; and in the market I have seen rails, larks, and wheatears. The yellow wagtail are sold by the natives at from one penny each, in the market, for the purpose of catching the flies in the houses, where they will live for several weeks, and answer the purpose as effectually as the chameleons do in Malaga. Olives are very much eaten by the Maltese, and oil enters largely into their cookery. The egg plant is regarded as a good vegetable by them, and when stuffed and roasted, it makes a palatable dish.

From Malta to Scotland, 1831

SIR WALTER SCOTT

This is a splendid town; the sea penetrates it in several places with Creeks formed into harbours surrounded by buildings and these again covered with fortifications. The streets are of very unequal heights as there has been no attempt at lowering them the greatest variety takes place between them, and the singularity of the various buildings leaning on each other in such a bold, picturesque and uncommon manner suggests some ideas for finishing Abbotsford* by a screen on the west side of the old Barn with a fanciful wall decorated with towers to enclose the Bleaching Green ornamented with watch towers such as these, of which I can get drawings while I am here.

---

* A plaque on St. Paul's Building, by St. Paul's Anglican Cathedral, records Sir Walter Scott's brief stay in 1831 in the former Beverley Hotel.

A necessary digression, 1927

F.N. WESTON

You have now reached St. John's Square with the church of that name that necessitates a digression from the route to inspect it.

St. John's Church, one of the most historic of Europe, was built in 1572–8 to form the conventual, or monastic, church of the Knights in the same way that most of the cathedrals of England were originally attached to the convent of some particular order, as St. John's was to that of the order of that name. The convent in this case consisted of the various separate Auberges, as the Universities of Oxford and Cambridge consist of the various colleges.

The church was probably at one time the richest of Christendom, as every galley had to give to it a part of its spoils, and each Knight on promotion presented some gift. For instance, the wonderful tapestries were presented by Perellos, and the green marble pilasters in the Nave by one of the Cotoneras, who also gave many vestments. Both the Cotoneras spent much money on the church, but took good care at the same time that their coats of arms and monograms were displayed liberally, as they were great self-advertisers. Most of the treasures disappeared when the church was looted by the French, who, however, soon lost their ill-gotten gains in the *Orient* – which was blown up at Aboukir (in Egypt).

From the guidebook, 1965

PETER MCGREGOR EADIE

St. John's Co-Cathedral, built in 1573–7 by Gerolama Cassar, and until 1798 the conventual church of the Order. The entire expense of its erection was defrayed by Grand Master La Cassiere and the church was consecrated on 20 February 1578. The building, which is remarkable alike for its historical associations, its architectural proportions, the richness of its decoration and the wonderful diversity of its treasures, was embellished by successive Grand Masters and further enriched by the *gioja* or present, which every Knight was bound by statute to make on promotion. All but two of the Grand Masters are buried here, their tombs affording a veritable museum of Baroque sculpture.

The interior, ornate but harmonious, consists of a single nave, 58m long with side chapels, the separating walls of which buttress the vault... The pavement is composed of some 400 sepulchral slabs laid in memory of the flower of the Order's chivalry. Made from marble of every hue, and adorned with the coast-of-arms, heraldic emblazonments, military and naval trophies, instruments of music and war, mitres and croziers, figures of angels, crowns and palms of martyrs, skeletons and other symbols of death, the floor produces the gorgeous and striking effect of a stone carpet.

The richness of St. John's, 1765

PATRICK BRYDONE

To the Protestant the ceremonies of the Catholic Church seemed very ornate and complex, and in Malta they were even more aware of the difference between the Catholic and Protestant services.

St. John's is a magnificent church. The pavement, in particular, is reckoned the richest in the world. It is entirely composed of sepulchral monuments of the finest marbles, porphyry, lapis lazuli, and a variety of other valuable stones, admirably joined together, at an incredible expense; representing in a kind of Mosaic, the arms, insignia, etc. of the persons whose names they are intended to commemorate. In the magnificence of these monuments, the heirs of the grand masters and commanders have long vied with each other.

We went this day to see the celebration of their church service. It seems to be more over-charged with parade and ceremony than what I have ever observed even in any other Catholic country. The number of genuflections before the altar, the kissing of the prior's hand, the holding up of his robes by the subaltern priests, the ceremony of throwing incense upon all the knights of the great cross, and neglecting the poorer knights, with many other articles, appeared to us highly ridiculous; and most essentially different indeed from that purity and simplicity of worship that constitutes the very essence of true Christianity; and of which the great pattern they pretend to copy, set so very noble an example.

A monument to power, 1806

GEORGE, VISCOUNT VALENTIA

I was very much struck with the magnificent church of St. John which still preserves the monuments of the illustrious Masters of the order. The silver rail of the altar, and the lamps, have, indeed, disappeared, the invincible Bonaparte having carried them with him to Egypt. The pavement is nearly covered by a beautiful mosaic, composed of the arms of the different knights who lie underneath. The revenues of the church are still continued to it, and its splendour must remain stationary, a monument of the power of the Order, and of its having passed away for ever.

The riches of St. John's, 1810

DR. CHARLES MERYON

The Church of St. John is a building, the imposing grandeur of which, when I first saw it, made a strong impression upon me. It consists of an immense nave, from which branch off, right and left, small chapels, each adorned with richly sculptures altars, beautified with everything that superstition can collect. The roof is arched, and painted in fresco by Matthias Preti, the Calabrian. The walls are also decorated with paintings by him and other masters; and the pavement is one uninterrupted piece of mosaic of coloured marbles. Some idea of its effect may be formed by imagining the pictures in the gallery of the Louvre in Paris to be taken from their frames, sewed together, and the spectator to be walking on them. The subjects are less lovely, certainly; because, in St John's Church, each mosaic picture covers the tomb of some Maltese knight, and consequently death and his emblems form the principal features in it; but they are not the less beautiful.

The church of St. John was built by the Grand Master, La Cassiere: its riches were, before their spoliation by the French, immense, from the donations made every five years by the master and the priors of the order, and by the piety of individuals. The carved ornaments were all gilt with sequin gold by the liberality of the Grand Master Cotoner.

✳

The beheading of St. John the Baptist, 1968

EDWARD SAMMUT

*In the Oratory of St. John's Co-Cathedral, built for Grand Master Wignacourt
in 1603 as a place of worship, is an extraordinary painting. There are seats
where one can sit and absorb the great work.*

At the back of the altar is to be seen what is probably the most important
painting in Malta, the "Beheading of St. John" by Michelangelo da
Caravaggio (1573–1610). This celebrated painter came to Malta in 1608,
having been obliged to fly from Rome in consequence of one of his
unsavoury escapades. During his stay in Malta, which lasted for less
than a year, he was received into the Order, commissioned to paint
two portraits of Aloph de Wignacourt, two paintings for the Chapel
of the Language of Italy and the "Beheading". Hardly had he finished,
when he was imprisoned in Fort St. Angelo for an unnamed crime and
effected a dramatic escape, only to be unfrocked and expelled from
the Order *tanquam membrum putridum et foetidum,* in a public assembly
held in the Oratory on the first of December, 1608.

This canvas, which is one of Caravaggio's last works, is also one of
his best, marking as it does the final, and the most important stage in
his art. The unusual composition, the well-knit group of five figures
in an almost perfect semi-circle at the side, and the oblique lighting
which leads the eye directly to the centre of attraction, leaving nearly
three quarters of the canvas practically blank, mark the climax of
an art which, in its time, had challenged every convention and had
revolutionized practically every tenet of painting.

The Church of St. John, 1844

WILLIAM MAKEPEACE THACKERAY

The Church of St. John, not a handsome structure without, is
magnificent within: a noble hall covered with a rich embroidery of
gilded carving, the chapels of the different nations on either side, but
not interfering with the main structure, of which the whole is simple,
and the details only splendid; it seemed to me a fitting place for this
wealthy body of aristocratic soldiers, who made their devotions as it

were on parade, and though on their knees, never forget their epaulets or their quarters of nobility. This mixture of religion and worldly pride seems incongruous at first... The church of the Knights of St. John is paved over with sprawling heraldic devices of the dead gentlemen of the dead order; as if, in the next world, they expected to take rank in conformity with their pedigrees, and would be marshalled into heaven according to the orders of precedence. Cumbrous paintings adorn the walls and chapels, decorated with pompous monuments of grand masters. Beneath is a crypt, where more of these honourable and reverend warriors lie... in the altar are said to lie three of the most gallant relics of the world: the keys of Acre, Rhodes, and Jerusalem. What blood was shed in defending these emblems! What faith, what endurance, genius and generosity; what pride, hatred, ambition, and savage lust of blood were roused together with their guardianship.

A thousand tomb-stones, 1857

WILLIAM C. PRIME

Prime, passing through Malta on his way to Egypt, visited Valletta with a knowledgeable monk, an acquaintance made on the journey. He was almost overwhelmed by the grandeur of the church of St. John, from whence he had to rush to catch his ship...

We left the crypt and walked over the splendid floor of the cathedral, which is inlaid with a thousand tomb-stones of Knights of the Cross. I glanced once more at the picture of the Beheading of John, which Caravaggio painted that he might be admitted to the order, and painted in fading colours (water some say) that the evidence of the debasement of the art and their debasement of the order, might disappear; and then, rushing out into the Strada Reale, and plunging down the steep narrow streets to the landing-place, over-turning a half dozen commissionaires, each of whom swore he was the man who said good morning the day previous, and became thereby entitled to his five francs ... I parted from Fra Giovanni with a warm pressure of the hand, a low "God bless you" and a long, earnest look out of those eyes of John the Saint.

Viewing portraits, 1841 and 1971

MICHAEL GALEA AND WILLIAM MAKEPEACE THACKERAY

A visit to St. John's (Cathedral) is almost always coupled with a visit to the former Grand Master's residence "in the lofty halls and corridors" of which "some portraits of the late Grand Masters still remain; a very fine one, by Caravaggio, of a Knight in gilt armour hangs in the dining room, near a full length of poor Louis XVI, in royal robes, the very picture of uneasy impotency. But the portrait of Vignacourt is the only one which has a respectable air; the other chiefs of the famous society are pompous old gentlemen in black, with huge periwigs and crowns round their hats, and a couple of melancholy pages in yellow and red. But pages and wigs and Grand Masters have almost faded out of the canvas, and are vanishing into Hades with a most melancholy indistinctness. The names of most of these gentlemen, however, live as yet in the forts of the place which all seem to have been eager to build and to christen; so that it seems as if, in the Malta mythology, they had been turned into freestone."

Annexed to the Palace building is the armoury, in which "thousands of pikes and halberds, little old cannons and war pieces, helmets and cutlasses, which the Knights or their people wore, are trimly arranged against the wall, and instead of spiking Turks or arming warriors, now serve to point morals and adorn tales."

The highest praise possible, 1831

SIR WALTER SCOTT

Tuesday, 29 November, 1831. At two o'clock Mrs Colonel Bathurst (wife of the acting Governor) transported me to see the Metropolitan church of St. John, by far the most magnificent place I ever saw in my life. Its huge and ample vaults are of the Gothick order, the floor of marble, each stone containing the inscription of some ancient Knight adorned with some patent of mortality and an inscription recording his name and family. For instance one Knight I believe had died in the infidels' prison. To mark his fate one stone amid the many coloured pavement represented a door composed of grates (iron grates I mean) displaying behind them an interior which a skeleton is in vain attempting to escape from by bursting the bars. If you conceive he has pined in his fetters there for centuries till dried in the ghastly image of death himself it is a ghastly imagination. The roof which bends over this scene of death is splendidly ornamented and gilded, is splendidly adorned with carving and gilding while the varied colours and tinctures both above and beneath, free from the tinselly effect which might have been apprehended, appear with greatest taste and solemnity in the dim religious light which they probably owe to the time which the colouring has remained.

Besides this main Aisle which occupies the centre there is added a chapter house in which the knights were wont to hold their meetings. At the upper end of this Chapter House is the fine Martyrdom of Saint John the Baptist, by a Caravaggio though this has been disputed.* On the left hand of the body of the church lie a series of subordinate aisles or chapels built by the devotion of the different tongues and where some of the worthies inhabit the vaults beneath; the other side of the church is occupied in the same manner.

---

* A fact no longer disputed. It was Caravaggio. Michelangelo Merisi di Caravaggio (1571–1610) fled to Malta from Naples in July 1607. He painted 'prodigiously' and even trained as a novice in the Order, and was admitted in 1608. He fell into further trouble, and left Malta abruptly.

The seven languages of the Knights, 1840

MALTA PENNY MAGAZINE

At a general chapter held in the year 1604, the several chapels on each side of the nave were assigned to the Seven Languages which composed the order of St. John in Malta.

The language of Portugal received that next to the entrance of the oratory.

The language of Spain, that adjoining the side door on the right of the church.

The language of Provence, that nearest to the chapel of the Holy Virgin.

The language of England and Bavaria, that enclosed with a brass balustrade on the left side of the church.

The language of France the next.

The language of Italy, that adjoining the left entrance to the church.

The language of Germany, that next the vestry.

With Protestant eyes, 1824

REVEREND JOHN HARTLEY

John Hartley was a missionary with the Church Missionary Society. He passed through Malta on his way to the Levant at the end of 1824. He had not visited a Catholic country before and deplored 'the Popish practices'. In a letter to the Society on 8 January 1825 he remarked about a procession: 'How painful, to view the religion of Christ Metamorphosed into so absurd a ceremonial!'

He visited the Cathedral of St. John several times, and one feels that he warmed to it, despite himself.

My visits to the church have now confirmed the first impressions which I received, viz., that as a whole it is a structure of very inferior kind, devoid of simplicity and consequently of taste. The style of Architecture is heavy Grecian. On entering many English cathedrals, the mind is laid hold of by very solemn and powerful impressions, and a feeling of awe is predominant. I find nothing of this kind produced in St John's... But if we proceed from a general view to a particular inspection, we find much that is exceedingly striking. Everything is sumptuous and ornamental in the highest degree. Vast sums have been lavished upon the several parts and upon the numerous instruments which are used in the Romish services. The pavement is an object truly splendid of the richest marble representing a vast variety of devices... To the left of the high altar are silver gates, painted over during the invasion of the French, in order to escape their rapacity. ... During my two last visits, I heard delightful Music. An organ whose tones I thought of unusual sweetness was accompanied by voices, which were singing those delightful compositions for which Italy and Germany are so distinguished.

At the end of his visits, Hartley felt 'a real tenderness for the multitudes whom Rome deludes and ruins. I prayed for the destruction of the Romish church but for the Salvation of its members...'

And the Protestant church, 1840

MALTA PENNY MAGAZINE

It had 'long been a matter of complaint with the English residents and with Protestant travellers, who are continually passing and re-passing this island, that they are almost entirely debarred from the privilege of attending public worship' as the only Protestant provision was in the Government Chapel, a room fitted up in the Palace and for the troops of the Garrison, amounting to 3,000, 'attend divine service in a room in the prison, which is also used as a public female school during the week.' At the end of 1839 the plans for the Protestant Church of St. Paul at Malta were public, and the Malta Penny Magazine *could publish a picture of the church as it would eventually be.*

The first stone was laid by Her Majesty, Queen Dowager Adelaide, on the 20th March, 1839 and "the front of the edifice would be adorned with a portico, supported by four Ionic pillars, and surmounted by a bas-relief illustrative of St. Paul's casting the viper off his hand into the fire immediately after the shipwreck (Acts xxviii.3). Each wing of the front will be ornamented with a statue of the two great apostles of the Christian church, St. Peter and St. Paul. The tower or steeple will be 130 feet high, terminating with the emblem of Christianity, the cross.

The dimensions of this building exceed those of any of the modern churches in London: the length of the area will be 110 feet, breadth 67 feet, and height 45 feet.

The Cathedral of St. John, 1927

HENRY JAMES FORMAN

The Cathedral was cool and empty except for a couple of workmen repairing the mosaic of a tomb worn beneath the feet of the worshippers, Grand Masters galore are buried here all up and down the nave in the chapels, corners and crypt. That is what is left of the Knights of Malta – dust under little oblongs of fine mosaic and names daintily embroidered in stone.

The different *langues* (languages) or nationalities had each its chapel, for the Knights of Malta were a sort of international soviet, and each *langue* vied with the others in making its chapel the most splendid in the cathedral – the *langue* of Provence, of England, of Portugal, of Spain, of Austria, of Auvergne and Italy. From being merely a monkish order of Hospitallers bent upon helping the pilgrims on their way to and from Jerusalem, they very soon donned the sword and mail and became a fighting order like the Templars. They were supposed to hold the Turk at bay. Anyway, they had a very good time fighting, ruling, collecting slaves for their galleys; and, if pilgrims did stop of Malta between Europe and Jerusalem, they were doubtless well entertained. But the way is so long and Malta is after all, only a dot in the Mediterranean.

A miserable remnant, 1835

EMMA ROBERTS

As soon as possible, we sallied forth to inspect the far-famed church of St John, and found our expectations were more than gratified by the interior of this gorgeous edifice. It was not, however, without melancholy feelings that we reflected on the miserable remnant of those valiant knights, who had made Malta celebrated throughout all history, and who, on the suppression of the order, were suffered to languish out of the remainder of their existence in obscurity. Mass was performing at the time of our entrance, and, seating ourselves in one of the side chapels until it should be over, we were at its conclusion accosted by a priest, who, finding that we did not speak Italian, sent another person to show the beauties of the church. Some Maltese ladies greet us very courteously, and, though perhaps we would rather have wandered about alone, indulging in our own recollections of the past, we could not help being pleased with the attentions that were paid to us.

The Palace, 1842

LADY GROSVENOR

We walked through the Lascaris Gate,* up a street of open fruit shops, and crossed a drawbridge over a moat, planted with orange and banana trees, which leads into the town through the second gate. Here a party of the Rifle Brigade were mounting guard.

The town is very clean, with well-built houses of Maltese stone, and the general effect of it is not unlike that of Cadiz, but on a larger scale.

Admiral Sir J.O. walked with us to the palace, which was under repair during the absence of the governor; it is a handsome building, with a fine suite of rooms, like a good English country-house, except that the staircase is a broad corkscrew ascent, with wide shallow steps, so constructed as to enable Knights to ride up and down on their mules. The appearance is bold and handsome.

Long corridors, with some bad pictures of old Grand Masters, conduct to various apartments, in one of which is some superb tapestry in excellent preservation; the subjects are chiefly Indian, with elephants, lions, ostriches, etc. The army contains fifteen thousand stand of arms well arranged, together with the portraits and armour of La Valette and Vignacourt.

---

* The city of Valletta is entered across a bridge from the great piazza which is, in effect, the bus station for the whole island. The city itself is protected by a dry ditch, 17 m deep and 9 m wide, which was gouged out of the solid rock by Turkish slaves, taken as prisoners at the Siege. This great 'ditch' surrounds the city centre for nearly 900 m. After crossing the bridge one enters the city properly through the Lascaris Gate.

The national library of Malta, 1806

GEORGE, VISCOUNT VALENTIA

The Library is a handsome building, and has a very valuable collection of books. It was accumulated from the private libraries of the different knights who died in the island, to whom the Order was heir. It also received, as presents, most of the splendid works which were published by the Catholic sovereigns of Europe. It contains about eight thousand volumes, and is chiefly deficient in English literature. It would be politic, as well as liberal, to appropriate a modern annual income to remove this deficiency. The Maltese should not be permitted to discover, in any one respect, an inferiority to their present monarch from their last. The splendour of their capital should be, by every means, increased, and not diminished. The present use of the books is inconvenient, access to them being allowed only from nine to twelve, during the summer months.

There is a small collection of medals annexed to the library, and some antiques of value, which are the more interesting, from having been found on the island. These, as well as the furniture of the palace, and every other article of value, would, probably, have been carried to Paris, had it not been for the closeness of the blockade, which precluded all retreat; till the capitulation put an end to the power of plundering.

The palace... and neighbourhood, 1927

F.N. WESTON

The Palace ... was the residence of the Grand Masters after the building of Valletta, and is now the main residence of the Governor, and the seat of the local government.

There are two charming courtyards, one containing the statue of Neptune which used to stand in the Fish Market fountain. Of the apartments open to the public the most interesting are the Legislative Chamber, hung with rich tapestries, and the Armoury.

The latter is very fine, although unfortunately much armour

disappeared after the departure of the Knights till the collection was arranged and catalogued.

Next to the Palace is Queen's Square. This was an orangery, and oasis of greenery and gorgeous fruit amid arid surroundings, till it was altered to its present uninteresting form in 1887 to commemorate Queen Victoria's Jubilee. At the back of the square is the "Bibliotheca", or Public Library, built a few years before the French occupation, and the last building created by the Knights.

Opposite it, and on your right, is the Auberge of Auvergne, built 1570–1, and now used as the Law Courts. ... After passing Sda. S. Giovanni you soon come to the Union Club, which was built in 1571–5 as the Auberge of the Language of Provence ...

The inside is outside, 1840

MALTA PENNY MAGAZINE

A visitor to Malta wrote of the impact of the place to the editor of the Malta Penny Magazine.

As we passed on, there seemed to be around us the stir and hum of great activity. One thing, however, struck us as very peculiar. It seemed as though all the in-door work of Valletta had come out into the streets this morning, to take an airing. The tailors, the shoemakers, the carpenters with the numberless chairs &c. and all the various mechanics, sat out of doors in front of their business with great apparent industry. This, I afterwards learned, was the common custom of the place. On our way to our lodgings we passed St. George's square, in the Strada Reale, in front of the governor's palace, where we saw crowds of Roman Catholic priests, with their three-cornered hats, tight small clothes, and loose outward robe – a multitude of gaily-dressed English officers – large groups of Scotch Highlanders, kilted, and in their usual military dress – numbers of the native Maltese, the men wearing a blue checked shirt, with a red or purple knit worsted cap, the top folding back; and the women, a black silk dress, with the faldetta thrown over the head, and reaching down the back like a shawl – clusters of ragged and impudent beggars, and dense masses of people, too numerous to be described, of every nation and tongue and variety of costume, mingling together, and presenting a most novel and picturesque appearance to the eye of a stranger.

An American view, 1929

ELIZABETH SCHERMERHORN

Aside from the ubiquitous British uniforms and the unsightly English signs that plaster the shop fronts, the intrusions of monuments to defunct British Governments on the 'proud bastions of the Knights', and of a painfully white statue of Queen Victoria, looking very small and complacent in her voluminous veil of Maltese lace as she sits in the dusty square beside the Grand Master's Palace – no city, perhaps, has preserved more unaltered and all-pervading the aspect and atmosphere of the past than Valletta, – and (almost) one could walk the streets of the Knights' city with the Grand Masters whose escutcheons are its chief ornament, undisturbed by the intrusion of any modern anomalies.

La Valletta from on high, 1843

ELLIOT WARBURTON

La Valletta is a sort of hybrid between a Spanish and an Eastern town; most of its streets are flights of steps, to which the verandahs of the houses are like gigantic banisters. Its terraced roofs restore to the cooped-up citizens nearly all the space lost by building upon; and there are probably not less than five hundred acres of promenadable roof in, or rather on, the city.

The church of San Giovanni is very gorgeous, with its vaulted roof of gilded arabesques, its crimson tapestries, finely carved pulpits, and its floor resembling one vast escutcheon; being a mosaic of knightly tombs, on which the coats of arms are finely copied in coloured marble and precious stones. The chapel of the Madonna in the Eastern side, is guarded by massive silver rails, saved from French rapacity by the cunning of a priest, who painted them wood-colour. Notwithstanding all the wealth and splendour of this cathedral, its proudest and most chivalric ornament is a bunch of old rusty irons, suspended on a crimson tapestry. These are the keys of Rhodes; and these the Order, overcome, but unconquered, carried away with them from their ancient seat, the bulwark of Christendom.

The Hotels of the different nations (or Tongues, as they were called), are palaces that bear testimony to the taste and power of their former proprietors. The principal are the Auberges de Castile, and Provence; and the palace of the Grand Master, now that of the British governor.

The others are converted into barracks; and probably the costumes of their olden time did not differ more from one another than those of its present military occupants – the dark green of the riflemen, the scarlet uniform of the 88th, and the varied garb of the Highlander "all plaided and plumed in his tartan array". Every costume of Europe, Asia and Africa, is to be met with in the streets, which swarm with the most motley and picturesque population.

The brilliant sunshine gives an almost prismatic effect to every object; from the gorgeously clad Turk to the beautiful parrot-fish, streaked with every colour in the rainbow; form the fruit and vegetables ranged on tables along the pave', to the roguish looking children that persecute you with flowers.

The Upper Barracca, 1851

W.H. BARLTETT

Passing round the southern line of the stupendous fortifications, and the noble "Auberge de Castile", we soon reach the Upper Baracca, a promenade raised upon a lofty angle of the city wall, overhanging the harbour, surrounded by arches, and formerly roofed in, once serving for the recreation of the Knights. Few prospects of the kind can be more striking than that which it commands, a prospect in which there is nothing of nature, save one solitary garden – where scarcely a tree or a blade of grass relieves the brilliancy of the glare; but exhibiting the *ne plus ultra* of military and naval grandeur – a mass of forts and batteries bristling with cannon, sheltering in their powerful arms an extensive harbour, studded with enormous ships of the line and steam frigates – an exhibition of power, which, associated with a sense of the great interests it protects, produces a feeling nearly allied to the sublime.

The Lower Barracca, 1973

JAMES MORRIS

Worth seeking out is this quiet memorial in a garden. The little Ionic temple which, high above the Grand Harbour at Malta, honoured the memory of Sir Alexander Ball, the first British Governor – built of Malta's soft golden stone, shaded by palms and hibiscuses, and looking so cool, so white, so small and poignant in that setting that it might have been a monument to homesickness itself.

One continued round of hospitality, 1813

JAMES SILK BUCKINGHAM

In the dinner and the evening parties which I had the pleasure to attend during my stay here, I found a happy mixture of English reserve and decorum, French vivacity and politeness, and Italian softness and languor, so tempering each other as to make a much more agreeable whole than either of them separately. The three languages were generally understood, though Italian was more current than French, and French better known than English. The dinner parties were less formal, less heavy, and occupied much less time than those at home, though chiefly given by the English. The evening receptions were in the French style, with no other refreshment than coffee, lemonade, and ices, but most agreeable and brilliant conversation; and the balls, notwithstanding the heat of the climate, as animated as those I had seen in the West Indies, and enjoyed more thoroughly than in London.

At home in Valletta, 1826

ANNE KATHERINE ELWOOD

Anne Katherine Elwood was on her way to India with her East Indian army husband. Their journey was a leisurely one and they spent the winter of 1825–6 in Malta.

The private houses are in a style of magnificence seldom to be met with; the rooms are large, spacious, and handsome, and the verandahs, flat roofs, terraces, courts, and fountains, evince the dubious situation of Malta, which required an act of Parliament to certify that it belonged to *Europe*. [*Much was there to remind her of the vicinity of Africa, though the English comforts and luxuries made her feel at home.*]

The British inhabitants sit over fires of Newcastle coals, "just as we do in England", and stir them into a brilliant blaze, with that peculiarly national-looking implement, a poker, ever accompanied with Anglo tongs and shovel; whilst Tripoli and Tunis, the Morea and Crete, are talked of as familiarly as Bath and Cheltenham: and a trip to Corfu, or an excursion to Sicily, are proposed for change of air, as we should recommend one to Brighton or Ramsgate. We had every reason to be pleased with our sojourn at Malta; we came in idea but for a few days, and, like St Paul, we tarried three months.

Theatricals, 1830

JOHN MADOX

Besides the opera-house,* there is an excellent English amateur theatre† built ... in 1810 (it having been suggested that the introduction of English theatricals would tend to facilitate the acquirement by the natives of the English language) ... (A company was procured "at a very considerable expense" from England.)

---

* Bombed in the siege of the 1940s and not rebuilt.
† He may be referring to the Manoel Theatre in Old Theatre Street, although this was completed in 1731, and is one of the oldest theatres in Europe; it is still in use, with its interior beautifully restored in 1960.

English theatricals were then introduced and the performances were such as might have merited the applause of a London audience. But the plague breaking out in 1813, the performers deemed it advisable to make their exit to old England.

An unexpected place, 1930

EVELYN WAUGH

Malta was quite different from what I had imagined. I expected it to be much more British and much more breezy. I expected a great many white flag-staffs and band-stands and very clean streets, and officers' wives with Sealyam terriers, and white-washed buildings with verandahs and little brass cannon and look-out towers with spiral iron staircases. I did not associate in my mind a naval base with baroque architecture, and, without giving much thought to it, I supposed the sailors were illimitably supplied with English nursery maids to walk with along the front and take to the cinema; it was odd to see them swaggering down precipitous alleys with prostitutes who talked a mixture of Arabic and Italian. I expected to find a Sabbath-keeping, undemonstrative Protestantism, one English church full of fairly recent memorial tablets, and a chaplain or two carrying tennis rackets. I found the most ardently Catholic people in Europe; a place where the Church owns a third of the soil, and monks, nuns, priests, novices, prelates, and religious processions emerge in serried masses at every corner. I daresay things seem different when the fleet is in; while I was there the harbour was empty except for a submarine, a target carrier, and the usual mercantile shipping. In these circumstances I got the impression of a place far less British than Port Said.

It is true that I saw a cricket match being played, and that Gieves have a shop in Strada Mezzodi, and that notices are displayed at the Customs House and the railway station advertising the addresses of local secretaries of the Society for the Prevention of Cruelty to Animals and the Girls' Friendly Society and that English money is used, and that the *cafe chantants* call themselves music-halls, and that instead of cafes there are public houses with a row of handles behind the bar and bar maids who draw up pint glasses of metallic-tasting draught bitter, but in spite of all of this there seemed something superficial about the British occupation. After all, we had only been there for a little over a hundred years, and we came, not as colonists among savages, but as the mandatories of an outpost of high European culture. But trivial as has been the English influence to alter the essentially Mediterranean character of the island, this tenancy by a first-class naval power has been the means of preserving almost the whole of its charm... Only the acquisitive instincts of British nineteenth-century diplomacy saved Malta from developing into such a thing as does not bear thinking of – a nightmare island combining and epitomising all the unendurable characteristics of Capri, Rye and Carcassonne. The occupation of the British Navy has prevented all of that; the fortifications have not been allowed to crumble and grow mossy; they are kept in good order, garrisoned and, whenever it was expedient, ruthlessly modified; roads have been cut through them and ditches filled up. Nothing, except the one museum in the Auberge d'Italie, has been allowed to become a show place; everything is put to a soundly practical purpose. There is a governor in the Grand Master's Palace, monks in the monasteries, marines and naval officials in the principal houses, a police station in the Knight's Hospital, a modern signalling station perched on the roof of the Auberge de Castille.

Valletta lives on, 1992

JEREMY LEWIS

I am bowled over by Valletta within seconds of coming through the gates: the buildings are high, handsome and made from honey-coloured sandstone, with ornate 18th-century doorways, and on each first floor, an Arabic-looking enclosed balcony, painted dark green and jutting out over the street. The pillar boxes are red, as are the old fashioned English telephone boxes, and most of the public notices and shop signs are in English; it's all pleasantly reminiscent of England in the Fifties.

The city of the warrior-knights, 1845

ISABELLA ROMER

Mrs Romer stepped ashore after a stormy journey on a moonlit night in October.

And beautiful it is, whether in the brightness of the noonday sun, when its streets are filled with a population rendered motley by the mixture of English uniforms and native costumes, that show there is no picturesque contrast, or, in the more subdued moonlight, when the oriental aspect of the buildings, half-illumined by the moonbeams, half-buried in shadow, assume the characteristics of an exquisite theatrical decoration, and scarcely a living creature is to be seen in the highways or the bye-ways to break the deep stillness of the scene. One might then almost fancy oneself transported two centuries back to the palmy days of the Knights of St John, and expect to be challenged from the bastions by some steel-clad soldier of the Cross, instead of the Highland sentinels passing backwards and forwards there. But, indeed, whether in sunshine or moonlight, such is the peculiar charm of Valletta, that I do not think it yields in beauty to the fairest cities of Italy or Spain.

An essential step, 1857

WILLIAM C. PRIME

Prime, a New York lawyer, travelled to Europe and Egypt in 1855, encouraged by distinguished persons in government service in Washington and at the Smithsonian Institute. At the theatre at Arles he met an Italian Franciscan brother and they travelled on together.

Sometime after that we were standing in the crypt of the cathedral of St. John's at Malta. That day we were to separate. I to go eastward, and he to travel he scarcely knew whither, on the work of his sacred calling. Before us, in the marble silence, lay the stout Villiers de l'Isle-Adam, and a little way off the brave Valletta, sleeping after his great battle with the Turks, who surrounded this, his rocky fortress.

He who goes to the East should always go by way of Malta. It is a proper stepping-stone between Europe and the Orient, where the last wave of the crusades rolled back from the walls of Jerusalem, and sank in foam.

"You will not find yourself always looking back to this little crypt in the middle of the sea, where your footsteps turn," said Fra Giovanni. "No place in the Mediterranean is so intimately connected with the history of the East as this island of Malta, and there is scarcely any part of the Orient in which you will not be reminded of it. This fact alone, that it is the place of the death and burial of that mighty order who for so great a period swayed the sceptre of power in Europe, is enough to connect it with Egypt and Holy Land, indeed with all the possessions of the Turks."

"Here, when Valletta was Grand Master, the arms of the Moslem had their first great check, and the followers of the false prophet learned that their boasted invincibility was a fable. Here, too, but yesterday, when the great leader of the French had garrisoned the island, your stout cousins of England, who followed his swift feet as the hounds follow after the deer, drove out his soldiery… There have been valiant deeds done on this rock…"

I don't know by my friend would have talked on all day, had not a gun from the harbour announced that the steamer was heaving up her anchor.

The English burial ground, 1840

MALTA PENNY MAGAZINE

There are burial grounds for foreigners, particularly the British, in Valletta. The Malta Penny Magazine wrote of one in 1840. It is situated 'on the north-west declivity between Valletta and Floriana, and occupies a great part of the fortifications in that direction.'

Numerous and some well executed monuments embellish the place, and the many shrubs and trees connected with the silence generally prevailing along the Quarantine Harbour, have rendered it an attractive promenade to the mind anxious to retire for a moment from the great bustle of earthly care and anxieties.

~

The sun had gone down behind the hills of Nasciar, when I took a lonely stroll to this region of the dead.... Tho' I had often shunned the spot, on this occasion I felt irresistibly led to climb the wall of the old burial ground, and took a posture by the tomb of my father...

The Protestant Cemetery, 1857

WILLIAM C. PRIME

Once more we visited the Protestant Cemetery, overlooking the Quarantine Harbour – the garden of the dead, – towards which, as to a common goal, each traveller naturally turns, – wherever he wanders through a world of sorrow and bereavement, – to contemplate the wrecks of frail humanity, and read the records of unavailing grief or manly admiration, from surviving comrades and friends.

Our last homage was paid at the tomb of one who died here in the prime of youth and beauty; and whom the mild zephyrs of the south were unable to rescue from insidious disease; though they now plentifully strew the hectic bloom of geraniums and other flowering shrubs, over her distant and lamented grave.

The Burial Ground, 1991

DEBORAH MANLEY

On our third visit to Malta we tracked down the Protestant "English" cemetery. The easiest way to find it is to ask in the Valletta Public Library, a short walk from the Phoenicia Hotel.

Over the years – and as a result of the second Siege of Malta – the cemetery had fallen into disrepair and had attracted vandals and litter. But a group of British residents in Malta had – as British will do – set up a voluntary organisation to research, resurrect and repair it. Part of the cemetery is carefully tended and as fresh and as green as the best British churchyard. Part was still under repair when we were there, but it was clear that this part too was, so to speak, rising from the dead.

In Guardia! 1991

DEBORAH MANLEY

Every other Sunday in the summer months a re-enactment of a military parade is staged in Fort St. Elmo. It is not to be missed. Volunteers in historic costume take over the fort and the parade ground and recreate in this wonderful historic setting, with cannon roaring, a military parade.

During the siege of World War II the bastions of Fort St. Elmo were manned by the Royal Malta Artillery; and within the fort is the National War Museum, where the actual George Cross awarded to the people of Malta is proudly on display.

Water for a city, 1926

SIR THEMISTOCLES ZAMMIT

Malta has always had to think about the supply of water and to nourish the water it has and plan for its care.

From a report written in 1723 by Fra Romeo Fortunata Casapecchia at the request of Grand Master Manoel de Vilhena, we learn that there were in Valletta and in Floriana 40 large water tanks, and 13 huge reservoirs, called *gebie*. Most of them were within the fortifications: 21 of them were open to the public. The more important of these were:

One in the ditch of Fort St Elmo, one near the old Bucceria at the eastern end of Strada Zecca, one at the Manderaggio, one at the top of Strada Zecca, one behind the Ferreria, between Sda. Fianco and Sda. Stretta, one opposite St. John's Church, one at the side of the church opposite the Auberge of Auvergne, one opposite the Public Library, one in Sda S. Paolo close to the University buildings, one close to the slave prison in Strada Levante; from this report we gather also that at the time 1037 water tanks were connected to private houses.

Departing from Malta, April 1848

EDWARD LEAR

Writing to his sister Ann, Edward Lear—after a very brief visit—had mixed views of Valletta...

I left Valletta on the evening of the 15th, at 5 p.m. – I cannot remember to have left any place with so much regret after so short a stay in it. Such extreme kindness I received is wonderful to think of. But I could not live in Malta – there is hardly a bit of green in the whole island – a hot sand stone, walls & bright white houses are all you can see from the highest places, excepting little stupid trees here & there like rubbishy tufts of black worsted. The harbours are very interesting, but I don't love the water well enough to portray such scenes characteristically. The street scenery – so white, so bright, so clean, so balconied, is really beautiful – but there the charm ends. The tapestry in the old palace is worth a visit; I never saw such anywhere; the Armoury too is fine...

ELSEWHERE ON MALTA,
AND THE ISLANDS

Malta's wonderful, though somewhat decrepit, bus service radiates out across the island from the large Triton fountain just outside the city gate of Valletta, taking the traveller into every town and village or dropping them off along the road. Past travellers went on horseback or hired a carriage, or *calesh*. For some years there was a small railway with 6½ miles of track, but it closed in 1931.

The buses of Malta are famed for their longevity and rattling efficiency. Each bus is said to be the responsibility of its driver, and he sees that it keeps going—for twenty or more years. The buses are bright yellow, mainly diesel-engined, mainly lacking air conditioning, and all with personal interior decoration: decorative religious scenes, family pictures, seasonal decorations, flags and other memorabilia. The seat covers are sometimes threadbare and the buses are usually crowded. It is said that the oldest buses are kept on the tourist routes—because the tourists admire them so enthusiastically as collectors' pieces; the newer buses are kept for the mainly Maltese-used routes—as they would rather have speed and comfort.

The bus is a great place to listen to the Maltese language—but with the additional benefit that everyone knows and speaks English and will be willing to help and advise you about where to get off and the times of the return buses.

The buses—which have no destination marked, but are numbered—spread out to almost every village. If you want to get off, tell the driver your destination; if you want to get on in a town or village or roadside, wave frantically and make sure the bus driver sees you. The buses stop in every village on their route—usually near the church. At Valletta the terminus is again the wide circle outside the main city gate around the Triton circle. Nearby there is a kiosk from which you can get timetables and information about bus numbers and destinations and where to queue.

Astonishingly the Malta yellow buses carry well over thirty million passengers every year.

~

Beyond Valletta the main 'lions' of the islands are Mdina and Rabat, the ancient tombs, the supposed place of St. Paul's shipwreck and then, beyond, the beautiful island of Gozo, reached today by land and ferry or direct from Valletta by sea.

Mrs. Elwood in 1825 and John Galt in 1812 described the *calesh*—she, always a romantic, comparing it to Cinderella's pumpkin. In Evelyn Waugh's day there was an 'absurd' railway to Mdina, now closed and turned into a stationary tourist attraction. Nassau William Senior in 1855 found the peace and freshness of Mdina a delight, as had Vivant Denon and James Silk Buckingham—and as do present-day travellers. Sarah Haight in 1843 and Lady Grosvenor in 1877 looked out across the island from the heights of Mdina.

W.H. Bartlett wrote of rumbling out into the countryside. There were a number of destinations. John Madox sought the Boschetto Gardens, Nassau William Senior drove along the 'fine bold coast' to St. Julian's Bay. The site of St. Paul's shipwreck was the destination of John Silk Buckingham, Bartlett and William Turner.

In 1839, before Isabella Romer was in Malta in 1845, archaeological excavations had already begun and she visited Hagar Chem and Gebel Keem. In 1812 Sir Robert Wilson and the young diplomat William Turner (en route to Constantinople with the ambassador Sir Robert Liston's entourage) had been to visit 'Hannibal's tomb'—with differing recollections of what they found. The colossal church at Mosta was an attraction in 1841, as it remains. Every village in Malta has its feast day, accompanied by fireworks and processions. In 1821 John Madox watched the feast of St. Grigorio at the village of Zeitun. Evelyn Waugh followed a walking guide rather erratically through Senglea, one of the three cities across the Great Harbour.

Gozo (or Goza) is the second island that makes up 'Malta'—perhaps, thought Elliot Warburton, Calypso's island. John Madox experienced the terrors of 'Fungus Rock'. Edward Lear had enthusiastic words for Gozo. The *Malta Government Gazette* in 1826 described a gracious visit to the island by the Governor and his family. Comino is the third island; it is small and barren and hardly populated—just as when Vivant Denon visited it in 1789.

Anywhere, on any of the islands, in a quiet corner, one might watch a lizard as Samuel Taylor Coleridge did in 1804.

✴

Mode of travelling, 1812

JOHN GALT

The common mode of travelling in Malta is in single-horse carriages, which hold two persons. They are called calishes (or caleeshes or karozzin), and are a very tolerable sort of vehicles. The driver never rides, but runs, all day, by the side of the horse or mule; and the fatigue which he will sustain, even under the influence of the scirocco, is almost incredible. Nor is he extravagant in his charges: for a dollar, a calish may be hired all the afternoon and evening. This carriage is the only thing in the shape of a machine that has struck me as peculiar to the Maltese. They are not, I suspect, a people remarkable for invention; on the contrary, they seem to have reached a Chinese state of self-sufficient perfection, and are satisfied with their attainments. They have the most beautiful breed of asses in the world; and they keep them in a handsome sleek condition.

How to travel, 1825

ANNE KATHERINE ELWOOD

The caleeshes, which, from the nature of the country, are almost the only vehicles in use, even with the English, are singular-looking conveyances. First of all comes, full drive, a wildish-looking little horse in shafts, and by its side, at a long swinging trot, runs the bare-footed caleesheer, his immense nightcap alternately sweeping one shoulder or the other, as the sun or rain requires the additional defence. Then, *not* upon springs, comes a sort of box or sedan chair, supposed to carry two, although that number is frequently doubled, nay, trebled. Last of all, like an after-thought, comes tearing away, a pair of wheels; and in this machine, off the traveller jolts, apparently to the eminent danger of dislocation either to his neck or limbs; but, though I frequently wished Cinderella's kind god-mother would have transmuted one of the enormous pumpkins sold in the market into a coach for my accommodation, I believe accidents are of very rare occurrence.

Across the harbour: Senglea, 1927

F.N. WESTON

To reach the three cities one needs to go round the Grand Harbour in a bus or taxi or across the Grand Harbour in a boat.

Senglea, with its spacious and symmetrical streets, had once hoped to emulate Valletta as "a city built by gentlemen for gentlemen" (as Sir Walter Scott described it); and many "dolphin" door-knockers – those emblems of Maltese respectability – may be seen upon the doors of the fine old-fashioned houses, in which still linger a few families of position. Vittoriosa was built earlier and otherwise, not for mere gallantry but hard fighting, with streets narrow and crooked to allow a handful of men to resist, in hand-to-hand encounter, an invading army.

The Three Cities attract many visitors to view the spots associated with the Great Siege, and everyone inspects in Vittoriosa the Column of Victory, the hat and sword of La Valettte in the Oratory of San Giuseppe, and the Palace of the inquisitor – a very important personage in his day, who could be exceedingly unpleasant to those who published an undesirable book, or took sides with the enemies of the Holy Church.

Composing the soil, 1789

VIVANT DENON

We went out of the town, without finding *the country*: for what is so called, is as much covered with buildings as is the city, and seems as strongly fortified by large continued walls, which hold up, or encase the little earth there is naturally on the island, and what is brought, or fabricated there; for by breaking small soft rock, and mixing it with the earth, filling the bottom with the best of it, and watering the whole, the indefatigable Maltese at length compose a soil, well suited at least to the cultivation of cotton, the most plentiful and most general produce of the island. They have abandoned almost every other species of culture for this, which is so advantageous both in point of quantity, and quality, as to supply the want of every other production, and to pay for the corn imported from the foreign countries to support them during nine months of the year, the island itself scarcely producing subsistence for three. They therefore make incredible efforts to increase their cotton, and are so convinced of the advantages they derive from it, that a peasant I found watering the plant, said to me, "We must still cultivate it, were we ever reduced to use oil instead of water."

So little soil, 1926

SIR THEMISTOCLES ZAMMIT

When viewed from a distance, both islands appear barren and rocky, owing to the scantiness of trees and to the stone walls which hide both soil and vegetation. On close inspection, however, one is struck by the number of fields, large and small, terraced on slopes, concealed in deep ravines and extending to every bit of ground upon which some soil can spread.

The quality of the soil necessarily varies with the geological layer on which it lies and from which is has been formed. On the Coralline limestone and the Globigerina the soil is of deep red colour, but in the marly districts it is whitish-grey or even bluish. The red soil is loose and granular and can be worked deep and with ease, the marly soil, on the other hand, is compact, heavy and difficult to break. Different crops thrive better in one soil than on the other and the Maltese husbandman is an expert in using the fields to the best advantage. Some villages, in fact, are renowned for certain crops which are never grown in other districts and many fruits only reach perfection when cultivated upon special lands.

The soil has little depth anywhere, except in the low-lying spaces at the mouth of valleys, where soil carried by rain water from high lands has been deposited for centuries. The fields in these places are well watered by springs from the hills and some of these at the Marsa, Fiddien, Saint Paul's Bay and Burmarrod are famous for their fertility.

The soil is almost everywhere rich in lime and phosphates derived from the disintegration of animal remains in the rocks.

The absence of trees from the fields is a feature which strikes the newcomer. Visitors are always ready to suggest that trees should be planted in every field and that shrubberies and groves should replace the hideous stone walls. The practical husbandman, however, knows very well that the shallow soil of the Maltese fields is not adapted to the growth of trees, for they impoverish the soil around them, and absorb all traces of moisture. In the valleys, and in well sheltered fields on the other hand, trees are grown with great care and with excellent results.

By train to Antonio Gardens, 1927

F.N. WESTON

For a period the traveller would turn to the little railway line to travel into the countryside.

This makes a most pleasant excursion that can be varied or shortened at will. You go first by train to Attard, and on leaving the station turn right by the Villa Bologne along Sda. S. Antonio, lined with trees. When the trees are on both sides look out for the two gates on the left marked "Governor's Private Gardens".

Inland, 1924

EVELYN WAUGH

I went inland one day on an absurd railway to Notabile or Citta Vecchia (Mdina), the old capital of the island. There I saw numerous ancient buildings, many of them of Norman construction, three churches, a cathedral containing a portrait of the Madonna painted by St. Luke and a good Della Robbia plaque, an infinitely boring Roman villa with a preserved tessellated pavement, a consumptives' hospital, the cave where St. Paul stayed on his visit to Publius (though this would seem anything but a courteous lodging), and a catacomb full of very dilapidated Byzantine frescoes which the custodian described as Phoenician – a term used among Maltese archaeologists to describe any work earlier than the Norman occupation.

The taxi and karrozin, 2007

SIMON GAUL

Maltese cabs only really serve the visitor. Cabs are clean white chariots of various vintages, a few are old Mercedes with huge ivory-coloured steering wheels belonging to the glory days of soft suspension. Most have shut-off meters (asking for them to be switched on is pointless). On the whole drivers are not particularly interested in advancing Maltese tourist relations, and the well-intentioned government tariffs are merely laughed at....

Taxis are to be found on ranks in the larger towns. Ask, haggle then agree the fare before getting in. Tipping is seldom offered or expected.

Karrozin are horse-drawn carriages that have plied the trade since 1856. They are a good way to see the sights especially in Valletta. The four person canopied bench-seats are high up and children enjoy the ride. Karrozin can be found outside most tourist attractions. Haggle with all your skill before boarding – the Maltese who use the karrozin on Sundays do.

One little building after another, 1917

VERA BRITTAIN

Sunday, October 15th. This really is a most fascinating place; I have not had much to do with it yet, but the more one sees of it, the more attractive it becomes. At present the ground looks all very parched & barren after the summer heat, & everywhere there is stubbly burnt-looking grass – though plots of this are frequently cultivated & ploughed, as if for the sowing of seed. The unbuilt-over part of the island would be one vast tract of this burnt grass were it not that all the land is divided up into plots the size of fields by low white stone walls...

The casals or villages, 1812

EDWARD BLAQUIÈRE

There are scattered about different parts of the interior twenty-two casals, or villages, and one city, Citta Vecchia or Notabile, the ancient capital (Mdina). The latter, though thinly inhabited, is surrounded with a strong rampart, and very agreeably situated. The villages are extremely well built, and have several fine churches, besides convents and consecrated spots. They are all, however, destitute of picturesque beauty, which is not, in fact, to be found in any part of the island. A Luogo Tenente, or civil governor, appointed by the civil commissioner, is placed over each casal to maintain order and regularity among the inhabitants. There is also a Casselano, not unlike our parish priest, nominated by the bishop, and who is a species of ecclesiastical governor.

The parish churches, 1927

F.N. WESTON

The principal building in a casal is the parish church, which generally stands upon a fine piazza, and has often been erected by the voluntary labour of the villagers – men and children carrying the stones from the quarry, and the women mixing the mortar for the masons. In this way was built the church at Mosta, resembling the Pantheon, the dome of which is said to be the third largest in the world.

The church in a casal, therefore, by reason of the personal bond, becomes an object of loving care to the inhabitants, who endeavour in adorning it to surpass the artistic efforts of their neighbours. On the festa of the village – commemorating a titular saint, legend, or historic event – the interior is, in addition to the usual elaborate altar decorations, embellished with green leaves and flowers strewn upon the floor and curtains of red damask upon the walls, which latter often mar the architectural beauty of the building, but the bright colour seems to charm the multitude, and, as it is their church, one cannot criticize. The people especially delight in the illuminations on the evening of a festa, when the facades of the churches are outlined by hundreds of lamps of coloured glass.*

---

* Today such lights are electric, but equally splendid.

Escorted by the Governor, 1805

GEORGE, VISCOUNT VALENTIA

As a visiting aristocrat and one who had been travelling for some years in India and then Egypt, Valentia was given a special welcome by Sir Alexander Ball, the first British Governor of Malta.

August 18: Sir Alexander Ball exerted himself to show me everything that was interesting in the island. I attended him to the races, where the horses were ridden by boys without saddles and bridles, but the crowd was great, and the spectacle altogether gay and interesting.

I also visited with him Citta Vecchia (Mdina) in the middle of the island, which has a handsome cathedral, shining with gold and painting, but without a picture a picture of any merit; and afterwards, a hunting seat of the Grand Masters', now used as a prison for the French officers. It is in a castellated form, and commands an extensive view of the island, broken into undulations, but ugly and unpleasing to the sight, from the want of timber. Near the castle is a deep glen, which formerly was covered with a forest, but the French destroyed it, and a few ancient orange trees alone remain in the garden. The soil is a rich red clay, which would well repay cultivation.

A country walk, 1841

GEORGE ANGAS

I have just returned from a walk in the country, where I have been to see Mr. Agius's villa and farm, accompanied by his two sons, Antonio and Tancredi. We left the city by the Marina gate, and walked along the shore of the Grand Harbour to Marsa, where there is a pillar erected on the beach. This spot commands a fine view of the harbour and the surrounding country. As we strolled along, the music from the men-of-war sounded clearly across the water, and broke the calm and pleasing stillness of the evening. The air was delicious; indeed the only time in this warm climate, suitable for walking, is either at sunset, or very early in the morning. When we had gained the summit of the hill, the sun was just setting behind a bank of resplendent clouds. The whole western horizon was tinged with a deep orange-yellow, and small clouds scattering their golden light along the sky, contrasted their exquisite beauty with the blue of the surrounding heavens. Occasionally we could see the gleaming lightning shine between the clouds, whose darkened edges became in an instant vividly bright, and added a glorious impressive grandeur to the prospect.

~

By and by we reached the farm, but it only resembled an English farm in name. We entered below a portly archway, painted with diverse strange representations of camels, goats and birds, and other creatures whose names I was unable to divine; above every doorway was a cow's head, carved in stone, and painted to resemble life. The cattle, of which there were nearly 300, were all tied up in rows outside long stone sheds, into which they were put at night, and in wet weather. These creatures were all undergoing the process of fattening, and some of them were really handsome: those from Barbary and Sicily I admired most, as the native Maltese cattle are all of a small size. It is from this farm that most of the men-of-war in Malta are supplied with beef... The sheep are also from Barbary, and of a very different breed from our own; they are frequently black and spotted; with long legs, and wool almost approaching to the structure and consistency of hair. But the most numerous and valuable which the Maltese possess are their goats, of which it is computed there are about 12,000 on the island; they are handsome creatures with very long hair, silky and of every variety of colour; black, white, dappled, and fawn being the most common. Their milk is plentiful and very good, though through the scarcity of water its price has of late been raised. The streets of Valletta are full of them, and it is the custom for the milkman to lead about his goats every morning and evening to serve his customers at their respective homes.

Horses which are scarce, are of the Barbary breed; the mules and asses of Malta and Gozo are remarkable for their large size and their elegant shape, and are the chief vehicles employed for draught and burden; they are very numerous, especially the mules, which are generally used for riding.

The race of the Maltese dogs, so renowned for their scarcity and singular appearance, is now nearly extinct, though they may still be obtained at an exceedingly high price. They are very small, with long glistening hair reaching down to the feet, and a turned up nose... Her Majesty Queen Adelaide (who supported the building of St. Paul's Anglican cathedral) procured one of these little creatures during her residence in Malta. It was carried to England, where it was greatly admired as being the only one of its race in the whole country.

We returned home by the light of the moon, and in passing through the suburban streets of Floriana we were serenaded by the chirping of numberless crickets. The Maltese seem greatly attached to these insects; they capture them as we would a bird, and hang them up in little wicker cages, full of leaves, outside their windows.

"Il fiori del mondo"—and ghosts, 1918

LADY FANNY BLUNT

In winter and spring Malta's rocky surface is covered with a velvety green carpet, interspersed with anemones, narcissus, blue iris and other lovely flowers, while in the gardens a perfect wealth of roses is to be seen practically all the year round. In autumn and winter the blossoms are pale and sweet, like a timid maiden receiving the first kiss of love, whilst in spring and early summer the buds develop into blossoms of deeper colour and sweeter perfume. The orange and lemon trees take their share in adorning the island, with their gold and yellow fruits reflecting the bright and shades of the stars above. All these beauties justify the Maltese in calling their island "Il fiori del mondi". Many people come each year to seek the winter warmth and sun in spite of the drawbacks, such as the absence of good hotels, and lifts to the many flats up long flights of stairs, and other minor discomforts felt by those who come from highly civilised countries.

Newcomers usually seek a home in Valletta, where the chief officials are quartered in fine old palaces and mansions built by the Knights of St John. Most of these lovely old auberges are full of paintings and decorations, relics of the Knights. Some of these fine houses are said to be haunted by the spirits of knights and others of bygone centuries, who occasionally visit their old dwellings. Some spirits are said to inflict marks of their displeasure on one or more of the present inhabitants they do not approve of. Others silently walk in and out of their old houses and give no sign beyond their passing apparition. The Maltese are naturally the most numerous inhabitants of the island, and it is mostly they who receive these mysterious visitors.

Wild flowers and much else, 1927

F.N. WESTON

One may follow the country roads – lined in spring and summer before the fierce August sun has parched them up, with all sorts of wild flowers, geraniums, the deep red thorn-rose, clumps of the dark carob-tree, and occasional cypresses – passing through orange and lemon groves, vine-yards, gardens of figs, peaches, pomegranates, medlars, apricots and pears.

Farther afield, a climb to the top of the Bengemma Hills will give a view of fields green with wheat, barley, and cumin, or streaked red with clover. The countryside from this height presents the appearance of a chess-board, the small fields and gardens being carefully enclosed by high walls or terraced at different levels to prevent the wind and the rain sweeping them away, so thin is the layer of soil.

One cannot, indeed, escape the stone. Malta has been described as a mason's earthly paradise, being in reality one vast quarry, the verdure with which it is covered in spring and early summer being due to the untiring energy of the inhabitants, the peasants in the country, like those in Gozo, living by agriculture, exporting to England and elsewhere early potatoes, beans, onions, melons, figs, oranges, especially blood-oranges, and lemons.

Thus the isles of Calypso abound with many interests over and above the fortifications, fever, and lace, with which alone they are frequently associated.

The appearance of Malta, 1810

DR. CHARLES MERYON

The general appearance of the island of Malta is the most unpromising for agriculture that can be conceived. Nowhere is the face of nature so uninviting. The surface of stone has, however, by the effect of industry, been powdered over with a soil, the general depth of which is said to be from six inches to a foot; yet, on this scanty bed, grow lemon, orange, pomegranate, fig, and other fruit trees, besides corn, cotton, lichen, kali, etc, in the greatest luxuriance. The vines spread wherever they are trained, and the oranges acquire the richest flavour.

Cotton is much cultivated in Malta. That which I saw most frequently was of a cinnamon colour when raw, and not like the white common cotton. Corn is said to yield from 16 to 60 for 1. The fruits are of exquisite flavour. Flowers are very fine, and I could not help fancying the roses more fragrant than in my own country. Malta honey is highly esteemed; but always remains in a liquid state.

Into the countryside, 1851

W.H. BARTLETT

A more lively scene is hardly to be found than the *sortie* from the walls of Valletta into the interior of the island. Rumbling under the long echoing gateway, with its guard house and red-coated sentinels, we emerge upon the bridge, which spans the tremendous ditch of the fortifications, cut through the solid rock, and averaging from fifty to eight feet in depth. Hence the road descending a long glacis or slope, passes through another rock-hewn line of defence, and emerges into the suburb of Floriana, within which has grown up another scattered town, with its usual complements – churches and convents, a beautiful botanical garden, and an extensive esplanade. All through these extensive lines of defence and suburbs, flows a perpetual and animated stream of life. The old fashioned caleches, rolling along at every moment, strikingly contrast with the more modern equipages of the English residents and officers – nor are their respective occupants more curiously dissimilar; the former containing, as it may happen, a quiet old-fashioned family of Maltese, from some country casal – brown-skinned, black-eyed, and ugly women, enveloped in the unchangeable black mantilla; while upon the latter are to be seen bright blue eyes and rosy cheeks and pretty faces of a northern clime, and the scarlet jacket of the officer, or the fashionable *négligée* of the Bond Street lounger. On clearing the fortified enclosure, we issue into the open country, over which an extensive and striking view suddenly bursts upon the eye. On a hot dry day and under a glaring sun, it looks almost like an arid desert of white stone, thinly veiled here and there with a patch of feeble verdure, or sparsely dotted over with round, black-looking carob trees; and one is utterly perplexed as to the sustenance of the dense population with which it evidently teems; for – look which way one will – large villages or *casals* everywhere salute the eye, solidly built, and invariably over-towered by large and handsome churches.

After the rains, however, this bare surface is suddenly carpeted with a most vivid green; and then, although there is nothing worthy of the name of scenery to be met with, it is really pleasant to peregrinate the island – the pleasure being mainly derived from the spectacle of industry triumphing over natural obstacles.

To the high ground, 1855

NASSAU WILLIAM SENIOR

Monday, 7 April, 1855: We drove with S. and his sisters to the Citta Vecchia, and thence to Verdala, one of the country houses of the Governor. We were there on nearly the highest ground in Malta, between three and four hundred feet above the sea. It bounded our view on all sides except the west, and we were high enough to see over the walls into the crops between; so that some blue and some green were mixed with the general grey. To the north we looked down into St Paul's Bay, the supposed scene of his shipwreck. I was delighted with the purity and freshness of the air. It seemed to be one in which no amount of exercise would tire.

Citta Vecchia contains, so far as I could discover, two great churches, eight or nine convents, twenty or thirty palaces, and one shop, tenanted by a greengrocer. Everything servile and commercial seems banished to the neighbouring town of Rabato. The three or four persons that we met in its streets and on its lofty ramparts, now disarmed, were priests.

"Here," I said to S, "if I were a Maltese I would like to live."

"Your taste is not singular," he answered. "Houses are dearer here than even in Valletta. The great ambition of the old Maltese families is to have a summer residence in Citta Vecchia. It is deserted, as you see, in winter, but in summer all these palaces are inhabited."

Verdala is a large square town, looking down on a narrow valley planted with oranges, lemons and olives, called the Boschetto. Here the Grand Master could walk for half a mile in the only leafy shade in the island. The English Governors neglected it, cut down many of the trees, and ploughed up the garden. Sir William Reid (the present Governor) inhabits the tower during the summer, and is gradually restoring the Boschetto.

Another town, 1813

JAMES SILK BUCKINGHAM

There is another town, called Civita Vecchia, or the old city, in the interior, which is still the seat of the Archbishop's see, and has several monasteries, nunneries and churches; but as there is no trade or commerce there, the grass grows in the streets, and the place has the silence of death.

The silence of the city, 1789

VIVANT DENON

From the catacombs (at Rabat) we entered the city (Mdina), fortified with large ditches and handsome walls, and equally well built with *La Valette*, but exhibiting a frightful solitude and depopulation; the only noise the traveller hears in the streets proceeds from himself. I thought I was entering a cloister after every person had retired to rest.

The landscape from the Citta Vecchia, 1843

SARAH HAIGHT

From the roof or terrace of the cathedral which is very spacious and formed of large smooth stones, we had a fine extensive view of the whole island, with its numerous villages scattered over it, each vieing with the other in the splendour of its cathedral, whose towers and domes form a beautiful feature in the surrounding scenery. Viewed from such a height, you look upon a carpet of vegetation that seems to overspread the country around. This is varied by extensive groves of olive, fig and orange which, with the different shades of their foliage, afford a pleasing relief to the eye. Valletta and its fortifications were distinctly visible, and afar off we could distinguish Etna with its snowy top, and the waters of the Mediterranean rolling between.

St. Paul's Cathedral, Mdina, 2007

SIMON GAUL

Of all the churches on the islands, St. Paul's Cathedral is the finest and most mature example of Maltese Baroque: not fussy and ornamental but the work of an articulate pen imbued with all the influences – Roman, Sicilian and Italian – from which the idiom evolved. From all perspectives, this monumental church with its bold swathes takes charge at the screen façade, from a distance, in silhouette and from inside.

Tradition states the cathedral is built on the site of the villa belonging to the Roman governor Publius, where the shipwrecked St Paul healed Publius' father and converted the grateful governor himself to Christianity. … The simple 12th century Norman structure of Count Roger was enlarged in 1419, and the present cathedral was built following the earthquake of 1693 which destroyed much of Malta. A new cathedral had been talked about before the earthquake: Lorenzo Gafa had added a new choir in 1679 and after the earthquake he was commissioned to create the new building. The site on the north-east corner of Mdina must have flattered Gafa's inspiration (this domed cathedral would be seen from afar) and the structure went up rapidly; five years after the foundation stone was laid in 1697 it was consecrated.

From above and below, 1877

LADY GROSVENOR

The appearance of the town (Mdina) reminded one singularly of the city in the Arabian Nights, of which the inhabitants had been changed to stone, – so grandly desolate and dilapidated it seemed.

The cathedral is handsome, and there is a view from the roof over the whole island, which, at least at this moment (September), is like an undulating plain of gravel and stone, intersected with stone walls, the sun gleaming and glaring over the whole. There is not a speck of green to be seen, but a solitary plantation of olives, no larger than gooseberry bushes.*

---

* This plantation is now well matured, and gives the appearance of a small, dense wood.

Under the adjoining suburb of Rabbato are extensive and spacious catacombs, excavated in the soft limestone. The tombs are commonly hewn out into chambers, calculated to contain two persons; and bones are frequently found. A large square chamber supported by rude pillars forms the termination of the passages, in the centre of which is a large slab on which the bodies are supposed to have been place previous to entombment. It is imagined that these sepulchres were the work and places of refuge of the early Christians.

We seated ourselves under a very pretty cross, just outside the gate of the town, and ate some excellent Muscatel grapes...

The greatest wonder of the Island, 1815

CLAUDIUS SHAW

Our next visit was to the great catacombs which may be considered the greatest wonder of the island. They were constructed by the natives as hiding-places from the Turks; they extend to a great distance underground, being divided into different apartments and streets. Sleeping places were cut out, of different dimensions: altogether they form a large subterranean town; at certain points being ovens, cooking-places, &c., &c. Only a small part is shown now, as there is some danger of being lost, if any one strayed too far; so stragglers are prevented by part being built up – yet sufficient is left to give a good idea.

Visiting the catacombs, 1789

VIVANT DENON

Our next visit was to the catacombs, the smallest and best preserved of any I had seen: being hewn out of white, sound stone, perfectly dry, they seem as if they had been formed but yesterday. There can be little doubt that the purposes for which they were designed were to inter the dead, to serve as a place of concealment, and to celebrate the mysteries of Christianity. If we consider the smallness of the galleries, in which one person only can pass at a time; their regular arrangement; their roof, which is arched, though cut out of the rock;

the chambers which are met with at different intervals; the plaster that still remains on many of them; the ornament of two fluted pillars in the largest apartment, and which seems to have been the principal; the contrivance of the little niches to receive the lamps that enlightened these subterraneous abodes; the regularity of the tombs, the greatest part of which were placed under square roofs, and had a sort of decoration representing a sarcophagus covered in the form of a pediment; we shall certainly find sufficient reason to conclude, that these catacombs are not, like others, mere excavations formed by chance, to get out stones, since the smallest of the galleries would have rendered that, if not impossible, at least very difficult; nor would the regular distribution which is seen, have been regarded, had nothing more been intended.

St Paul's Catacombs, Rabat, 1990

DAVID TRUMP

The largest group, the so-called St. Paul's Catacombs, are in government ownership and form a popular tourist attraction.

A steep flight of steps is cut into the rock, with small *loculus* graves for children in either side. At the foot of the stairs, one is confronted by a pillar left in the solid rock. To the left of it, at a slightly lower level, is the room interpreted as the chapel. An altar reported by early writers has since disappeared. To the left of this chapel, a grave has been restored with material from elsewhere; the catacombs themselves were despoiled many centuries ago.

On the other side of the pillar is another imposing hall, obviously the centre of the whole monument. At either end is a so-called *agape* table, a common feature in the Maltese catacombs. It consists of a circular table, carved from the rock, with a bench at the same level on all sides except where a niche allows direct access to the table. This is thought to have been for the funeral feast or wake, part of the ceremony of final leave-taking. Scratched into the roof of this hall can be made out crosses and coast of arms, probably souvenirs of visitors in the Knights' period. Passages lead off from these halls in several directions into the bewildering galleries of tombs.

Across the Grand Harbour, 1610

GEORGE SANDYS

On a steep Rock stands the Castle of St. Angelo, whose strength appeared in frustrating those vile Batteries, (being next besieged by the *Turk*) whereof it yet beareth the scars. At the foot of the Rock are certain Cannons planted, that front the mouth of the Haven. This Castle is not only divided by a Trench cut from though the Rock, from the Burgo, a little City that possesseth the rest of that Promontory, being all Rock, hewn hollowed within for their better defence, and disjoined by a great deep Ditch from the Land.

South of this on the next Promontory, stands another Town, which is called La Isula, on the point whereof there is a Platform, and at the other end the strong Fort of St Michael, yet inferior in strength to that of St Angelo. Here remember we the piety of a Mahomedan, descended no doubt of Christian Parentage, and favouring our Religion, who in the time of the strictest siege, and smallest comfort to the besieged, leap'd into the Sea; and maugre all the shot that was made at him, swam to this Fort; where first requiring and receiving Baptism, he made known unto them the secrets of the Enemy, advised how to frustrate their purpose and bravely thrust himself forward in every extremity.

Across the Great Harbour, 1840

MALTA PENNY MAGAZINE

The Naval Hospital was built in 1830–2 at an expense of full £20 000 to the English Government... The hospital is capable of containing two hundred and fifty patients, having two small and four large wards, besides rooms for officers in each pavilion. One of the best things in the establishment is a corridor, ten feet wide and one hundred and sixty feet long, which runs through the centre of each wing, ventilating it in all directions. The officers belonging to the establishment have comfortable houses within its walls. It receives about 8 per cent of the ships' companies of the fleet yearly; being, with ten thousand men, about eight hundred within the year.

The village churches, 1972

NIGEL DENNIS

There is, Nigel Dennis describes, a similarity in church architecture on Malta which can be attributed to the necessities of the materials available to the architects and builders. This gives an explicable distinctive style to the country churches.

Mdina had always the stamp of a city and grew its Baroque out of a medieval township; lesser places like Zejtun are much closer to the countryside, and the little cubes that surround their churches derive from a far more rural, far more ancient way of life. It is difficult to say how ancient this derivation is, because much of the building was done under the protection of the Knights, but in a manner that was already traditional.

The manner is appropriate, inflexible, and capable of infinite repetition. It is based on the simple fact that where there is no timber to make beams, all roofs must be of solid stone and provision made, in the walling, to support the weight above. This support is provided by very thick walls into which heavy arches are deeply embedded, sometimes down to ground level, as in the little chapel of Maqluba. These arches, in turn, support the slabs of the ceiling. The distance between the arches, in any given length of building, is decided absolutely by the invariable nature of the slabs above these cannot be more than seven feet long, or they may crack and split, succumbing to summer heat, occasional earth tremors, and their own weight. Two of this seven feet must rest on the flat tops of each pair of arches, thus, there can never be more than five feet of ceiling between arches, and the arches themselves must always be at least two feet in width. Out of these plain necessities, the room of the characteristic Maltese farmhouse building, the older type of church, and the simple town house have grown always a cube, to sustain the heavy arches; always preponderantly arched, to sustain the slabs; always flat-roofed, to avoid the extra weight of a dome. So engrained is this method that even where the architect has risked a slight rising curve in his roof, the better to throw off storm-water, he has been careful to edge his roof with a low parapet that hides the curve, thus maintaining at least the appearance of the severe traditions.

✳

Mosta compared, 1879

REVEREND WILLIAM LOFTIE

The Dome of Mosta, a village some four miles from Valletta, was an object I wished very much to see. The history of the church has often been told. The villagers finding their place of worship too small for the requirements of an increasing population, determined some fifty years ago to build another. The priest and village mason seem to have been enterprising people. They resolved that the new church must be built, but the old one could not be removed until another was ready.

The site of the two churches must be the same. The apparently inconsistent propositions were ingeniously reconciled. The new church was built over the old one, and as soon as it was ready the old church was carted out, so rapidly that not even a single Sunday service was omitted.

The dome was built without scaffolding within; yet it is one of the largest in Christendom. Here is a list of the principal domes of the world, and the importance of Mosta may be seen from it in an instant:

The Pantheon at Rome is only 146 feet high, but the interior diameter is 142 feet.

St. Peter's is 333 feet in height, and the interior diameter is 137 feet.

St. Maria, Florence, height 275 feet, interior diameter, 137 feet.

St. Paul's, London, height 220, diameter 108 feet.

Santa Sophia, Constantinople, height 182 feet, diameter 107 feet.

The dome of Mosta is not less than 200 feet in exterior height, 160 feet in interior height, and 124 feet in diameter, so that it is 16 feet wider than St Paul's.

Internally the extreme plainness of the Mosta dome greatly increases its appearance in size. It is perfectly smooth, and if the exterior was as simple as the building would be much more satisfactory. But it is disfigured by a number of large coarse honey-coloured scrolls, calculated to dwarf it to the utmost, and the Ionic or quasi-Ionic capitals which support the portico are in a style too debased to be even picturesque.

The village is small and miserable, but built, like the dome, of the beautiful yellow stone of which the whole island consists.

The colossal church at Mosta, 1841

MALTA PENNY MAGAZINE

The great domed church at Mosta is an important stop on the tourist route, and as one stands, head back astonished by the dome, the guide will tell you of the enemy bomb that fell on the church one Sunday in 1941, skittered along the floor away from the congregation and exploded—harming no one...

The main body of the Church consists as a perfect circle of about 200 feet in the extreme diameter. Two additional portions stand out from this at opposite points: presenting each a front of about 125 feet. The front projection facing the square of the village forms the portico, which is recessed between the two Bell Towers. .... The columns are of the Ionic order with engaged columns behind, with niches between some, and the three entrance doors between the others. The two Bell

Towers are complete, and the great height of the building may be judged of, from these towers being only two thirds of the contemplated height of the central door. ... The total height of the edifice will be about 200 feet.

On comparing the church at Mosta with the Pantheon of Rome, we find the diameter of the former equal to that of the latter, when the thickness of the walls is included in both cases in the calculation. ... The elevation of the temple at Mosta is greater than that of the Pantheon, which is as broad as it is high.

The village of Mosta is about five miles from town and is sited in rather a pleasant valley. It numbers about 6000 inhabitants, almost all of the poorest class, and the contrast between the houses which form the sides of the village square, and the front of the temple now erecting is, we would say, painful and saddening. ...

✳

A favourite walk, 1841

MALTA PENNY MAGAZINE

It was once a favourite walk of ours which we gladly recommend to those who are fond of long excursions on foot. – Let them visit the church at Musta, following the ravine of Uied il Hasel where the hermitage of St. Paul and its cool spring may detain them in pleasing yet deep thought for a while, they should reach the heights of Naxaro just as the sun sets. The view from these is grand, nor does the wide expanse of sea, which presents itself, add little beauty and grandeur to the scene. Ere the last ray sets, let them again look back at the bell towers of the church in Musta, then all around; while resting, let them muse for a short time upon the many associations connected with the places before them, and we are confident they could not return home repeating that all is barren from *"Dan to Bethsaida."*

The Bosquetta estate, 1765

PATRICK BRYDONE

From this we went to see the Bosquetta, where the Grand Master had his country palace; by the accounts we had of it at Valletta, we expected to find a forest stored with deer and every kind of game, as they talked much of the great hunts that were made every year in these woods. – We were not a little surprised to find only a few scattered trees, and about half a dozen deer: but as this is the only thing like a wood in the island, it is esteemed a very great curiosity. The palace is as little worth seeing as the forest; though indeed the prospect from the top of it is very fine. The furniture is three or four hundred years old, and in the most Gothick taste that can be imagined: But indeed the Grand Master seldom or never resides there.

The Boschetta Gardens, 1822

JOHN MADOX

I visited the orangery of the Boschetta Gardens in company with an English artist. Here is a beautiful grotto and fountain, in the former of which parties frequently dine. We passed on through the valley, shaded by groves of trees, and by the rocky mountains, and in returning, we visited what is called the Palace of the Inquisitor … the interior is a total ruin. The walls and ceilings of the great hall and of some other apartments are curiously painted in fresco. From the top of the palace there is, I think, the finest view of the island. Much delighted with this little trip and with the fineness of the climate, though at times the heat was excessive, we left it with regret and returned to Valletta.

To St. Julian's Bay, 1855

NASSAU WILLIAM SENIOR

Saturday, March 22: I walked with S. round the Quarantine Harbour, through Sliema to the fine bold coast of St. Julian's Bay. A south-east wind drove the breakers over the rock headlands in vast masses of spray. The country all around the road is undulating; never rising high, but never level. A few – sometimes very few – inches below the surface is the rock. This thin stratum of soil is in constant danger of being washed away by the rain of the southern climate. To protect it the fields are built up by stone walls into a succession of terraces. The walls are high enough to conceal, at a short distance, the flat strips of ground within them. So that, unless you look down from a hill, you see nothing but grey wall over wall. There is no grass, no hedge, no tree except sometimes a solitary olive or palm, or the cypress which rise over the lofty garden walls. Churches of the grandest Renaissance architecture; grand domes behind shallow porticoes with heavy pinnacles on each side of them, are everywhere dotted about, and the suburb of one town almost joins that of the next.

Off St. Paul's Bay, 1813

JAMES SILK BUCKINGHAM

Drawing nearer to the chief city of Malta, we passed also the creek called "The harbour of St. Paul", in which it is believed that the great apostle of the Gentiles was wrecked, in his memorable voyage from Caesarea to Rome, were he was going to appeal to Caesar against the unjust sentence of the colonial governor of Judea, as related in the Acts of the Apostles.

St. Paul's Cave, 1815

CLAUDIUS SHAW

Not far from this is St. Paul's Bay, where the saint was shipwrecked: a small chapel is erected over where the cave is, and a good statue of marble, with the viper on its hand, is shewn. The priest who shows it, recommends you to take away a piece of the stone of the cave, as a specific against shipwreck; he said "Take away as much as you please you will not diminish the cave." – I said, "I think not" – he smiled and turned away.

To the site of St. Paul's shipwreck, 1851

W.H. BARTLETT

After an early breakfast we started in a caleche, and passing out at
Port Bomb, reached the summit of the hill at Casal Nasciar, where,
between two antique small forts, an extensive view suddenly opened
over the greater part of the island, St. Paul's Bay being among the
most conspicuous features. A little distance on the left was a deep
rock dell with a cavern, the spot to which the Apostle traditionally
retired after his shipwreck for prayer and meditation – a tradition
which, smacking as it does of the cave mania of Palestine, and being in
manifest opposition to the practical tone of the Apostle's mind, which
would rather have led him to dwell among his fellow men, than to
exclude himself in an ascetic retirement, did not induce us to deviate
out of the direct road to the Bay.

The Grotto of St. Paul, 1812

WILLIAM TURNER

About eight miles from Valletta ... a small chapel, dedicated to the
same saint (St. Paul), is built over the grotto in which the Maltese say
he dwelt three months; and the man who served it bade me carry
away a piece of chalky stone of the grotto, as an infallible preservative
against the bite of vipers or any venomous insect, denouncing
vehement curses on all who disbelieved its efficacy.

Near Citta Vecchia I was also shown some catacombs of considerable extent, in which it is said the Saracens took refuge, and
which certainly were well calculated for concealment and defence.
Apartments, tombs, ovens, and even a small church, were hewn out of
the subterranean rock, which was quite a labyrinth, and out of these
habitations branched a passage, also subterranean, which I was told
extended two miles.

St. Paul's Bay, 1840

MALTA PENNY MAGAZINE

The bay is about three miles in length, and two in width at the entrance, gradually decreasing towards the extremity. At this point the beach is sandy, and differs from the general appearance of the coast round the harbour, which is rugged and rocky. To the north-west of the entrance is a small oblong island, called Salmone or Selmoon, separated from the mainland by a narrow straight. A tower and other fortifications in the vicinity serve to defend the bay, and were raised for that purpose by the Knights of Malta.

The only object of interest worth noticing in this place is a small chapel, built upon the supposed site where the inhabitants lighted a fire to warm the shipwrecked crew. It contains a few old paintings, illustrative of the events connected with St. Paul in this quarter.

Sliema as it was, 1834

GEORGE WARING

The little village of Sliema (which word, being interpreted, signifies "peace") consists principally of summer residences of inhabitants of Valletta, and is situated, as you will see from the map, close to the sea, on the north-western side of the quarantine harbour. Most of the houses in the village are built on the top of the hill facing the sea, for the benefit of the refreshing breeze, for the summers are generally intolerably hot and oppressive, and the heat is increased by the reflection of the sun from the light-coloured walls and roads. Our house is pleasantly situated close to the harbour, and is sheltered from the cold northerly winds by a rising ground at the back, on which account it appears more suited for a winter than for a summer residence.

~

We often take long rambles along the coast and into the interior, and in these excursions we never confine ourselves to roads or footways, but climb over walls, and pass through fields and gardens without rebuke or molestation from any person, as though the garden were our own private estate. The Maltese are certainly very good-natured to trespassers, for though in these cross country rambles we are continually falling in with men at their work, no notice is ever taken of us. In one of our first excursions in this area, we were delighted by finding some beautiful large blue anemones, the same species we cultivate with so much care in our English gardens.

Malta of the classics, 1831

GEORGE PERCY BADGER

An ancient author writes concerning this island: "Malta is furnished with many and very good harbours, and the inhabitants are very rich, for it is full of all sorts of artificers among whom are the excellent weavers of fine linen. Their houses are very stately and beautiful, adorned with graceful eaves, and pargetted with white plaster. The inhabitants are a colony of Phœnicians, who, trading as merchants, as far as the western coast, resorted to this place on account of its commodious ports, and convenient situation for maritime commerce; and by the advantages of this place, the inhabitants frequently became famous both for their wealth and their merchandise." (a) From this quotation it appears that the Phoenicians were very early, if not the first settlers of this island, and the learned Bochart considers them the same with the Phœnicians, mentioned by Homer, generally taken for the aborigines of Malta. Several other quotations from Cicero, and particularly from Homer, who mentions the island under the name of Ogygia, together with the preceding, if not decisive proof, go far to establish the early settlement of the Phoenicians in Malta.

To Hannibal, 1812

WILLIAM TURNER

It was the opinion of Sir William Drummond* that Hannibal had been buried on Malta. William Turner rode with a small party, including Sir Robert Wilson, to the village of Benlisa, at the eastern extremity of the

---

* Sir William Drummond was a Scottish scholar and philosopher who in 1810 published an essay on a Punic inscription found on Malta relating to one Hanni-Baal.

island, 'rather with the view of seeing the country, than with the idea of realising so wild a vision'.

We found some ruins of a small pyramidical building (the base of one side of which was in good preservation), that had evidently been a tomb, whose foundations, enclosing two distinct chambers, were still very distinguishable. Round it lay several hewn stones, with circular serpentine ornaments sculptured on them, and the old man who accompanied us said that he remembered an old church standing near there, in which it was said, that some great man of old lay interred.

Visiting Annibal's tomb, 1812

SIR ROBERT WILSON

On Monday, I resolved to visit Annibal's tomb. In vain endeavoured to acquire information on the subject in Valletta, until an old book was provided, which afforded a clue to the neighbourhood of its site. We passed over "impassable rocks", and, after great difficulties, succeeded in finding an old man who undertook to show us what, he had heard, attracted many years ago the attention of some travellers, and the remains of a building which the tradition of the Island reported to have been the monument of a very great ancient warrior.

He first showed us some ornamental entablatures of a temple, and then carried us to the mound, or sepulchre, where we found the distinct foundations and compartments of two chambers, with two faces of one of the angles nearly entire. The building was evidently of a pyramidal form, constructed with large blocks, and in one of the chambers was lying a great hewn stone, like the top of a sarcophagus, which we endeavoured in vain to lift, but which I think it would be well worth while to raise.

… Whether this is the actual tomb of Annibal, the most illustrious of great captains, or not, it is undoubtedly an ancient sepulchre,…and the possibility of its having been what it is now presumed…to have been, produced a train of thought that amply indemnified me for a very severe ride of twenty-two miles, of which half a dozen were trials for the nerves, as the rocks were slippery as glass.

Hagar Qim, 1990

DAVID TRUMP

The village of Quendi's most famous site is Hagar Qim.

This temple stands in a commanding position with the ground falling gently away on all sides. This is only one of the features in which Hagar Qim differs from the other temples, and it in turn explains the second. The ridge is capped with globigerina limestone which, being the only stone locally available, was used throughout in the construction of the temple. The effect can be clearly seen in the outer southern wall, where the great orthostats, exposed to the sea winds with their corrosive salt content, have been whittled away by surface flaking over the centuries. ...

Into prehistory, 1845

ISABELLA ROMER

A mile and half from the village of Casal Crendi, Mrs. Romer visited 'the greatest antiquity and the greatest novelty contained in the island'.

Within the last five or six years excavations were made there under the direction of the late governor, Sir Henry Bouverie, which brought to light the remains of what is supposed to have formed part of either a Phoenician Temple, or a place of sepulchre, – probably both, since the human bones and the rude stone altars discovered by some of the chambers would infer that it had been devoted to either purpose. No inscription has been found to give any data of these remains, but their Druidical form (or, what is technically termed, Cyclopean architecture) argues the remotest antiquity.

The chambers are oblong in form, and the larger ones rounded at one end; the walls and partitions composed of huge blocks of stone placed upright on the ground; the windows and doors are of the rudest construction, and there are no attempts at either architectural or sculptural ornament, beyond the surface of the stone of which the altars and the seats are composed being irregularly punctured with small holes.

The spot where these remains were discovered has, from time immemorial, been indiscriminately called by the Maltese, *Hagiar Chem*, ('the stones of Chem') and *Gebel Keem* ('the mountains of worship'). The latter denomination proves the existence of some traditionary record of their original purpose, and corresponds with the opinion pronounced by most of the scientific men who have visited the place, namely, that Hagiar Chem was the religious temple of some Phoenician city, which once existed in the immediate neighbourhood, and the vestiges of which may hereafter be brought to light as this curious remnant of bygones ages has been.

What is this place? 1851

W.H. BARTLETT

Bartlett, visiting Hagar Qim not long after it had first been excavated in 1839 under the direction of Sir Harry Bouverie, Governor of Malta, could only guess at the purpose of this building, far older than Stonehenge, and older than the Pyramids.*

But whatever they were, no one could look upon them as we did, in the profound stillness of a summer noon – unbroken but by the hum of the gilded fly, or the rustle of a lizard as he furtively made forth, and then disappeared again from among the chinks of the masonry – by the soft waving of the scented wild flowers and silken rye grass – or wandered about their grey avenues of stones, with the wild and desolate landscape around, and the blue sea, upon which imagination pictures the barks of the roving Phoenicians, to whom tradition assigns the structure, – without a feeling of intense curiosity, and almost of awe, which perhaps no other description of edifice is, in an equal degree, calculated to call forth.

Bartlett gave a detailed and measured description of the temple, further explained with detailed drawings. He summed it up thus:

In general, it may be said that this singular edifice appears to be a curious stage between the most primitive style of building – the

---

* Modern archaeologists now date Hagar Qim at about 3400 BC.

Fig. II.

Fig. III.

Fig. I.

Fig. IV.

mounds and earthworks, and Druidical circles and avenues of stones, found in our own country and elsewhere – and the earliest forms of masonic architecture known to us.

General description of the ruins, 1840

MALTA PENNY MAGAZINE

The colossal remains of ancient architecture, styled by the natives of Malta *Hagiar Chem* or *Cham*, situated in a stony district towards the south-east extremity of the island, about twenty minutes' walk from Casal Crendi, have often excited the curiosity and raised the conjecture of several learned antiquarians, who from time to time have visited them. Until very lately, however, nothing beyond hypothesis was ever attempted upon the evident work of human art which appeared in the regular connexion of massy stones several feet above the surface, and the honour is due to His Excellency Sir H. Bouverie of being the first to direct, that further investigation should be made, and satisfactory information obtained, of the extent and nature of these extraordinary remains.

The superintendence of the excavation was committed to Mr. Vance, and in the course of three months the rubbish which choked up the cavities was all cleared away, and the work completed. The once irregular rows of hewn and unhewn blocks have given place to a regularly constructed building, exceeding in the style of its architecture, and the variety of its furniture, anything yet discovered in this island, and even more interesting than the so called *Giant's Tower* at Gozo.

Megalithic sanctuaries, 1926

SIR THEMISTOCLES ZAMMIT

Involved in the early archaeological work on the temples, Zammit had a very special contribution to make to their description.

There are in Malta a number of highly important megalithic monuments which are thought to have been sanctuaries. They are usually extensive, but probably some of them consisted originally of single chambers to which other rooms were added at a later period. The whole structure would thus represent centuries of human activity. Most of these buildings have a large elliptical forecourt paved with coarse slabs, and are enclosed by a high wall of monoliths, with the main entrance to the centre of the forecourt. The chambers, which are either oval or semi-circular open on to a common corridor.

The internal walls are concave, so as to support a roof or dome, the horizontal courses being corbelled, each course projecting slightly beyond the one below it. The large amount of debris found close to the ruins suggests that the buildings were further covered with stones so as to form one large pile, binding the various parts into a huge mass.

There is an apocryphal story at Hagar Qim that the archaeologists in the inter-war years were planning to re-instate one of the great blocks. They told the Maltese labourers that this would be done on the next morning. The archaeologists arrived next day with modern lifting tackle and other equipment to complete the task. The great stone was already lifted and in place…

To the ruins of Hajar Kim, 1841

GEORGE ANGAS

Upon leaving the village of Crendi, our road lay over a rocky path, which was in some places very abrupt, and more fitted for mules than for the slight and graceful barbs which bore us. When we reached the summit of the hill we had been ascending, I was agreeably surprised by a sudden view of the sea below us, which burst unexpectedly upon our sight. It was blue – deep hazy blue – as far as the weary eye could reach towards the shores of Tripoli. In the distance the rock of Filfila arose darkly from the sapphire plain, for the shades of evening already began to blend the garish tints of day into a mellow and sombre hue. I shall never forget the refreshing sight of that deep blue sea, after a day's toil among the parched and arid rocks of Malta.

We reached the first ruin of Hajar Kim, after crossing a scorched plain studded with golden rod and other bulbous roots…we proceeded on foot to examine the ruins. They consisted of two separate chambers of an oval form opening into each other by a doorway composed of two large upright stones, with a third placed crosswise on the top.

Communicating with these chambers are several smaller ones, in one of which are the remains of a fire-place. There are also several curious, but rudely carved relics scattered around. One of these in the largest apartment seemed to have been an altar for religious purposes. The whole was in the rudest style of primitive architecture, and is supposed to have been the work of the Phoenicians, who occupied this island many ages since.

They continued on to the second site.

As the twilight was fast approaching we hastened up the hill to rejoin our horses, where they were waiting for us, as the first mass of ruins we had visited. Here and there we roused a solitary quail, the lone possessor of this silent and sterile spot.

✳

To Hagiar Kim, 1927

F.N. WESTON

Mr. Weston's walking guide to Malta often approached sites from rather different directions than did more formal guides.

I always prefer to approach Hagiar Kim from this direction rather than through Krendi, in order to avoid the hordes of begging children that pester one, and are so difficult sometimes to get rid of. It is desirable, however, to arrange for a *carrozin* to meet you at the gate of Hagiar Kim, as it is not always possible to pick one up at Krendi.

This walking is extremely interesting, and in parts beautiful if you follow the whole of the route described. – (which led past old houses, "and you should miss no opportunity of peeping into open doors, as many of the gardens and courtyards are very pretty, especially when there is the glint of sunshine on them." – and along varied paths ...)

As you drop towards the sea, Filfola Rock comes into view.

There is more scrambling described until:

Scramble up the rocky slope till you reach the cart-track by the quarries, and follow it towards the sea. A watch-tower soon comes into sight, and then Mnaidra below us, with the ruins of Hagiar Kim against the sky just to the left. The country about here is much spoiled by quarries. On the top of the slopes on the left, above Mnaidra, there are some ancient water-tanks from Phoenician, or even prehistoric, times, which are still in use.

After examining the ruins you can take the paved path to Hagiar Kim, but if you have time you should first follow the path that runs towards the watch-tower. It makes a circle round the hill, giving a good view of the bold cliffs on the other side of Wied Babu. On reaching cultivated ground, do not go round the head of the field, but continue straight along the track between walls, which leads into the road a little to the right of Hagiar Kim. (Entrance fee 6d.)…

The discovery of the Hypogeum of Hal Saflieni, 1902

DAVID TRUMP

The Hypogeum is in every way unique … it is an unpromising district for ancient remains, which adds to the impact it makes on visitors. It was discovered in the course of housing development in 1902, when workmen cutting cisterns for the new houses broke through its roof. Unfortunately, the knowledge of it was deliberately hushed up until the houses were complete, by which time considerable and avoidable further damage had been done to the upper levels.

The next chapter in its story is a little more cheerful. Investigation of the site was entrusted to Father Magri, S.J., who cleared the central chambers but then left for missionary work in the East. Though most of his finds were preserved, no record of their context or associations survives.

The work was completed in a much more scientific manner by Dr. (Themistocles) Zammit in 1905–9.

To the Hypogeum, 1927

F.N. WESTON

Much as Hagiar Kim and Mnaidra appeal to the imagination, largely owing to their romantic situation, the finest and most interesting remains are those discovered in recent years.

These remains were excavated as recently as 1915–16, having been buried and largely destroyed by former generations, and then forgotten altogether until 1914 ...

You will see from the model in the Valletta Museum that they consist of three sets of apsed compartments, these probably representing three different temples, erected at various times in the late Neolithic period. They afterwards fell into disuse, and three feet of soil collected over the pottery and other objects of the Stone Age, but in the layer above this were discovered bronze daggers and other remains of the Bronze Age.

Professor Zammit, who supervised the discovery, wrote:

"The building in question was erected in the late Neolithic Age, and was very probably used as a sanctuary. Before the full development of the Bronze Age this sanctuary fell into oblivion, and the various rooms and courts were gradually filled up with dust and other light debris such as are usually carried by natural agencies.

... The high walls, still standing, gave excellent shelter to the funeral pyres, and the spaces, enclosed by lower walls, made a convenient depository for the ashes of the dead. ...After the burial ground was abandoned and completely forgotten the destruction of the building followed, first for the sake of the good stones of which it was built, and, later on, for turning the place into an arable field.

～

On leaving these ruins ... the next turning on the right, called Catacomb Street, you come to the Hal Saflieni Hypogeum. It was discovered in 1911, and is the most wonderful thing in Malta, being probably unique of its kind in the world.

Above it there was at one time a megalithic building like the others of which the ruins still exist, but nothing now remains of it. From this there was a passage to a system of chambers in two storeys cut out of the solid rock. These are very much on the plan of what the exterior building must have been like, with doorways and niches of the dolmen type. It is conjectured that they too formed a sanctuary, or perhaps a school of initiation. ... In later days the chambers were used as an ossuary, for the remains of thousands of skeletons were found there. Being below the ground, the Hypgeum is naturally in the best state of preservation of any of the ancient monuments of Malta, and is excellently lit by electric lamps arranged and screened so none can be seen as one advances along the passages.

The Hal Saflieni Hypogeum, 1926

SIR THEMISTOCLES ZAMMIT

When the Hypogeum was discovered, in 1902, it was full of rubbish, and the lower rooms contained water. It was cleaned out, and found to consist of four sets of caves and galleries cut at different levels in the white calcareous rock. No trace of natural caverns can be seen in any part of the hypogeum and although advantage was taken of natural fissures, this extraordinary monument was dug throughout in the solid rock.

Numerous flint implements and stone objects were discovered in the course of the long excavation, but no bronze or other metal. This fact confined with the marks left by flint tools on the rock surface, and with the personal ornaments and pottery collected, leads us to the conclusion that the monument was dug out in prehistoric times.

The original entrance was through a doorway now buried under Hal Saflieni Street; the present one is in Catacomb Street, and was made when the place was being cleared. Descending the modern stairway, one lands in the middle storey of the Hypogeum, which contains a kind of passage with a trilithon in front; a series of caves are on the left and several others are at a higher level on the right. The first cave on the left of the entrance is roughly circular, and at a level lower than that of the passage. The curved wall on the left of the door has three large niches, cut in the rock, the central one being enlarged into a small cave.

"Cart-ruts" across the land, 1990

DAVID TRUMP

One of the most intriguing aspects of Maltese archaeology is that of the so-called cart tracks. These are parallel grooves in bare rock representing traffic long before the present landscape pattern was established. They run in pairs, sometimes for long distances, often forking or combining like railway sidings, until they disappear beneath fields, rods or houses, over cliff edges or into the sea.

... Tracing the ruts across country for plotting onto a large-scale map is a very satisfying sport, more humane than most, particularly on bright winter days with their invigorating blend of warm sun and cool air. Much of the new information [here] comes from such excursions, in my case disguised, if only very thinly, as work.

A common pattern—one cannot say rule—is for them to climb from the cultivated valley, cross a ridge by the most convenient place, and descend to vanish below the fields of the next valley. This is why they are so frequently found beside modern roads, which are, of course, doing exactly the same thing, short of vanishing. The prominent group running from Salina, past Tal-Qadi and up to San Pawl tat-Targa might have carried salt, or any other sea product. Most can be explained by regular agricultural activities.

Where they run over cliffs (Gihar Zerrieg, Ras il-Pellegris) or into the sea (St. George's and Mellieha Bays), they reappear within few score yards, and cannot be quoted as evidence for land-bridges. In some places, as near San Lawrence on Gebel Ciantor, ruts start off clearly across bare rock, but become progressively fainter until they disappear. In the absence of evidence for erosion of the rock, this must indicate the former existence of soil cover, since swept away.

There are many questions the reader may want answered about the cart-ruts which cannot be answered here, and for which the archaeological studies of Malta can answer. Here is David Trump's explanation of their function.

The pairing of ruts, and their behaviour relative to the topography, make them certainly a means of vehicular communication. ... At St. Pawl tat-Targa, one rut has been tapped to carry rain run-off into a cistern, but this must be secondary. ...

The bells of Malta, 1960

EDWARD LEOPARDI

One of the sounds connected with our island are the bells which ring from the belfries of our churches. The visitor may wonder at the different peals and frequency of the ringing: the Maltese initiated in the language of the bells understand every stroke and the reason for the ringing. However, some of the younger generation have no more knowledge than strangers to the island.

The towns in Malta are especially noted for the consistency and correctness in bell ringing; these are Qormi and Birkirkara, which have kept the old rule of informing the faithful of events through the bell. At 4 a.m., or 4:30 a.m., the *Pater Nostra* is sounded with 33 strokes, 33 being the number of years Our Lord spent on Earth. Other peels common throughout the island are at 8 a.m., midday and sunset. Many recite the *Angelus* at the ringing of this bell.

Since the hour of sunset varies with the season, the evening bell does likewise. It gains 15 minutes on the 1st and 15th day of each month in the first six months and loses 15 in the last six. An hour after the evening *Angelus* is another short peal known as the *De Profundis* to mark the first hour of the night.

Mass is announced by a few strokes of a bell 15 minutes before – this giving time for the faithful to gather in church. The bells of a Collegiate Church ring a two-toned peal for 15 minutes prior to the meeting of the Chapter for matins and vespers. A bell which has become rare today is that of the dying. This was nine strokes of the bell followed by three strokes every hour or until the passing bell was sounded. The passing bell would be followed by the death bell. The last two are still common in Malta and, on hearing these bells, the faithful utter a prayer.

On festive occasions the bells ring out in unison for periods short and long. Before High Mass and Vespers on the occasions of a first class feast there are four periods of ringing and three for a second class feast. A sermon is announced by the stroke of a bell at measured distance.

Life today has many diversions but our ancestors living in Malta before the First World War had ample time to listen to the bells they understood, thus following the happenings around them. There was a special bell known as the *Gloria* – this was a lively peal – at the burial of an infant...

The procession, 1821

JOHN MADOX

*Madox attended the Feast of St. Grigorio in the village of Zeitun on 26 April
1821. Every Maltese village and town has at least one feast or festa in honour
of its patron saint. The villagers and their priests, and their band clubs, plan
the celebrations, arrange fireworks, and gather in their flamboyant finery to
process and enjoy the occasion. John Madox witnessed a procession that was
more significant than many, bringing people in from far and wide.*

The procession was grand, its length extending for some miles,
it was composed of the country-people from all the surrounding
villages, who formed themselves into companies or fraternities, each
devoted to a particular saint or lady-patroness. Everyone in the train
was dressed in gay attire, and all appeared cheerful and happy; some
carrying crosses and banners of various colours, denoting the order
of fraternity to which they belonged. Thus they proceeded to the
church, the rear being brought up by the bishop and cannons in costly
mantles, accompanied by half a dozen priests, miserably scraping
some cracked violins and a crazy violincello or two.

Somewhere else, 1929

EVELYN WAUGH

I spent too little time in Malta. Most of my days were spent in exploring
Valletta, with the aid of a small book called *Walks in Malta* by F.N.
Weston, which I bought for two shillings (10 pence) at Critien's, the
big stationer's shop. I found it a slightly confusing book at first until I
got used to the author's method; after which I became attached to it,
not only for the variety of information it supplied, but for the amusing
Boy Scout game it made of sightseeing. "Turning sharply to your
left you will notice..." Mr. Weston prefaces his comments, and there
follows a minute record of detailed observation. On one occasion,
when carrying his book, I landed at the Senglea quay, taking it for
Vittorioso, and walked on for some time in the wrong town, hotly
following false clues and identifying "windows with fine mouldings";
partially defaced escutcheons"; "interesting ironwork balustrades",

etc, for nearly a mile, until a clearly non-existent cathedral brought me up sharp the realization of my mistake.

The country houses of the Knights, 1765

PATRICK BRYDONE

Our banker, Mr. Poufilach, was here before we were up, inviting us to dine with him at his country-house, from whence we had just returned. He gave us a noble entertainment, served on plate, with an elegant dessert, and great variety of wines.

After dinner we went to visit the principal villas of the island; particularly those of the grand master, and the general of the galleys, which lie contiguous to each other. These are nothing great or magnificent; but they are admirably contrived for a hot climate, where, of all things, shade is the most desirable. The orange groves are indeed very fine, and the fruit they bear are superior to anything you have seen either in Spain or Portugal.

The aspect of the country is far from being pleasing: the whole island is a rock of very white free-stone, and the soil that covers this rock, in most places, is not more than five or six inches deep; yet, what is singular, we found their crop in general was exceedingly abundant. They account for it from the copious dews that fall during the spring and summer months; and pretend likewise, that there is a moisture in the rock below the soil, that is of great advantage to the corn and cotton, keeping its roots perpetually moist and cool; without which singular quality, they say they could have no crops at all, the heat of the sun is so exceedingly violent.

The fruit of Malta, 1765

PATRICK BRYDONE

The orange trees of Malta are one of its surprises and pleasures. Many houses have a tree in their garden, so, as one walks down a street through much of the year, either the scent of orange blossom or the excitement of the golden-orange globes amongst the green leaves is a frequent pleasure.

The Maltese oranges certainly deserve the character they have, of being the finest in the world. The season continues for upwards of seven months; from November till the middle of June; during which time, those beautiful trees are always covered with abundance of this delicious fruit. Many of them are of the red kind, much superior, in my opinion, to the others, which are rather too luscious. They are produced, I am told, from the common orange-bud, grafted on the pomegranate stock. The juice of this fruit is red as blood, and of a fine flavour. The greatest part of their crop is sent as presents to the different courts of Europe, and to the relations of the chevaliers. It was not without a good deal of difficulty that we procured a few chests for our friends at Naples.

✳ GOZO AND COMINO ✳

Reaching Gozo, 1839

THOMAS MACGILL

Separated from Malta by a narrow channel of about five short miles, is Gozo, the fabled island of Calypso. In mid-channel is the little island of Comino, at present farmed by an English gentleman. The island of Gozo is about twelve miles long, and from six to seven in breadth, and is prettily diversified with hill and dale – the highest hill is called *Delegi*.

The coast is bold and precipitous in most parts; there are, however, in the ravines, two pretty good landing places, also one or more of lesser note, into which boats can run in stormy weather. The principal landing place is called Migiarra and is on the east end of the Island, facing the western point of Malta called Marfa. Here there is a fine sandy beach where boats from Malta unload their cargoes and passengers. On a height, to the right of this little bay, stands a small fort for its defence, and on another, to the left, is the fine fortification called Chambray, founded by a knight of that name, about the middle of the last century. Chambray is the headquarters of the garrison of Gozo – the outworks of the fort are extensive, enclosing a large space, as a retreat for the inhabitants of the vicinity, with their cattle, in case of any sudden invasion.

Gozo can boast of no rivers, but she may vaunt of having no morasses or marshes. She is however abundantly supplied with rich springs of fine water, which run in rivulets, enriching the soil as they pass. Some even run to the sea.

The climate of Gozo is remarkably healthy, her robust, industrious and abstemious inhabitants live to a very great age; and, standing high, the air in summer is considered two degrees cooler than that of Malta. The physicians of Malta recommend the fine climate of Gozo, to people in delicate health.

In different parts of the island there are pretty groves and plantations of orange and other fruit trees.

The productions of Gozo are the same as those of Malta, but more abundant – all the surplus goes to the market of Valletta. ... The Gozo race of jack-asses is remarkably fine. So great has the demand for them been, for England and America during the last forty years that it is with difficulty that a first rate trumpeter can be procured on the Island.

✳

Victoria, or Rabat, and the Citadel, 2007

JOSEPH ATTARD TABONE

The Gozitans always call it Rabat. It is the only town in Gozo and was named Victoria in 1897 on the occasion of the Diamond Jubilee of Queen Victoria. It is in the centre of the island and has been the capital of Gozo probably from the time of the Romans. The Romans built defensive walls around their town which the Arabs continued to reinforce after they took over in 870 AD. Nothing structurally very old has survived, but one can see in the irregular twisting lanes and alleyways of the town the splendid balconies and other features of local architecture.

The main Government offices are scattered in the centre of the town, while the banks, the main police station, the Bishop's Curia and the Government Secretariat for Gozo are at Republic Street.

The Citadel is on one of the many flat-topped hills in the centre of Gozo. Its origins can be traced to the late Middle Ages. At one time all the population of Gozo had to take shelter within these walls after sunset. The walls themselves date from the 16th to 18th centuries. Most of the buildings inside the Citadel are in ruins but the Old Courts of Law and the Old Governor's Palace are still being used as the Law Courts of Gozo. There are also the Old Prison and the Armoury of the Knights, the Archaeological, Natural History and Folklore Museums. The Cathedral, the Bishop's Palace and the Cathedral Museum dominate the Citadel.

Over the abyss, 1822

JOHN MADOX

On the far side of the island from where Madox landed is 'Fungus Rock' or Il-Gebla tal-General, the General's Rock, a 60-metre high monolith at the entrance to a lagoon. It gained its nickname from a fungus-like plant with supposed medicinal properties that grew on its summit. To protect the rock from would-be collectors, it was declared out-of-bounds in 1746, with a guard and a precarious 50-metre long cable and box-car to the mainland.

There were ropes from which was suspended a small square wooden box, large enough for one person, which was pulled across with the aid of blocks or pulleys. When seated in the box, you are carried with great velocity mid-way across; you are then pulled the remaining way by two stout fellows, and the greatest danger is apprehended in getting out of the box, and crawling to the summit of the rock. If the attendants see you in any state may to a great measure be attributed to these labours of the Sabbath.

Fungus Island, 1815

CLAUDIUS SHAW

One object of curiosity on the south side of the island, is a rock, on which grows a kind of fungus, which is used as a styptic. The passage to this rock is rather curious, if not dangerous; two ropes are made fast on each shore, on which a box with grooves on its edges passes over. A Maltese first works his way across, then the person desirous to go over draws the box back and seats himself in it, when he is hauled over by the guide; in this manner as many as please can go, one at a time. It is not a very pleasant sensation to be suspended some hundred feet above water, and if there is any wind, the movement of the box is anything but agreeable, and all that can be obtained are a few pieces of FUNGUS! I was well pleased to be back again, and made a determination never to risk my precious carcase in that conveyance again. It seems very strange to be swinging up in the air between two rocks, with sea gulls and other aquatics flying about below you.

Comino, 1789

VIVANT DENON

This isle is so named from the cumin it produces, and which grows, if I may say so, on the stone…

Unable to enter Malta at night and seasick from a rough crossing from Sicily, Denon and his party spread their cloaks on the ground and endeavoured to take some repose…

Disappointed by Calypso's island, 1765

PATRICK BRYDONE

The distance of Malta from Gozzo [sic] is not above four or five miles, and the small island of Comino is betwixt them. The coasts of all the three are bare and barren, but covered over with towers, redoubts, and fortifications of various kinds.

As Gozzo is supposed to be the celebrated island of Calypso, you may believe we expected something very fine; but we were disappointed. It must either be greatly fallen off since the time she inhabited it, or the Archbishop of Cambray as well as Homer, must have flattered greatly in their painting. We looked, as we went along the coast, for the grotto of the goddess, but could see nothing that resembled it. Neither could we observe those verdant banks eternally covered with flowers; nor those lofty trees forever in blossom, that loft their heads in the clouds, and afforded a shade in the sacred baths of her and her nymphs.

We saw, indeed, some nymphs; but as neither Calypso nor Eucharis seemed to be of the number, we paid little attention to them, and I was in no apprehension about my Telemachus. Indeed, it would have required an imagination as strong as Don Quixote's, to have brought about the metamorphosis.

Finding our hopes frustrated, we ordered our sailors to pull out to sea, and bid adieu to the island of Calypso, concluding, wither that our intelligence was false, or that both the island and the inhabitants were greatly changed. We soon found ourselves once more at the mercy of the waves: Night came on, and our rowers began their evening song to the Virgin, and beat time with their oars. Their offering was acceptable, for we had the most delightful weather.

The centre of the villages, 1995

JOSEPH ATTARD TABONE

Every village has its own parish church, which is usually in the centre of the inhabited part of the village with its dome and belfry dominating over the rest of the building. A different titular saint is venerated in each church, whose festa is celebrated on a Sunday in summer. The statue of the saint is carried shoulder high along the main streets of the village or town while brass bands play, bells peel and fireworks crack.

These churches are embellished with many rich works of art testifying to the great religious devotion of the Gozitans of today as the prehistoric temples do to that of the early inhabitants of this island. It seems even that the 'cyclopean' mentality is still persistent. One can see this at the Rotunda of Xewkija. The enormous and newly built church has replaced a much smaller uncommonly pretty 18th century one, and this in turn replaced a prehistoric megalithic temple. Its dome is now the third largest church dome in Europe, relegating Mosta to fourth place.

Every Gozitan thinks that his village is better than the neighbouring one and the parochial attitude culminates during the festa season with demonstrative rivalry. This is perhaps more deeply rooted in Victoria between the two rival band clubs. The town is divided into two parishes: the Assumption of St Mary at the Cathedral and Saint George close to the main square, 'It Tokk'. Each has its supportive band club which is responsible for the organisation of the open air festivities of its respective patron saint. These clubs are the hub of activity during weekends for both town and village folk.

The Giant's Tower of Gozo, 1870

ANDREW ADAMS

Inland about two miles, on the side of the Sciacca plateau, overlooking the fertile valley of Ramala, which opens on the bay of the same name, is situated the so-called Giant's Tower, – the most cyclopean of all the Maltese monumental structures. It is built on the same principle as the others, so that a description of Hagiar-Kim will suffice for the general elucidation of their modes of construction and style of architecture. It has been a subject of frequent remark, considering the rude workmanship displayed on the buildings, that the modes of conveyance must have been very effective, to have transported huge monoliths of a very friable rock for long distances; but this is more apparent than real, inasmuch as I found that there are few if any of the monuments which have not been constructed from rocks in their immediate vicinity, as is well seen on the sandstone about Hagiar-Kim, where the ancient trenches around the mass of stone to be removed were dug in the exact same way as now practised by the Maltese.

It has always appeared to me that the transport of the largest blocks is more suggestive of the number of inhabitants on the islands at the same time than remarkable for their modes of conveyance and machinery used in placing them in their present situations. In the case of the Gozo monument, it must however be stated that the nearest possible situation where the sandstone blocks could have been obtained is fully half a mile distant.

The Ggantija, 1990

DAVID TRUMP

The Ggantija, or Giant's Tower, is easily the most impressive of the island's [Gozo's] temples. It stands on the lip of the Xaghera plateau, facing, like so many of the temples, towards the south-east. Its presence has been known for a long time, and even before any excavation was done on it, Jacques Houel in the late 18th century was able to give quite a good plan of it. Clearance of the site (excavation would be a misleading word in the context) was undertaken in 1827, and we are extremely fortunate to have a series of watercolours of the site printed within a year or two of that date by the German artist Brocktorff. The paintings are now in the Royal Malta Library in Valletta, and are practically our only record of the work.

On closer inspection, the pile of masonry can be seen to enclose not one but two temples, both built in the Ggantija phase. The southerly one, on the left, is the older and better preserved. The façade towards the left-hand corner still stands, unrestored, to a height of six metres. Note here the contrast between the rough coralline limestone of the external walls and the softer well-tooled globigerina employed in the walling of the entrance passage and elsewhere inside the monument. The great stone threshold slab deserves mention too.

Touring Gozo, 1881

MURRAY'S GUIDE

This egg-shaped island, lying W. of Malta, is about 24 m. in circum-ference, and is considered superior to Malta in fertility and salubrity. Three or four days may be spent here pleasantly, especially in the spring during the season for quail-shooting when the country is especially gay with countless wild flowers. There is a daily omnibus, which carries the letters, starting from Saliba's stables, S. Mercanti at Valletta, the fare being two shillings to the landing place at Gozo. To reach this we pass St. Paul's Bay, and the prettily situated village of Melleha, almost an hour's drive beyond. In the church is a picture famous for its miracles, and full of votive offerings, commemorating escapes from shipwreck and pestilence. On the opposite side of the valley is a statue of St. Paul, and near at hand is one of the supposed grottoes of Calypso, who delayed Ulysses. Another hour over a rough road brings you to Marfa, the place for embarkation. In the channel, or Straits of Freghi, lie the small islands of Comino and Cominetto. The Gozo boats are very sea-worthy, but the length of time in crossing from Lata to Gozo (4 to 5 m.) necessarily varies greatly according to wind and weather, while occasionally the passage is impossible. Or the excursionist may take passage in one of the numerous boats plying between Valletta and Gozo.

The island of Calypso? 1789

VIVANT DENON

The isle of Gozzo [sic] has been imagined by many of our modern antiquaries to have been the island of Calypso; but this opinion has now been out of fashion for some years, and though there is nothing at Malta which in the least resembles the description of that island by Homer and Fenelon, they have now transferred to that island the residence of the amorous nymph, and placed her palace at the bottom of the harbour of *la Melleha*.

We traversed the whole island to discover this bay or harbour, in the recess of which, and half way up the hill, there is in fact a fountain of four inches breadth of water, conveyed from off the rock by an aqueduct of four hundred feet in length. Into this aqueduct I entered, to examine if I could discover any buildings, but found nothing but the rock carelessly excavated, without any kind of ornament.

Calypso's island? 1831

ELLIOT WARBURTON

One or two uninhabited little islands, that seem to have strayed from the continent and lost their way, speck the sea between this pleasant penal settlement (Pantellaria) and Gozo, which is also a claimant for the doubtful honour of Calypso's isle. Narrow straits separate it from the adjoining rock, which represents the island of Malta.

Drawing Gozo, 1866

EDWARD LEAR

Edward Lear visited Malta on more than one occasion in transit to other places. He spent longer there in the winter of 1866, but was not happy. In March, having 'drawn all Malta', he went to Gozo and 'drew every bit of that'.

The scenery of Gozo may truly be called pomskizillious and gromphibberous, being as no words can describe its magnificence.

A gracious visit to Gozo, August 1826

MALTA GOVERNMENT GAZETTE

The Noble Family (the Marquess of Hastings, Governor of Malta), who had been residing a short time at Marfa, for the enjoyment of the refreshing sea breezes and the benefit of sea bathing, disembarked on the soil of Gozo, amidst the *Vivas* of the people collected from the neighbourhood to witness their arrival; and, accompanied by a guard of honour, from the Rifle Brigade under the command of Major Gray, proceeded to Rabbato. His Excellency was met at the approach to the town by the Principal Civil Officers and a Deputation of the Clergy; where, alighting from his carriage, he walked to the house of Mr Somerville, who, in the absence of the Lieutenant Governor, had the honour of expressing to His Excellency the great gladness of the people of Gozo at seeing HIS LORDSHIP amongst them. Indeed nothing could equal their own expressions of happiness and contentment as the LADIES passed through the crowded streets. High and low, old and young, testified the earnest desire of beholding, though the day was near to its close, those who they had so often heard spoken of with admiration and gratitude; and the gentleness and generous expression with which her LADYSHIP and DAUGHTERS received these demonstrations, animated the people of Gozo, as dutiful and respected by nature as their fellow subjects of Malta, to an unbounded and sincere utterance of attachment so justly due to the family of our excellent GOVERNOR.

✳ THE END OF THE DAY ✳

Anywhere that one wanders in the countryside of Malta and Gozo, one may pause and watch a lizard, just as Coleridge did.

Watching a lizard, July 1804

SAMUEL TAYLOR COLERIDGE

Lizard half-erect stands still as I stop – I stop a long while – he turns his head & looks sidelong at me – Crawls two or three paces by stealth – stops again. I walk off briskly, turning my head tho' and looking at him – he is too cunning – & has not moved – at length I really move away – and off – he is gone!

Glide across the sunny walk like shooting Stars, grey, speckled exquisite grace of motion all the delicacy of the Serpent and a certain dignity from even just the increasing erectness of it to its hind paws – Dragon flies, 1 purple, & 2 most common, a deep crimson – Not so long in the *Sheath* as our finest ones in England. Butterflies glorious ones but their flight unwieldy – I could catch them with ease – the Lizard's motion and the Dragonfly's – both darting and angular, yet how different – the Dr's always & naturally angular, the Lizard's only by choice.

Lizard green with bright gold spots all over – firmness of its *stand-like* feet, where the *life* of the *threddy* Toes makes them both seem & be so firm, so solid – yet so very, very supple. One pretty fellow, whom I had fascinated by stopping & gazing at him as he lay in a thick network of Sun and Shade, after having turned his head from me so as but for the greater length of its Tail to form a crescent with the outline of its body – then turned his Head to me, depressed it & looked up, half-watching, half-imploring, at length taking advantage of a brisk breeze that made all the Network dance & Toss, & darted off as if an Angel of Nature had spoken to the breeze – Off! I'll take care, he shall not hurt you! – I should like, if I could know what they eat, or if they eat bread, to tame one –

Lizard driven headlong before a gust into the Harbour – turns his head & innocent eye sidelong towards me, his side his forepaw throbbing with a visible pulse – a minute & then a slow timid creep off for an inch or so – then stops.

The end of the day, 1765

PATRICK BRYDONE

We were delighted on our way back to the city, with the beauty of the setting sun; much superior, I think, to what I have ever observed in Italy. The whole of the eastern part of the heavens, for half an hour after sun-set, was of a fine deep purple, and made a beautiful appearance. This the Maltese tell us is generally the case every evening, at this season of the year.

Serenaded home, 1841

GEORGE ANGAS

We returned home (from the countryside) by the light of the moon, and in passing through the suburban streets of Floriana we were serenaded by the chirping of numberless crickets.

The Maltese seem greatly attached to these insects; they capture them as we would a bird, and hang them up in little wicker cages, full of leaves, outside their windows.

✳ AND FINALLY, FAREWELL ✳

Farewell to Malta, May 26th 1811

GEORGE GORDON, LORD BYRON

Adieu, ye joys of La Valette!
Adieu, sirocco, sun, and sweat!
Adieu, thou palace rarely enter'd!
Adieu, ye mansions where I've ventured!
Adieu, ye cursed streets of stairs!
(How surely he who mounts you swears!)
Adieu, ye merchants often failing!
Adieu, thou mob for ever railing!
Adieu, ye packets without letters!
Adieu, ye fools who ape your betters!
Adieu, thou damned'st quarantine,
That gave me fever, and the spleen!
Adieu, that stage which makes us yawn, Sirs,
Adieu, his Excellency's dancers!

Adieu to Peter -- whom no fault's in,
But could not teach a colonel waltzing;
Adieu, ye females fraught with graces!
Adieu red coats, and redder faces!
Adieu the supercilious air
Of all that strut "en militaire"!
I go – but God knows when or why,
To smoky towns and cloudy sky,
To things (the honest truth to say)
As bad – but in a different way. –

Farewell to these, but not adieu,
Triumphant sons of truest blue!!
While either Adriatic shore,
And fallen chiefs, and fleets no more,

And nightly smiles, and daily dinners,
Proclaim you war and woman's winners.
Pardon my Muse, who apt to prate is,
And take my rhyme – because 'tis "gratis."

...

And now, O Malta! since thou'st got us,
Thou little military hot-house!
I'll not offend with words uncivil,
And wish thee rudely at the Devil,
But only stare from out my casement,
And ask, for what is such a place meant?
Then, in my solitary nook,
Return to scribbling, or a book,
Or take my physic while I'm able
(Two spoonfuls hourly by the label),
Prefer my nightcap to my beaver,
And bless the gods I've got a fever.

BRIEF BIOGRAPHIES

Andrew Adams (1827–82) served in India and then in Malta as an army surgeon with the 23rd Regiment. He admitted that 'in the absence of war or pestilence' an army surgeon had time for ramblings and alternative interests. His were natural history, archaeology and geology—and, for these, Malta (in 1861–8) was a perfect setting. He is described as being a naturalist 'in the best Victorian tradition'. For a time he concentrated on exploring the island's caves and discovering, among much else, the remains of pygmy hippopotami and miniature elephants.

George Angas (1822–86) came to Malta in 1840 when he was just 19 years old. He was an artist and zoologist who travelled widely, wrote often for journals and became a fellow of various British learned societies. His book on Malta provides sensitive insights useful to the traveller.

Joseph Attard Tabone is a Maltese from Gozo who, after a career in the Maltese police, has become an authority on the pre-historic history of the islands, in particular discovering the Brockdorff Circle in Xaghra, after which he was awarded the Midalja ghall-Qadi tar-Repubblika.

Douglas Austin was born in Malta in 1934 and is the author of *Churchill and Malta: A Special Relationship* (2006).

George Percy Badger (1815–88) was an Arabic scholar and printer who spent his youthful years in Malta and from there travelled in Arabia. Becoming a priest in 1842, he visited the Eastern churches, and became Government chaplain in Bombay, and Chaplain to the Persian expedition of 1856–7 and on a mission to Zanzibar in 1872.

Francisco Balbi di Correggio (1505–89), a foot soldier in the Knights' army, recorded the forces and actions of the Great Siege. His work, originally in Spanish, was translated for the Folio Society by Ernle Bradford in 1965—to celebrate the four hundredth anniversary of the Siege.

W.H. Bartlett (1809–59) started life as a topographical artist, working in Britain and then overseas. He travelled widely in the Near East and both wrote the text and illustrated a number of books about the region. He visited Malta twice while returning from the East, but, sadly, on his second journey, from Malta to Marseilles, he died and was buried at sea.

Samuel Bevan (fl. 1849) was an adventurous young man who travelled through Malta to Egypt and wrote of his experiences in his book *Sand and Canvas*.

Malcolm Billings is the BBC's most experienced archaeological broadcaster, presenter of the series *Crossing Continents*, and has written *The Cross and the Crescent; The Crusades; History of the English*.

Edward Blaquière (1779–1832), an author and philhellene, was the author of *Letters from the Mediterranean*.

Brian W. Blouet is a specialist in geo-politics and geo-strategy, and author of *The Story of Malta*.

Lady Fanny Blunt (1840–1926) Grand-daughter of Constantine Zohrab, Fanny's father was a representative of the East India Company in Constantinople, her mother the daughter of a princely Persian family. She married Sir John Elijah Blunt KCB (British Consul at Salonika and Boston) but the break-up of the Ottoman Empire led to the Blunts' removal to America, Britain and eventually Malta where she wrote *The People of Turkey*.

Louis de Boisgelin (1758–1816) was a French Knight of St. John who wrote about ancient and modern Malta (1804). He had travelled widely in Europe before settling in Malta, but from 1793 lived in England. He wished Malta to be returned to the Knights after the French invaded and then the British took over. He published the final volume of his history in 1809.

Ernle Bradford (1922–86) was a popular writer on many subjects from antiques to sailing, from jewellery to the Greek islands, Hannibal to Constantinople, but may be best remembered for his historical work *The Great Siege of Malta* (1961).

Lady Annie Brassey (1839–87) was a traveller who wrote about her long sea journeys with her husband and children on their sailing ship the *Sunbeam*. She died at sea near Brisbane.

Vera Brittain (1893–1970) was a writer, a pacifist and a feminist. She is remembered for a number of thoughtful novels. She worked as a nursing assistant in Malta in World War I, and was an active pacifist in World War II. Her book, *Testament of Youth*, was based on her war experiences and losses.

Patrick Brydone (1736–1818) started travelling as a tutor and then extended his travels to Sicily and Malta (1765). He later lived in Scotland, published books about his travels and wrote papers on electricity.

James Silk Buckingham (1786–1855) was at sea for several years from 1796. In 1818 he became a journalist in Calcutta but was expelled for criticism of the government. He then travelled in Syria, Palestine and Malta, returning to England as a journalist in 1824–30 and becoming Member of Parliament for Sheffield 1832–37. He then travelled in America for three years. He wrote about his travels and an autobiography.

John Lewis Burckhardt (1784–1817) was born in Switzerland, and went to England in 1806 to study Arabic at Cambridge University. He went on to travel widely in the Near East, passing through Malta en route. In his travels in Egypt he became the first European to record seeing the great temple at Abu Simbel.

George Gordon, Lord Byron (1788–1824), the Romantic poet and English peer, travelled to and around the Mediterranean, sometimes with John Galt. Together they reached Malta on 31 August 1809. In the heat of summer, Byron spent hours in the public library in Valletta, going sailing and dining and celebrating with acquaintances.He returned for a few weeks in 1811. Byron became involved with the Greek War of Independence and died in Greece. His time in Malta was brief, but phrases in his poem 'Farewell to Malta' have echoed down the years.

Samuel Taylor Coleridge (1772–1834) is best known as a poet and philosopher, but, after a shaky start was supported in his erratic life and despite his opium habit, by being appointed as secretary to the British Governor of Malta (1804–5), from where he wrote sensitive letters home. His erratic life and poetic output continued and he became a 'lion' of London literary circles. He was clearly a charmer...

Nigel Dennis (1912–89) worked as a journalist and freelance author and, later, playwright. He lived in Italy and then in Mdina in Malta. His essay on Malta, illustrated by Osbert Sitwell, was a plea for the better care of the Maltese countryside.

Vivant Denon (1747–1825) was a French antiquary, artist and diplomat who joined Napoleon's team of *savants* who worked on the Commission on Egypt to study the background of the French invasion of Egypt. Somewhat surprisingly he had already visited Malta before the French invasion of the island in 1785. He returned to France and rose to become Director of National Museums.

Peter Dietz is an educationalist and writer who served as an officer in the Royal Marine Commandos and then worked for the Royal Army Education Corps.

Benjamin Disraeli (1804–81) who would become a Member of Parliament, a novelist and first British Prime Minister of Jewish origins, travelled in the East as a young man, briefly visiting Malta.

Peter McGregor Eadie is a travel writer and editor who edited four editions of the *Blue Guide to Malta and Gozo*, and also wrote other travel guides.

Anne Katherine Elwood (fl. 1843) the wife of an East India Company official, she travelled with him, stopping for several weeks in Malta en route to Egypt, and wrote perceptively about all she saw there, and, later, in India. On her return to England, she became familiar with women writers and wrote *Memoirs of the Literary Ladies of England.*

Henry James Forman (1879–1966) was an American writer who wrote a number of varied titles on literature and travel.

Michael Galea was a Maltese historian of the Knights of Malta, and short story writer.

John Galt (1779–1839) was an employee in a mercantile house, but also a poet and novelist and friend of George Byron, with whom he travelled from Gibraltar and Malta and onward to the East. His account of his travels was published in 1812 and he also wrote fictional travel accounts. He spent some years in Canada working on the purchase of Crown lands.

Simon Gaul is a veteran sailor and the author of *Malta, Gozo and Comino*.

Lady Elizabeth Mary Grosvenor, Marchioness of Westminster (1797–1891) wrote *A Narrative of a Yacht Voyage in the Mediterranean during the years 1840–41*, published in 1843. In 1819 she had married Richard Grosvenor, 2nd Marquess of Westminster, and had thirteen children.

Alec Guinness (1914–2000), the actor, served in the Navy during the Second World War, and wrote about it in his autobiography, *Blessings in Disguise*.

Sarah Haight (fl. 1846) was the wife of a rich New York businessman with whom she travelled to the Mediterranean, Egypt and the Near East.

Reverend John Hartley (1796–1843) was a clergyman and writer who travelled around the Mediterranean and the Near East in 1830.

John Howard (1726–90) is famed as a prison reformer who visited city and county gaols and worked for their improvement. He also considered the experiences of being incarcerated in the Lazarettos of the Mediterranean, and in 1785–6 travelled round Europe to experience them personally.

Reverend William Jowett (1787–1855) worked for the Church Missionary Society in Egypt and the Near East while living with his family in Malta.

Dun Karm (1871–1961) was a priest and respected writer about his homeland, Malta; he is now often known as 'the bard of Malta'.

Alphonse de Lamartine (1790–1869) was a French author and traveller who passed through Malta on his way to the East.

Francesco Laparelli (1521–70) was an Italian-born architect sent by Pope Pius V to mastermind the reconstruction of Valletta in 1565.

Jean Parisot de La Valette (1494?–1568) was born into an eminent French aristocratic family and rose to become the most illustrious Grand Master of the Knights Hospitaller in 1557. He led the resistance to the Ottoman Turks in the siege of 1565 and gave his name to the rebuilt capital city.

Edward Lear (1812–88), the artist and somewhat eccentric writer and poet, travelled widely around the Mediterranean painting the scenery. He wrote home to his sister and his letters were later published.

Edward Romeo Leopardi, an historian, was the author of *Malta's Heritage*.

Reverend William Loftie (1839–1911) was a clergyman, collector and writer who travelled widely in Egypt, becoming a keen Egyptologist. He also wrote about British art and architecture. Travelling to Egypt through Malta, he wrote of his experiences there.

Sir Harry Luke (1884–1969) was a colonial civil servant who held senior office in a number of countries including Malta and Cyprus, and wrote about his experience of these countries.

Thomas Macgill (fl. 1839) wrote a handbook and guide for visitors to Malta, published in 1839, and other accounts of travel around the Mediterranean.

John Madox (fl. 1834) set off to travel in the Levant in 1821, visiting Malta en route and travelling in Upper Egypt and Syria over the next six years. He later published an account of his travels.

Malta Penny Magazine (14 September 1839–18 December 1841) was published in Valletta. Each issue was 4 or 8 pages long in two columns on quarto paper with line illustrations. The content ranged through articles describing the sights of Malta to descriptions of other Mediterranean areas and what might be regarded as matters of interest to any reader—from the new Thames Tunnel to carrier pigeons—plus poems and thoughtful quotations. Some articles, like that on the boa constrictor—with a nightmarish illustration—were lifted from other sources. The editor and main writer was David Richardson.

Dr. Charles Meryon (1783–1877) was doctor and loyal travelling companion to Lady Hester Stanhope, and recorded her travels in the Mediterranean and the Levant.

Lady Mary Wortley Montagu (1689–1762) was an English aristocrat, traveller and early authority on the Orient.

Murray's Guides provided the most detailed information about the means of travel and what should be visited and experienced in travelling in many parts of the world. The series was started by one of the publishing Murray family, and the guides were published by John Murray Ltd.

Admiral Horatio Nelson (1758–1805), the great naval hero was serving in the Mediterranean in the 1790s, harrying the French and Spanish. He followed Napoleon's French fleet to Egypt in 1798 and hammered them in Aboukir Bay and then directed the blockade of Napoleon in Egypt and Malta, until 1800 when he returned home and to his later duties.

David Niven (1910–83) joined the British army and served in Malta, where he soon decided he had made a wrong career choice. He left Malta and the army and made a living as a film extra and eventually a star. He wrote about Malta in his autobiography.

Stewart Perowne (1901–89) was a diplomat and writer about the ancient world and the Roman Empire, and the history of Christendom, but also published *The Siege within the Walls (1940–1943)* in 1970—an account of the Second World War siege of Malta.

S.E.G. Ponder (fl. 1937) served in various territories and wrote about his experiences and the contemporary life he saw.

Whitworth Porter (1827–92) was a major in the Royal Engineers and author of *History of the Knights of Malta* (1858).

William C. Prime (1825–1925) was an American historian who recorded his journeys around the Mediterranean in his *Tent Life in the Holy Land* (re-issued in 1977).

David L. Richardson (1801–62) was a writer and journalist who worked in India and Bengal and, for a period in the early 1840s, created and ran the journal the *Malta Penny Magazine*.

Emma Roberts (1794–1840) was a writer who in 1828 travelled to India, writing of the experiences of her journey, including when she stopped over at Malta, and of India where she died. She was editor of the *The Oriental Observer* and published several accounts of her travels and life in India.

Isabella Romer (1805–52) separated from her husband and went travelling to the East, and in 1846 published an account of her experiences. She is regarded as an authority on the Kurna villages on the Nile.

H.J. Ross (fl. 1849) Ross was an archaeologist associated with the discovery of Sennacherib's palace at Nineveh; he also has striking memories of his childhood encounter with Disraeli.

Edward Sammut was the author of guides to the Co-Cathedral of St. John and to Valletta, the capital of his country.

George Sandys (1578–1644) was a son of the Archbishop of York who, in 1610, set out travelling and spent a year in Turkey, Egypt and Palestine, visiting Malta en route. He later became interested in the colonial expansion of the period, and went to America in 1621, but returned to England, where he died. His papers are held by the Ashmolean Museum, Oxford.

Elizabeth Schermerhorn was an American scholar and author of *Malta of the Knights* (1929).

Sir Walter Scott (1771–1831) In 1831 the great Scottish writer Sir Walter Scott, author of *Ivanhoe*, visited the Mediterranean and Malta for his health, accompanied by his daughter, grandson and two servants. Familiar with the Knights' history from his interest in the medieval world, Scott went sightseeing in Valletta and across the island. 'Papa,' his daughter wrote in her diary, 'never tires of the tombs of the Knights...' He planned a novel with this background, but wrote only a quarter of it before he died.

Nassau William Senior (1790–1864) was one of the commissioners appointed in 1864 to inquire into popular education in England. In the later years of his life, during his visits to foreign countries, he studied with much care the political and social phenomena they exhibited.

Claudius Shaw (fl. 1875), author of *Malta Sixty Years Ago*, which was also a synoptic sketch of the Order of St. John of Jerusalem, from its first formation till the evacuation of Malta; to which was added a short sketch of the Crusades and a concise history of the Knights Templar.

Reverend Charles Swan (fl. 1826) published moral tales and sermons, and in 1825 travelled to Malta and around the Mediterranean.

William Makepeace Thackeray (1811–63) had a somewhat misspent youth travelling, taking up various interests, spending his inheritance and writing for journals and then, in his thirties, began to write about his travels in the popular *Cornhill to Cairo* (1846) and then published novels, for which he is remembered.

Joanna Trollope, a descendant of Anthony Trollope, and also a novelist, wrote her novel *The Brass Dolphin* (under her pen-name Caroline Harvey) based on her experience of living in Malta during the war. She is famed today for her 'Aga Sagas'—novels based on contemporary, mainly rural, life.

David Trump, Curator of Archaeology at the National Museum of Malta, oversaw the initial excavations of the unique underground Neolithic burial complex.

William Turner (1792–1867) was a diplomat who was able to travel widely in the East from his first appointment in Constantinople. He wrote about these travels, which included Malta. He was envoy to Colombia in 1829–38.

George, Viscount Valentia (1770–1844) travelled widely in Africa, India and Egypt in 1802–6, together with Henry Salt, later British Consul General in Egypt and an important collector for his nation. They returned home via Malta, experienced the Lazaretto, and later enjoyed the sights of Malta.

Philip Vella wrote the history of the Second World War as far as it affected the Maltese islands—using contemporary photographs to show the impact on the islands.

Elliot Warburton (1810–51) was a Cambridge-educated Irish barrister and author of *The Crescent and the Cross* (1844), an account of his travels in the East.

George Waring (fl. 1843) was the author of *Letters from Malta and Sicily, Addressed to a Young Naturalist.*

Evelyn Waugh (1903–66), the novelist and traveller, is best known for his *Brideshead Revisited.* He visited Malta as a young man on a Mediterranean cruise.

F.N. Weston (fl. 1920s) published his guide to Malta while working there in the 1920s.

John Gardner Wilkinson (1797–1875) was an explorer and early Egyptologist who wrote about the daily life and customs of the early Egyptians as interpreted from the tomb paintings. In the 1840s he wrote the Murray's *Handbook to Egypt,* including information about the journey through Malta.

Sir Mark Wood (1750–1829) was an army officer and engineer who supported the British colonisation of Malta.

Sir Themistocles Zammit (1864–1935) was a medical doctor, and major Maltese historian and archaeologist, who published extensively on his researches of the Maltese temples and other prehistoric finds in Malta, both in English and his own Maltese language.

BIBLIOGRAPHY

Adams, Andrew, *Notes of a Naturalist in the Nile Valley and Malta*,
    Edinburgh, 1870
Anderson, Aeneas, *A journal of the forces which sailed from the Downs in April
    1800 with a particular account of Malta*, J. Debrett, London, 1802
Angas, G., *A Ramble in Malta and Sicily in the Autumn of 1841*, Smith Elder,
    London, 1842
Anon., *Journal of Queen Adelaide's visit to Malta*, Malta, 1838
Arberry, A.J., *A Maltese Anthology*, Clarendon Press, Oxford, 1960
Arberry A.J., and Grech, P., *Dun Karm: Poet of Malta*, Cambridge University
    Press, 1961
Attard Tabone, Joseph, *Gozo: The Island of Calypso*, Plurigraf, 1995
—— *The Ghosts of Malta*, Publishers Enterprise Group, 1997
—— *The Knights of Malta*, Publishers Enterprise Group, 1995
Austin, Douglas, *Churchill and Malta: A Special Relationship*, Spellmount, 2006
Badger, George Percy, *Description of Malta and Gozo*, Valetta, 1838
Balbi di Correggio, Francisco, *The Siege of Malta 1565*, Folio Society,
    London, 1965
Bartlett, W.H., *Pictures from Sicily*, London, 1853
Bedford, W.K.R., *Malta and the Knights Hospitallers*, Macmillan, London, 1890
Bevan, Samuel, *Sand and Canvas: Narrative of Adventures in Egypt*, London, 1849
Billings, Malcolm, *The Cross and the Crescent*, The History Press, Stroud, 2000
Blaquière, Edward, *Letters from hte Mediterranean*, London, 1813
Blouet, Brian W., *The Story of Malta*, Faber hardback, Progress Press
    paperback, 1984
Blunt, Lady Fanny, *My Reminiscences*, London, 1918
de Boisgelin, Louis, *Ancient and Modern Malta*, 3 vols, London, 1804
Bradford, Ernle, *The Great Siege: Malta*, Hart Davies, London, 1961
Brassey, Lady Annie, *A Voyage in the Sunbeam*, London, 1878
Brittain, Vera, *Chronicle of Youth*, HarperCollins, London, 1981
Brydone, P.A., *A Tour through Sicily and Malta*, 2 vols, London, 1773
Buckingham, James Silk, *Autobiography*, London, 1855
Coleridge, Samuel Taylor, *Literary Remains*, Project Gutenberg
Dennis, Nigel, *An Essay on Malta*, John Murray, London, 1972
Denon, Vivant, *Travels in Sicily and Malta*, London, 1789
Dietz, Peter, *The British in the Mediterranean*, Anova Books, London, 1994
Disraeli, Benjamin, *Home Letters 1815–1834*, Cassell, London, 1886
Eadie, Peter McGregor, *The Blue Guide to Malta and Gozo*, A & C Black,
    London, 2000

Elwood, Anne Katherine, *Narrative of a Journey overland from England*, Vol. 1, London, 1830

Forman, Henry James, *Grecian Italy*, Jonathan Cape, London, 1927

Galea, Michael, 'The Captain' in J.A. Arberry, *A Maltese Anthology*, Clarendon Press, Oxford, 1960

—— *Malta Historical Sketches*, Veritas Press, Malta, 1970

—— *Malta: More Historical Sketches*, Veritas Press, Malta, 1971

Galt, John, *Voyages and Travels in 1809–11*, London, 1812

Lady Grosvenor, *Narrative of a Yacht Voyage in the Mediterranean during the years 1840–1*, London, 1843

Guinness, Alec, *Blessings in Disguise*, Hamish Hamilton, London, 1983

Haight, Sarah, *Over the Ocean, or glimpses of travel in many lands*, New York, 1846

Hartley, Reverend John, *Researches in Greece and the Levant*, London, 1831

Harvey, Caroline, *The Brass Dolphin*, Doubleday, London, 1997

Howard, John, *An Account of the Principal Lazarettos in Europe*, London, 1789

Jowett, William, *Christian Researches in Syria and the Holy Land*, London, 1825

Kininmonth, Christopher, *The Brass Dolphins: A description of the Maltese Archipelago*, Secker and Warburg, London, 1957

Lear, Edward, *Letters of Edward Lear*, ed. Lady Strachey, Fisher Unwin, London, 1911

Leopardi, E.R., *Malta's Heritage: selections from the writings of E.R. Leopardi*, Progress Press, Valletta, 1969

Luke, Sir Harry, *Malta, an account and an appreciation*, Harrap, London, 1949

MacGill, Thomas, *A Hand Book or Guide, for Strangers Visiting Malta*, Malta, 1839

Madox, John, *Excursions in the Holy Land, Egypt etc*, London, 1834

Malta Government Gazette, Department of Information, Valletta

Malta Penny Magazine, Valetta, 1840–1

Dr. Meryon, Charles, *Travels of Lady Hester Stanhope*, Colborn, London, 1846

Murray, J., *A Handbook for Travellers in the Ionian Islands, Greece, Turkey, Asia Minor, and Constantinople*, John Murray, London, 1840

Niven, David, *The Moon's a Balloon*, Hamish Hamilton, London, 1984

Perowne, Stewart, *The Siege Within the Walls: Malta 1940–43*, Hodder and Stoughton, London, 1970

Ponder, S.E.G., *Mediterranean Memories*, S. Paul and Co., London, 1937

Porter, Whitworth, *History of the Knights of Malta*, London, 1858

Prime, William C., *Boat Life in Egypt and Nubia*, Harper Brothers, New York, 1874

Roberts, Emma, *Scenes and Characteristics of Hindustan*, Caxton Press, London, 1835

Romer, Isabella, *A Pilgrimage to the Temples and Tombs of Egypt*, Richard
    Bentley, London, 1846

Sammut, Edward, *The Co-Cathedral of St. John, Formerly the Conventual
    Church of the Order of Malta, and its Art Treasures*, Progress Press,
    Valletta, 1950

—— *Notes for a history of art in Malta*, Progress Press, Valletta, 1954

—— *Valletta: a guide to the capital of Malta*, Progress Press, Valletta, 1968

Sandys, George, *A relation of a journey begun in 1610*, London, 1621

Schermerhorn, Elizabeth, *Malta of the Knights*, Heinemann, London, 1929

Senior, Nassau William, *Conversations and Journals in Egypt and Malta*,
    London, 1882

Shaw, Claudius, *Malta Sixty Years Ago*, London, 1875

Sonnini, Charles, *Voyage dans la Haute et Basse Egypte*, Paris, 1799

Sultana, Donald, *Samuel Taylor Coleridge in Malta and Italy*, Progress Press,
    Valletta, 1969

—— *The Journey of Sir Walter Scott to Malta*, Progress Press, Valletta, 1980

Sultana, Joe, *A New Guide to the Birds of Malta*, BirdLife Malta, Valletta,
    1982

Swan, Reverend Charles, *Journal of a Voyage up the Mediterranean*, London,
    1826

Thackeray, William Makepeace, *Sketchbooks: Notes of a Journey from
    Cornhill to Cairo*, London, 1846

Trollope, Joanna, see Caroline Harvey

Trump, David, *Malta, an Archaeological Guide*, Faber, London, 1990

—— *Malta: Prehistory and Temples*, Oxbow Books, Oxford, 2002

Turner, William, *Journal of a Tour in the Levant*, London, 1820

Valentia, Viscount, George, *Voyages and Travels, 1802–6*, London, 1809

Vella, Philip, *Malta: Blitzed but not Beaten*, Progress Pres, Valletta, 1985

Warburton, Elliot, *The Crescent and the Cross, or romance and realities of
    Eastern travel*, London, 1844

Waring, G., *Letters from Malta and Sicily*, London, 1843

Waugh, Evelyn, *Labels: a Mediterranean Journey*, Duckworth, London, 1946

Weston, F.N., *Walks in Malta, an archaeological and historical guide*, Daily
    Malta Press, Valletta, 1925

Wilkinson, J.G., *Handbook for Travellers in Egypt*, John Murray, London, 1847

Williams, P., *Recollections of Malta, Sicily and the Continent*, Edinburgh, 1857

Wortley Montagu, Mary, *The Complete Letters*, ed. R. Haisband, 2 vols,
    London, 1965–7

Zammit, Sir Themistocles, *Malta the Islands and their History*, Malta Herald
    Office, 1926

ACKNOWLEDGEMENTS

The editor and publisher acknowledge with thanks the use of material in this book to the following: Caroline Harvey for excerpts from *The Brass Dolphin* published by Doubleday. Reprinted by permission of the Random House Group; Malcolm Billings for excerpts from *The Cross and the Crescent* published by BBC Books. Reprinted by permission of Random House Group Ltd; Joseph Attard Tabone for excerpts from his writings on Gozo; Brian Blouet for excerpts from *The Story of Malta* published by Progress Press, Valletta; E.R. Leopardi and *The Times of Malta* for excerpts from *Malta's Heritage*; John Murray Publishers and Hachette UK for excerpts from *An Essay on Malta* by Nigel Dennis; Somerset Books for excerpts from *Blue Guide Malta and Gozo*, 5th edition; Anova Books for excerpts from *The British in the Mediterranean* by Peter Dietz; Philip Vella and *The Times of Malta* and Progress Press, Valletta, for excerpts from his *Malta, Blitzed but not Beaten;* Edward Sammut and *The Times of Malta* and Progress Press for excerpts from *A Guide to the City of Valletta;* the Wylie Agency for excerpts from *Labels: a Mediterranean Journey* by Evelyn Waugh; Joe Sultana, Charles Gauci and Birdlife Malta (formerly the Malta Ornithological Society) for excerpts from *Bird Life in Malta;* Donald Sultana for excerpts from *Samuel Taylor Coleridge in Malta*, Barnes and Noble, New York, 1969, and *The Journey of Sir Walter Scott to Malta*, Progress Press, 1980; the heirs of Elizabeth Schermerhorn for excerpts from her *Malta of the Knights;* the heirs of Alec Guinness for the excerpt from his *Blessings in Disguise;* the heirs of Sir Harry Luke and Harrap for excerpts from his *Malta, an account and an appreciation;* the heirs of Stewart Perowne and Hodder & Stoughton for the excerpt from *The Siege within the Wall;* J.A. Arberry and the Clarendon Press, Oxford, for excerpts from his *A Maltese Anthology;* David Trump and Faber for excerpts from *Malta, an Archaeological Guide;* the Folio Society for excerpts from Francisco Balbi's *Siege of Malta* translated by Ernle Bradshaw; A.M. Heath and Co. Ltd for excerpts from *The Great Siege of Malta* by Ernle Bradshaw. The excerpt from Vera Brittain's *Testament of Youth* is reprinted by permission of Mark Bostridge and Timothy Brittain-Catlin, Literary Executors for the Vera Brittain Estate, 1970.

The editor and publisher have made every effort to track down copyright material, and regret the use of any material included for which we have failed to locate the owners.

INDEX

Lightning Source UK Ltd.
Milton Keynes UK
UKOW04f2214040218

317361UK00001B/40/P